In the

COMPANY

of

ANIMALS

STORIES OF EXTRAORDINARY
ENCOUNTERS

D0792839

EDITED BY PAM CHAMBERLAIN

NIMBUS
PUBLISHING LTD

Nimbus Publishing Limited
3731 Mackintosh St, Halifax, NS B3K 5A5
(902) 455-4286 nimbus.ca

Printed and bound in Canada

NB1131

Cover and interior design: Jenn Embree

Library and Archives Canada Cataloguing in Publication

In the company of animals : stories of extraordinary encounters / editor, Pam Chamberlain.
Issued in print and electronic formats.
ISBN 978-1-77108-224-2 (pbk.).—ISBN 978-1-77108-225-9 (html).—
ISBN 978-1-77108-226-6 (mobi)

1. Animals—Anecdotes. 2. Animal behavior—Anecdotes.
3. Human-animal relationship—Anecdotes.
I. Chamberlain, Pam, 1970-, editor

PS8323.A5I5 2014   C813'.0108362   C2014-903178-5
                                                 C2014-903179-3

Nimbus Publishing acknowledges the financial support for its publishing activities from the Government of Canada through the Canada Book Fund (CBF) and the Canada Council for the Arts, and from the Province of Nova Scotia through Film & Creative Industries Nova Scotia. We are pleased to work in partnership with Film & Creative Industries Nova Scotia to develop and promote our creative industries for the benefit of all Nova Scotians.

to
the ones who taught me to love animals—
my father
Ralph George Chamberlain
and
my grandmother
Kathleen (Bunny) Chamberlain, née Rackham
(1913–1998)

TABLE OF CONTENTS

Introduction

Animals fascinate us. We decorate our babies' nurseries with images of birds and bunnies. We read our children stories about a bear named Pooh and a pig named Wilbur. We drive Broncos, Beetles, and Rams, and we cheer for the Blue Jays, the Tiger-Cats, and the Lions. Animals and their images surround us.

I grew up on a farm in the company of animals. There were cows, horses, sheep, pigs, rabbits, and all kinds of poultry in the farmyard. Barn cats and cattle dogs roamed freely. Beyond the farmyard, in the pastures and in the bushes, there were coyotes, deer, black bears, foxes, jackrabbits, badgers, porcupines, skunks, and plenty of gophers. There were hawks, owls, crows, magpies, grouse, grosbeaks, and many little birds I couldn't name.

I loved animals. I loved to tame and snuggle kittens and rabbits. I had no qualms about picking up the tiger salamanders that lived in our dirt cellar. We all learned to ride horses, and when I was eleven, my grandmother gave me the gift of a lifetime: a palomino mare named Brena. I rode bareback—I loved the physical connection between Brena and me. I rode whenever I could: with my dad to move cattle, with my grandma to pick wild crocuses or to picnic by the dam, and with my friend Hannah, whose family raced chuckwagons and who was an excellent rider. What I lacked in horsemanship skills, I made up for in enthusiasm.

As a teenager, I helped my dad with our sheep herd. One spring, a ewe was injured while birthing a large lamb, and she gave up on caring for it. Dad tried to get the lamb to suck, but the ewe was wild, ill, and uncooperative, and Dad eventually gave up too. Two hundred other animals

My mom, my brother and sister, and me (in the cowboy hat), bottle-feeding calves, 1980.

on the farm needed his attention. I wouldn't give up, though. I cornered the ewe in a stall in the barn, pinned her neck against the rails with my left elbow, pressed the crown of my head into her flank to keep her still, and with my right hand, guided the baby toward the teat. I repeated this daily until eventually—oh joy!— the lamb was strong enough to suck on her own, and the mother was well enough to let her. I'd spent hours in the barn and I had ticks in my scalp, but I was thrilled to know that I—*I!*—had saved the life of a lamb. Dad rewarded me by giving me the lamb, whom I named Julia, and I had the beginning of my own sheep herd.

It wasn't all sunny, though. Although I could never bear to kill an animal myself, the reality was that we kids were contributing members of a farm family. As soon as we were old enough, my brother and sister and I took part in "doing" chickens. Dad beheaded the chickens with an axe, Mom dunked their bodies in boiling water, and we kids helped with plucking the feathers and "cleaning out" the birds—our small bare hands fit easily into the chickens' body cavities to pull out the intestines, gizzards, and other organs. Afterward, the house was filled with the stench of dead birds as my mom "processed" them for the freezer. As members of the local 4-H club, my siblings and I raised, tamed, and trained steers. We did this not only to learn animal husbandry skills, but also to earn money: the steers were sold for beef. Each year, after the Achievement Day sale, I would sob my heart out over my betrayal of my bovine friend.

Although I wouldn't trade in my childhood on a farm, it was, in many ways, hard for me to grow up surrounded by animals in the midst of birthing, living, and dying. I fell in love with animal after animal, and I cried over their deaths. To me, my father embodied the paradoxes of farm life. He shot gophers and problem coyotes, and he butchered pigs and steers near the barn. But I also saw him cover a newborn lamb's nose and mouth with his lips, breathing for the lamb until it took a breath on its own. The first time I saw Dad cry was when his faithful cattle dog, Smokey, was fatally injured in a fight with a neighbour's dog. Even today, Dad gets tears in his eyes when he talks about a particular cow's devotion to her calf.

As a teenager, I struggled to come to terms with the role of animals on the farm and with the contradictions I saw in farm life. I was often sad and angry about the plight of farm animals (even though the animals on our small, traditional farm had much better lives than animals in large, commercial operations did). Years later, I took a university course on animal theory, and I began to understand the discomfort and the questions I'd had all those years. After years of *feeling* about animals, I finally learned how to *think* about them. In an essay by cultural critic John Berger, who describes a farmer being both fond of his animals *and* (not "but") happy to eat them, I finally understood my father. He loved his animals—he was their midwife, their caretaker, their doctor, and their guardian—*and* his livelihood depended on their deaths.

I've long wanted to do a book about animals, and I knew to adequately reflect the diverse relationships with animals in our society, I would need multiple voices and viewpoints. The writers whose stories are included in this book are people who spend time in company of animals, in the role of pet owner, farmer, veterinarian, artist, landowner, game warden, and hunter. Some stories I chose because I could relate to them: I saw my lamb Julia in Nellie, the lamb Mary Ellen Sullivan rescues in "Raising Nellie," and I saw my beloved Brena in Poteet, the horse that rescues Charlotte Mendel in "Grass Can Get Greener." However, I also included stories by writers whose perspectives are very different from mine: unlike David Adams Richards or Marcus Jackson, I will never hunt wild game or collect roadkill, but their stories expand my understanding of the complexities of human-animal relationships. The stories in this collection explore what animals mean to us in their many roles—as our companions and our workmates, our symbols and our totems, our possessions and our food.

An encounter with a wild animal is often interpreted as a gift, one in which we try to find meaning. In "Discourse with a Mountain Lion," Michael Lukas struggles to understand the significance of an encounter with a cougar. As Christine Lowther writes in "Living Light," her story about swimming with a seal, when we encounter wild animals we experience "a longing that makes us reach from our limited, tame, human selves. We want to belong to a place in the way they do...We yearn to slip out of our skins and into theirs, or, failing that, at least secure their blessing." We revere wild animals because they symbolize nature and wilderness, and they reflect to us our own animal nature.

Some wild animals are so elusive that we can know them only in death. In "Learning to Love Coyote," Marcus Jackson's discovery of a dead coyote on the highway sparks a journey of self-discovery. In "Heart the Size of a Small Car," Mark Ambrose Harris's encounter with a beached whale helps him grieve the loss of a friend.

No matter how much we love the *idea* of wild animals, we sometimes come face to face with animals that are considered pests. What is an animal lover to do when rodents move into her house? Melody Hessing explores this question in her humorous story, "Home Invasion," as she ponders whether her love for wildlife includes rats.

For years, domestic animals were our workmates, and in "*Ein Gutes Gespann*," Catherine R. Fenwick recalls the essential role horses played on the family farm. Nowadays, though, most people's primary experience with animals—aside from eating them—is with pets. We invite our pets to share our food and our beds, we take them on vacations, and we dress

Me with my dad and his horse, Paddy, 1972.

them in costumes. Collectively, we spend billions of dollars each year on them. We develop close relationships with them, and devoted pet owners often find themselves caring for pets when they are no longer cute or convenient, as is the case with Grover the cat in Andrew Boden's "Mad King Grover." But our pets take care of us, too. In "I'm Here for You," Jean Ballard recalls how her dog Muffin watched over her as she recovered from a car accident, and in "Counterparts," Rose-Marie Lohnes explains how her cat Raven protects her from cancer.

Pet owners understand that their pets are individuals with personalities. As the legendary primatologist Jane Goodall said, "You cannot share your life in a meaningful way with any kind of animal with a reasonably well-developed brain and not realize that animals have personalities." For many pet owners, the death of a pet means the loss of a family member. Farley Mowat writes a moving account of the death of his childhood companion, Mutt, in "April Passage," and Ruth Edgett writes about letting go of her beloved horse Maggie in "They'll Only Break Your Heart."

Although we spend much time and money coddling our pets and protecting wildlife, we tend to give less thought to the lives and deaths of the millions of farm animals living in Canada—as Chris Nichols illustrates in "Shipping Day," his recollection of working on a chicken farm— and many of us are unwilling to shell out the extra dollars on our grocery bills that would be required to ensure that "livestock" live comfortable lives. However, farm animals are individuals, too. Paul Beingessner's "Old One-Eye" reveals that even a rooster is capable of forming a relationship with a human. In "The Dominant Sow," Anny Scoones introduces us to Buster, a pig who loves his new owner a little *too* much.

This book is about extraordinary encounters with animals. At first glance, we might be tempted to assume that these extraordinary encounters occur because the individual *animals* are extraordinary. We might think that not any rooster would bond with a man like Old One-Eye did or that not every pig is capable of loving a woman the way Buster did. I suspect, however, that these individual animals are typical of their species, and it is, in fact, the *human* in each of these stories that is extraordinary for seeing an animal as individual and being open to a deeper relationship with it. In other words, these extraordinary encounters are very possible, and could even become quite ordinary, if we humans were to view and interact with animals in a new way.

The writers in this collection know that animals have lessons to teach us. In "Apparition," for example, David Weale finds meaning in his unlikely sighting of a cougar on Prince Edward Island. Many of the writers explore the boundary between human and animal and suggest that such a boundary is imaginary. Paul Beingessner describes the moment when he understood the actions of Old One-Eye: "The barrier between us had been shattered once and for all."

In the philosophies of Aboriginal cultures, the importance of animals is clear. In an essay titled "The Animal People," Richard Wagamese explains:

When Creator sent Human Beings to live in this reality, he called the Animals forward and directed them to remain our teachers forever. Their teachings showed the Human Beings how to relate to the world and how to treat the earth. What the Ojibway know of ourselves as people, such as our need to live in harmony with each other, came to us from the Animal People.

And, Wagamese explains, animals are more than teachers:

We are all related. That's what my people understood from the earliest times....[We are] brothers, sisters, kin, family. Ojibway teachings tell us that we all come out of the earth, that we belong here, that we share this planet equally, animals and people.

Michael Lukas echoes this idea as he reflects upon his encounter with a mountain lion, writing that he and the big cat acknowledged a "shared world," one that humans and animals are "constantly renegotiating." Perhaps Aboriginal philosophies hold some keys to success in this nego-tiation. And success is essential: the fates of humans and animals are inextricably linked.

We humans like to imagine that we are separate from the other animals on this planet. The stories in this book invite us to question that assumption. Perhaps if we spend enough time in the company of animals, we will realize that we and the other animals are, after all, kin.

—Pam Chamberlain

I'm Here for You

Jean Ballard

A co-worker begged me to take him, that little five-month-old pup who was being brutalized by her abusive husband. Last night, she said, he had kicked the dog down the stairs, screaming at him for peeing on the floor by the back door. Though my friend was not ready to leave the man, she knew she had to protect the dog.

Living in a small town in the Northwest Territories, my friend had few options. There was no SPCA, no pound, no vet, no rescues, no shelters. This was a town of just a few hundred people living in a cold northern climate, five hours by road to anywhere—and then only to another small town. Sick animals were shot, and unwanted ones were left to fend for themselves, even in the long harsh winters. And so I agreed to meet Muffin.

He was a scruffy little pup, white and tan, with wavy fur that never looked tidy—a Slave River terrier, as the northerners jokingly said. There were dozens just like him along the nearby river. He was a mix of who knows what, the result of years of unplanned breeding of mutt to mutt until the genetic roots could no longer be discerned. Yet did it matter? He was an animal in need, a shivering, quivering, unassuming four-legged furball who needed a safe place to land. I knelt down beside him and reached out my hand. "I'm here for you," I whispered.

When Muffin came to live with me, I didn't really know much about dogs. Though he was not my first, I had never taken the time to educate myself about animal care or training. I fed Muffin some kibble, I took him

Muffin.

for walks, I taught him to sit. It was not until many years and several dogs later that I began to take a deeper interest in animal behaviour and to learn, from books, trainers, and the dogs themselves, how to better meet the needs of traumatized animals. Despite my ineptitude as a canine caregiver, Muffin quickly bonded with me and became my faithful companion. He loved to play ball, de-stuff stuffies, and chase me around the yard.

But for the rest of his life, Muffin would have a reactive temperament that led him to lash out unexpectedly, sometimes with his bark and sometimes with his bite, at almost anyone who came too close. His cute Muppet-like looks and wagging tail invited strangers on the street to reach for him, unaware that they risked losing a finger or two by doing so. His daily walks were exercises in caution as we crossed and re-crossed roads in order to avoid oncoming pedestrians. Even family members still bear the scars of his sudden changes of disposition when hands reached too close.

When I moved back down south, Muffin, of course, came with me. We drove in my battered old car, Muffin riding shotgun as I travelled mile upon mile of unfamiliar roads, through the Northwest Territories, across northern Alberta, and down through British Columbia to the west coast. There, in the Fraser Valley, we made our new home.

Always leery of strangers, always protective of me, Muffin had to give tacit approval to any potential mate of mine. It was not surprising, therefore, that when I began living with Harry, Muffin merely tolerated his presence in my life, and remained bonded only to me. That bond became very apparent when circumstances brought about drastic changes to both our lives.

It was the summer of Muffin's thirteenth year when his health began to fail. In October, his medical tests confirmed what I had feared: liver cancer. He had a few weeks, a month at most, the vet said. There was nothing I could do except keep him comfortable until it was time to let him go. Muffin had reached the final leg of his life's journey.

He was still alive almost one month later when my vehicle was broadsided by another and I ended up in hospital, both hip joints broken, my pelvis fractured in seven places. With a long period of hospitalization ahead, I feared I would never see Muffin again. But I underestimated the strength of both the canine-human bond and Muffin's determination to be there for me as I'd been there for him.

When Harry took my clothes home from the hospital, Muffin sniffed them thoroughly. Pawing frantically at the heap of material, he began crying and whining and showed all the signs of a stressed and grieving dog. For a week, he would not eat. When Harry was away from the house, Muffin scratched at the door, howled, and lost control of his bowels and bladder. When Harry was home, Muffin stayed right beside him though the two had never interacted much before. After about a week, Muffin began to settle down, to eat, to relax—but he still stayed close to Harry and he slept near the bedroom door rather than downstairs in the family room where he'd always slept.

Muffin was still alive a month later when I was finally released from the hospital. With my bones still requiring immobilization, I was confined to bed, where a nurse looked after me by day and Harry looked after me at night. Muffin lay beside the bed, leaving me only when ordered to by my caregivers, to eat, or to go outside. He was quiet and watchful and very, very still. His tail seldom wagged, and he never barked or whined. When I cried in pain or frustration, he was there to comfort me. And when I reached out my hand and laid it on the soft fur of his head, his tail softly thumped the floor. *I'm here for you,* he told me.

And he was still alive the next month when I graduated to a wheelchair. Learning to maneuver in a wheelchair was a challenge for me, and learning to stay clear of the wheels was a challenge for Muffin. The long hairs of his bushy tail were often run over as I backed up or turned around without first telling him to move. But we adjusted, he and I, and for three more months he stuck by my side, quiet, watchful, concerned.

And so it was that Muffin was still alive when I began the process of learning to walk again. The nurse arrived with a walker, and Muffin watched with curiosity as I cautiously rose from the wheelchair, grabbed the top rung of the walker, and stood for the first time in five months. He stayed right beside me as I shakily took those first steps—just ten at first, five away and five back. Each hour that day, I rose from the chair and took a few steps. By the end of the day, I was more sure-footed, and I felt confident that I would soon be liberated from the medical equipment around which my life had revolved. As I slowly shuffled across the room, Muffin's tail wagged vigorously for the first time since the accident.

That evening, I lay on the floor beside Muffin, stroking his fur as he gave my face happy little kisses. Suddenly, I noticed a change in him. His breathing became laboured, his heart began to pound, and he looked at me with sad brown eyes. I told him I was okay. I told him he was a very good dog. I told him I loved him. He sighed deeply, and with his body curled next to mine and my hand resting gently on his fur, he slowly closed his eyes and silently slipped away.

Perhaps it was just coincidence that Muffin lived until the very day I regained the use of my legs. After all, veterinary prognoses in canine cancer cases are, at best, informed guesses. He may well have survived those long six months regardless. But I'm convinced Muffin felt it was his duty to make sure I was going to be okay, to be there for me as I had been for him. And until that day when he saw me walk and sensed my optimistic state of mind, he simply couldn't leave me.

The bond between human and canine can be as strong as any human-to-human bond. And nowhere is that bond forged so deeply as when two hearts say to each other, *I'm here for you.*

A Perfect Ten

Leslie Bamford

"**M**eow!" Blackberry wails as I open yet another can of cat food. I dole out a serving of chicken and rice in gravy and put the plate down on his kitty placemat, holding my breath as he approaches the food. Will he finally eat? It is his favourite flavour, always a hit no matter how finicky he is feeling.

Blackberry sniffs the food, takes one lick, then backs away. "Meow!" he wails again, looking up at me with round yellow eyes.

"What's wrong with you? Why won't you eat?" I say, looking at the ten cans of open cat food that line the kitchen counter.

Finicky is one thing—this is something more.

I call the vet for an appointment. Then I go downstairs to inspect the litter box. A clump of litter indicates that Blackberry is at least still peeing. But there is no poo in the box. There hasn't been any for days. I walk slowly back upstairs.

"I am supposed to be on sick leave this week," I say to Blackberry, who lies on his side in the hallway, a heap of black fur. "But now it's all about you, isn't it?"

Blackberry raises his head off the floor at the sound of my voice, then closes his eyes halfway, a look of despair on his face. I hate to see him like this, his usually sweet personality shut down by something he can't explain to me. No more kisses when I come home and pick him up to say hello. No more nose nips in the morning when I wake up. No more purring.

Summer wasn't supposed to be like this. My husband Bob and I were planning to spend our time around big water, something Bob's soul requires regularly. We were planning to go to Midland for a week, and then move on to Kingston for another week so Bob could get his annual fix of looking at boats in marinas.

I love the water myself. I love the rhythm of the waves, the colours that are always changing, the sun glinting off white hulls in the distance. I love swimming in Lake Huron and listening to the sound of the surf as the sun sets in a ball of orange on the horizon. For me, big water is soothing and regenerating. But however much I love it, Bob loves it even more. He is drawn to water like a sandpiper to a shoreline. Sometimes when I look into his eyes and see that yearning for the sea, I think I married Poseidon's son.

But vacation is on hold. The brochures for Midland and Kingston lie on the coffee table, unopened. I have been sick since June with fatigue and recurring low-grade fevers. I worked through my symptoms for several weeks, as if denial would make them go away. But I felt continually worse, and finally went to the doctor for blood tests. They came back more than fine—apparently I have the blood work of a twenty-five-year old Olympian athlete. My kidneys are fine, my liver is fine, my thyroid is fine. I have normal blood sugar levels, low cholesterol, and even low blood pressure. "Must be post-viral syndrome," my doctor said. "Rest is the only cure." He wrote me a note for a week of sick leave.

"Some rest this is," I mutter as I sweep the cat food cans off the kitchen counter into the garbage bin.

A few hours later, Bob and I drive Blackberry to the vet where he has x-rays and blood tests. When the vet calls later, there is good news and bad news. The bad news is the vet doesn't know what is wrong with Blackberry. The good news is his blood tests show no diabetes. His liver is fine and his kidneys are functioning better than they have in years. But why won't he eat or poo?

The vet doesn't know. ·

The next day there is a torrential downpour. The rainwater comes up over the curbs of our street, the storm drains unable to keep up. Soon there is water in the basement. I spend two hours with the Shop-Vac, keeping the flood at bay. While I vacuum, my ears ringing from the roar, I contemplate my life. When I dreamed of summer in the dark days of last winter, I pictured something completely different. We were going to travel, write, and golf. Why am I always getting blindsided by uninvited threshold guardians? I like it so much better when things work out the way I plan. I am tempted to lie down on the floor, kicking and screaming like a little kid. Instead, I take a deep breath and keep on vacuuming.

Once the flood has subsided, I go upstairs and, one by one, open five more cans of food for Blackberry. He eats one bite of can number five, then walks away, meowing pitifully. I go down to the basement and check the litter box. Again, no poo. I put the harness on Blackberry, inviting him to go out in the garden, usually his favourite activity. He lies at the top of the steps, head down, not moving. The only way to get him outside is to carry him. He perks up a bit, then slumps on the grass where he lies until I carry him indoors again.

I try to escape the stress by picking up the book I was reading before my illness began. *By the Grace of the Sea*, the story of a woman who singlehandedly sailed around the world on a poorly equipped boat, is a tale of near-death experiences. The book distracts me for a while, until Blackberry's meows from the kitchen interrupt. I hurry in and offer him a special kibble treat, which he normally loves. He takes it in his mouth, and I think he is finally eating. But then he spits out the treat and lies down in the middle of the floor with his ears back. My pats do not comfort him.

The next day, Bob and I take Blackberry back to the vet for more tests. Nothing conclusive comes of this except the bill, which is now over $500, the price of five nights in a motel in Midland.

That evening, my fever spikes, and I collapse in front of the TV to watch the Beijing Olympics. So far, Canada wins no medals. We seem to

Blackberry and me.

have a national affinity for being fourth. Not that fourth in the world is bad—it's fantastic. But the way the Olympic Games are set up, fourth is disappointing to many athletes and to most of the nation, particularly the reporters, if you read the papers.

Somehow my lack of energy, our inability to help Blackberry, and seeing our finest athletes *just* miss the podium all meld together, leaving me feeling powerless and despondent. As I watch, I feel a particular affinity for the hurdlers. Their sport is like my life: something is always in the way.

"Want to go for a bike ride?" asks Bob the next morning. He has recently purchased a Thule bike rack for the car and hopes to take our mountain bikes somewhere interesting for regular rides, now that we can't go to Midland or Kingston. By interesting, he means somewhere around water.

"The doctor says I'm supposed to rest," I say.

"Of course, we should stay home," he replies, trying to sound like he means it. But his voice is an auditory version of Blackberry's face, full of sadness.

Two despondent loved ones in the house at one time is more than I can bear. "I could go for a short ride," I say, wanting to see him smile again.

We drive to Hamilton and ride along the harbour through parks that wind around several marinas. Lake Ontario gleams azure in the sunshine. The trail is lined with wildflowers, in glorious yellows and purples. Swans and gulls swim near the tiny islands in the bay, joined by cormorants who sit on the rocks and spread out their wings, drying them in the breeze. Thanks to Bob, my gloom lifts for a while. Then I start getting tired, and I start worrying about Blackberry again.

"We really should get home," I say after a two-hour ride. Bob agrees. I sleep in the car while he drives. Back at the house, Blackberry is lying in the hall where we left him. I run down the basement stairs to see if he has been in the box. The litter looks clean but I dig around with the scoop, hoping to find something. Nothing.

I come back upstairs. "He hasn't eaten or pooed all week," I say, unnecessarily, to Bob.

"We have to take the poor guy back to the vet tomorrow," Bob says. He looks as worried as I am.

That night it pours again. More water comes into the basement. This time Bob brings me a glass of wine while I work with the Shop-Vac and he tries to figure out exactly where the water is coming in. Then we collapse in front of the TV. Canada still wins no medals, but we watch in awe as Michael Phelps wins another gold in the pool.

I hear another clap of thunder and wonder if we are in for more rain. Images of Phelps swimming his next race in our basement flit through my mind. Just then, Bob announces that he is going to tear the panelling off the wall in the front room tomorrow and find the damnable leak once and for all. This means emptying two large cabinets full of things we haven't used for years and moving them out of the way.

That will be my job.

The next morning, we take the cat back to the vet. Blackberry sits on my lap, trembling and grumbling, as Bob drives. He'll spend the day at the vet's, where he'll have an enema, in case he is blocked internally, though the x-rays don't show anything of this nature. As the vet carries Blackberry out of the examination room to the treatment room, the cat looks ahead at what is to come, not back at us. He is braver than I am. Tears fill my eyes as I wonder if this is the end of the trail for Blackberry. Who knows what is really wrong with him? Before we leave, the vet promises to phone in two hours.

I pass the time at the house vacuuming. Blackberry hates the vacuum, so by doing the vacuuming while he is out, I can spare him the trauma of hiding from the hateful machine. Two hours pass. Two hours and ten minutes. Two hours and thirty minutes. The vacuuming long done, I pace the house, willing the phone to ring, my chest tight with worry.

"I thought you were supposed to rest," Bob says as I pace past the door of his home office, where he has been distracting himself by looking at expensive boats for sale in faraway places.

"Fat chance of that!" I say. Just then, the phone rings. Seeing the vet's number on call display, I answer quickly, my heart in my mouth. What has he found? A tumour? A ruptured bowel?

But there is good news. The vet reports that an enema was not required. Turns out Blackberry had blocked anal glands and the vet "expressed" them, whereupon Blackberry's bowels moved twice in quick succession. The vet says he thinks this was the problem all along.

"You can pick him up again in an hour. He should be fine now, with all systems functioning," he says, sounding relieved.

When we arrive at the clinic, we find Blackberry sitting in the very back of a dark cage. He shrinks away from us, staying out of reach. The vet's assistant has to crawl into the cage to pull him out. Bob puts the harness on the cat and takes him to the waiting room while I pay yet another bill.

We are now paying with Kingston hotel money.

As I wait for my debit card transaction to be processed, a young couple comes into the waiting room with a large bulldog, unleashed, following behind. The bulldog takes one look around the waiting room and spies the only thing of interest—Blackberry, who is lying beside Bob on the bench. The dog lunges at Blackberry, who hisses, sending the brute on a run around the waiting room. As the vet yells to the couple to leash their dog, the bulldog races back to Blackberry, confronting the cat with at least ninety pounds of muscle and out-of-control energy. Bob reaches down, about to scoop Blackberry up out of danger, but there isn't time— instead, Blackberry whacks the dog on the head with one paw. The huge dog sinks down on the floor in a pose of submission, unhurt but cowed by an eighteen-pound feline with no front claws. In fact, Blackberry is so confident he has not felt it necessary even to rise to his haunches or puff up his fur. Instead, he has won the match with a single blow. It is an Olympic gold performance.

That night, Blackberry eats a small meal. We pour a couple of glasses of wine to celebrate and watch the Olympics again. Still no medals for Canada. But another gold for the amazing Phelps.

The next day, Bob tackles the panelling in the basement and finds a long crack in the foundation of the house. No wonder the threshold guardians got in.

By nightfall, there is still no kitty excrement in the box. What if the vet missed something? What if Blackberry isn't really better?

The next day, Blackberry eats two small meals, but still produces nothing.

As I sift the litter box again on the third day and find nothing, I feel myself becoming unglued. Waiting for a week for a cat to have a bowel movement is not my idea of rest and recuperation. It's like *Waiting for Godot*, only more excruciating. I think of rewriting Beckett's classic and calling it *Waiting for Godot to Have a Shit*. Then I shake my head. I am really losing it.

"Want to go for another bike ride?" says Bob.

"Sure, why not. I'm not resting anyway. Maybe Blackberry is waiting for us to go out to use the box."

We drive to Burlington and bike along the waterfront. Today, Lake Ontario is a mixture of navy and cerulean with small whitecaps under a sky billowing with puffy white clouds. A few sailboats pass close by, and I can see a trawler in the distance. We bike twenty kilometres, stopping for a beer at a watering hole along the way. It feels good to move, to pedal, to push myself. I feel almost athletic, despite the virus. Perhaps it's not an Olympic performance, but I have energy, and we both smile in the sunshine, trying to breathe life back into our stressed-out bodies.

On the way home, I think about Blackberry. He is brave in a crisis, and when he is sick, he suffers mostly in silence except for some yowling at mealtimes. I could learn a lot from him. I am often fearful, and I have a tendency to complain. I call it venting. Bob calls it ranting.

Back in the car, Bob drives home while I sleep through my spiking fever. At home, I am the first out of the car. I unlock the back door and open it. Blackberry is right inside the door, waiting. I pick him up and he begins to nibble on my chin, making kissing noises. I kiss him back. He nips my nose gently and purrs. I put him down and almost run down the basement stairs to the laundry room. Rounding the corner, I look into the litter box. This time, there is a clump of something brown in the middle. It's the most beautiful sight of my week: a pile of healthy cat poo.

Once the litter box is cleaned and Blackberry has eaten a serving from the first can I offer him, Bob and I open a bottle of French champagne that we were saving for a special occasion and stand in the kitchen beaming at each other, toasting the wonder of kitty bowel movements.

"Here's to Blackberry and his Olympic litter-box performance," I say, smiling at Bob.

"What did the vet call that treatment?" Bob asks.

"Expressing his anal glands."

"Here's to expression, anal or otherwise. Time to get back to writing," says Bob, eyes twinkling. We clink our glasses.

That evening, we watch the Olympics again, sitting side by side on the futon in the rec room while Blackberry snoozes on his favourite recliner, the one with the old ObusForme on the seat, which suits the contours of his bulky body. Michael Phelps continues to win medals while Canada does not. But there is no more gloom weighing on my heart. The world is full of bright colours again, the Olympic athletes stunning to watch, whatever country they come from. I feel myself begin to relax. Perhaps the threshold guardians are finally loosening their grip.

The next day, Canada wins gold, silver, and bronze. The day after that, more medals. Suddenly, Canada has thirteen medals. And there are still many more of our athletes who have yet to compete.

Vacation is over now. It didn't turn out as planned. But the leak in the basement has been sealed. The vet bills have been paid. Blackberry is feeling well again, and I am getting my energy back. Bob's soul has been replenished by waterfront bike rides. In the meantime, I learned a lot about being in the moment, about patience and acceptance, about giving up control and going with the flow. Or lack of flow, depending on how you look at it.

Tonight I pick up *By the Grace of the Sea* again. I want to learn more about courage. It seems to be required, whether you sail around the world or stay home. I open the book and start reading the first chapter again: "I recognized that life happens best on the days when I didn't know what to expect."

Looking at it that way, our summer has been a perfect ten.

THE RABBIT KING

K. BANNERMAN

When I first spied Renny, locked in a lonely cage at the back of a pet store, the prospect of owning a rabbit was the furthest thing from my mind.

My husband and I had stopped in at the store to admire the tropical fish when I spied a small cage, half hidden behind sacks of dog food. Inside the cage was a brown-and-white lop-eared rabbit hunched over his food bowl with a depressed dullness in his chocolate eyes. He ignored me as I crouched next to him. The crime that warranted his solitary confinement was nothing less than the felony of growing old—a new shipment of spring bunnies had arrived. The adult lop-eared rabbit, the last of his litter, had been moved aside. Someone had taped a handwritten sign to his cage that read FIVE BUCKS.

I paid for him, brought him home, and let him out to stretch his stubby legs. He immediately raced around the apartment, leaping in the air with glee, and thanked me for the open space by politely using the litter box I'd bought him.

We named him Renny, and within a week he had settled into his new, quiet life as a house-bunny. He explored the corners of our apartment, nibbled on strawberries, and slept on a cushion on the floor.

Renny demanded attention by bumping his nose against my toes. When pleased, he made a curious buzzing sound, halfway between snorting and purring. He also developed a strange loyalty towards my right foot, and would jealously protect it from my left. When I stood in the kitchen, he would hop in a tight circle around my right foot, and when I sat down, if my left foot got too close, he would push it away with his nose. Crossing my ankles was impossible.

Renny enjoyed comfort, but he was neither delicate nor shy. He was bold, brash, and stubborn. As weeks passed, it became clear that Renny ruled our apartment; he never hid from strangers, and he would jump onto the couch, then onto the top of its back, to better survey his territory. This was his favourite place to recline, and when guests sat on our couch, he would snuggle along their shoulders like an affectionate, buzzing fur stole.

But Renny never bit or kicked or scratched. If he felt slighted, he preferred to use guilt, and would sit with his back to me in the greatest disdain. He denied me his love until, magnanimous, he allowed me to grace his presence again.

He feared nothing, neither vacuum nor open doors nor dogs. When my husband and I adopted a Great Dane, Renny was quick to make clear his station in life: King of the Living Room. He gave the dog's paws a haughty sniff, gamboled between its lanky legs, and promptly began bumping his head against its ankles in a demand for adoration. When the requested affection was not forthcoming, Renny sat in a huff in the corner, his back to the confused canine.

One morning, I discovered a gelatinous lump on Renny's jaw. My husband and I took him to the neighbourhood veterinarian, but she told us it was nothing serious: a spider bite, perhaps, or an allergic reaction. Given time, it would disappear. "And if it doesn't," she said with a shrug, "Well, it's just a rabbit."

We waited for the swelling to disappear, for the allergic reaction to run its course, but it soon became clear that the situation was getting worse. The lump swelled to the size of a golf ball, and Renny's face was stretched into a grotesque parody of its previous cuteness. He refused

Renny.

to eat anything but his favourite foods—bananas and oats—and he cowered in the corner, shivering and miserable. His weight melted away. His bones protruded through his matted fur. His lop ears hung huge and limp against his misshapen head. We asked friends, trolled through books, and searched the Internet, but found no information about his ailment.

At last, the lump cracked and oozed a custard-like pus. Now desperate, we decided to remove the abscess ourselves, so, with the experience of our rural childhoods and a book on bunny anatomy, we drained the pustule and cleaned out the hollow it had formed. Tears coursed down my cheeks as I hugged Renny close. He was too weak to move and lay in my arms like a boneless rag doll, his face distended.

For days we watched, waited, and monitored any change in his position or breathing. We tended his every need, brought him a mash of bananas and strawberries, morbidly sure that each day was his last. Then, slowly, he crept to his food and water of his own accord. His flesh began to knit itself together. One morning, as I sat on the floor reading by his side, Renny bumped his head against my right foot again, demanding love.

Many years later, while taking a course on equine biology, I recognized the symptoms of *Streptococcus equi* as those that Renny had suffered. After class, I pulled aside my professor.

"Yep, rabbits can get *Streptococcus,*" he replied. "It's called 'Snuffles.'"

I told him of our frantic treatment, wringing my hands, worried that he would deem me to be barbaric and cruel.

Instead, he gave an efficient nod. "Well done," he said. "They often die from Snuffles. How long ago was this?"

"Eight years," I replied.

"And how long did the little guy live afterwards?"

I blinked, confused that he'd consign Renny to the grave.

"Oh, he's still alive," I replied, which earned me a surprised look in return.

Ten years have passed since I found Renny alone in the back of a pet store. He no longer jumps on the couch, preferring now to be placed there, and his lips have an Elvis-like snarl from the scarring on the inside of his jaw, but otherwise he's as spry and tenacious as ever. He joins us on vacation, lounges in the backyard when I garden, and cuddles close to my right foot when I sit typing at the computer. He continues to rule the dog, who cowers close to the carpet trying to look as small as possible whenever the Rabbit King hops by. Renny still buzzes happily when lavished with adoring attention, as most of us probably do.

I suppose he's a testament to the benefits of a healthy diet, lots of exercise, and minimal stress, but I wonder too if his longevity is a reflection of his determined will. Renny refuses to believe that he's at the bottom of the food chain, and he will never be subservient to anyone or anything. Renny simply turns his back on death and ignores it.

OLD ONE-EYE

PAUL BEINGESSNER

As love stories so often do, this one began in springtime. I never noticed him at first. He wasn't the type who stood out from the crowd. Content to lead the irresponsible life of the young, he wandered aimless until fate struck him a cruel blow.

I never actually saw the crime, but I can imagine how it happened. He may have bumped into one of the others in a careless moment. Perhaps he merely absorbed the unchannelled rage of a crowd hungry for stimulation. There is a viciousness about a crowd that you'll seldom find in an individual. A demented individual, perhaps, might act out his savage fantasy alone, in secret. But the most average of creatures, normal, respectable in all ways, is quite capable of acting, as part of a mob, in ways that would bring him feelings of revulsion and horror were he to contemplate committing the same act in solitude.

It was some time before I noticed the missing eye. With two hundred chickens running around the farmyard, it's not surprising that he could escape my attention. But a rooster with a missing eye is a target for every other rooster out to prove his masculinity.

The pile of flapping chickens in the corner was the first sign. At the bottom of such a pile, you will always find some hopeless victim. With this foreknowledge, I waded into the melee, flinging roosters aside, administering a few well-placed boots to little chicken derrières. He looked up at me in surprised relief and scurried away. As he ran, I noticed a flash of opaqueness on the right side of his head.

Chickens are not gifted with large brains—or so is the popularly held belief. Indeed, visual observation of a chicken will reveal a head far too small for its oversized body, a reminder of the sad plight of the dinosaur. That small cranium must carry all the instincts for survival and reproduction. Could there possibly be room for complex thoughts or deeper emotions? Observation of the activities of a flock of chickens would not lead one to think so. If left to roam freely, a chicken spends its time searching out and consuming food, dust-bathing, quietly roosting, and occasionally running madly across the yard toward the chicken house, squawking wildly, for no apparent reason whatsoever. A chicken whim, perhaps.

The monotony of this life is relieved occasionally when a group of chickens spots a weakness in one of their fellow creatures. A small scratch, a drop of blood, a few missing feathers, or a slight limp will arouse a primeval sort of rage in a chicken flock. En masse they will attack, and if the hapless victim can't escape by running or finding a place to hide, he or she will be reduced to a small beaten clump of feathers and cannibalistically consumed.

Raising chickens is not a job for the faint-hearted.

If you are someone who believes in the nobility and gentleness of nature, you may be tempted to write off this behaviour as the result of man's intervention in the evolution of chickens—the unnatural rearing practices, the genetic selection that undermines the laws of Darwin. I must remind you, however, that humans select for manageability, for gentleness, not for self-destructive behaviour. And a free-ranging chicken displays these characteristics no less than a chicken confined to a pen. And while on one hand I cannot understand why a creature would display such cruelty toward its own kind, I am struck by the uncanny resemblance this type of chicken behaviour bears to a group of children on a school playground.

I will, in fact, contend that chicken comportment is akin to the basest type of behaviour humankind is capable of. The activities of a flock of roosters consorting with a group of hens brings to mind visions of Attila the Hun's men stumbling across a harem. Attila would have blushed at the rooster's enthusiasm for his game.

I've raised quite a few chickens over the years. From tiny, fragile chicks to fledglings with all the grace of gawky, pimpled teenage boys to mature, mindless fowl. When my kids were small, they would search the white flock for a sign of individuality, a mark that would distinguish one chicken from another. On discerning a slight variation of colour in the feathering, they would immediately christen the chosen bird with a name and set out to develop a personality for it. "See how Rusty looks at me, Daddy?" The bird would be picked up, squeezed, and petted for a while until pinfeathers overwhelmed his downy cuteness. He was then forgotten and gradually blended in with the flock as full feathering occurred.

I've tried to recognize some spark of individuality in adult chickens. Tried with the sincerity of a druid wanting to believe in and appreciate the essential equality of all life, the creaturehood of all who walk and crawl. Nope. "All you guys look the same," said the bigot.

But *he* was different.

The missing eye had healed completely over by the day I intervened to protect him. The hundred hens and hundred roosters that roamed the yard were coming to maturity. The roosters' combs were beginning to grow, and they were developing that awful arrogance that produced the word *cocky*. (The resemblance to teenage boys was unmistakable.) The hens were beginning to look maternal, filling out, preparing for the onset of the never-ending but totally unnatural flow of eggs that would begin at their twentieth week.

Old One-Eye (for so I named him, in a flash of clarity and insight that occurs only rarely in one's life) was definitely different. For one thing, he had already survived the blinding blow and the daily abuse that his imperfection brought him. For another, although he was a rooster, he never developed the large red comb of his roost-mates. Just as it is with humans, not all roosters are equally endowed. But Old One-Eye had no comb at all.

He grew large enough; his long legs were probably the reason he made it to adulthood. But he had none of the aggressive nature of the other roosters, none of the powerful, primeval sexual urges, none of the strutting arrogance. It seemed that his manliness had been removed along with the eye that so offended the one who had plucked it out.

I began to watch for him as I crossed the yard, did chores, or worked at the never-ending task of repairing senescent machinery. He did his best to stay away from the crowd but would occasionally forget himself in his cyclopean pursuit of an insect, venturing close enough to another rooster to be recognized for the invalid target that he was. Then the flight was on as he tore across the yard, squawking in terror. This bit of self-defeating behaviour only served to attract more pursuers. On those occasions when he was cornered, unable to escape, I'd rush to the rescue, all the while cursing chickens' inhumanity to chicken.

As I vanquished the aggressors with lumps of dirt and steel-toed persuasion, Old One-Eye would right himself, fix me momentarily with a beady-eyed stare, and scurry away to safety. Mere seconds later, all was forgotten as the chickens returned to their hunt-and-peck existence and I returned to my work. I never thought much about these incidents. When you raise chickens, rescuing the weak and lame is a common occurrence. One day, however, shocked me out of the stupefaction of the daily routine and changed my image of chickens forever.

I came out of the house and was crossing the yard without thought or care. A shrill squawk broke through my inattention, and I looked up to see a tall white chicken running for his life. Three maniacal roosters, unmistakably part of the chicken mafia that ruled the yard, were in hot pursuit. Without hesitation, Old One-Eye ran straight toward me and came to a breathless halt, two inches from the scuffed steel toe of my workboot.

For a moment or two, his legs continued to pump up and down as he ran on the spot. His tormentors practically crashed into us, so single-minded were they. A sharp word from me and they scattered, some vague memory of a swift kick resurrected briefly in their vestigial brains.

Old One-Eye continued to stand by me for a few minutes until, assured that his attackers had dispersed, he too ambled away, leaving me dumbfounded. My rooster had reasoned. He had related. He had recognized me as his protector. He was more than a ball of feathers, more than a gizzard with legs. The barrier between us had been shattered once and for all.

Many times during that summer he sought me out as his bodyguard. He would lurk in the trees until I entered the yard, then rush from his hidden spot to stand by me. Other farmers may have had a faithful dog, a loving cat. I had Old One-Eye.

As the summer progressed, the other ninety-nine roosters became more and more obnoxious. The point came, as it always does, when the attacks on the hens became so frequent and so violent that they had to be stopped. And so the roosters were confined to a small fenced pen to finish their short lives growing fat on grain and grumbling half-heartedly about their lot.

Except, of course, for Old One-Eye. These were his glory days. He soon realized that he was entirely safe from the mob. He and the hundred pullets were free to roam, unscathed by the venom of the roosters who stomped continually along the fence, occasionally voicing their frustrated lustful intentions. At night, Old One-Eye would retire to the henhouse to roost alongside the young hens, serene and content. He didn't, however, develop any of the passions of his more able brethren. That part of him seemed forever lost, but he carried himself with a newfound dignity.

As they approached nine months of age, the pullets began to lay. The first small eggs appeared in the henhouse, but before long they were turning up everywhere, and my kids had the pleasure of a daily egg hunt.

Now I began to close the henhouse door at night after all the chickens were safely inside. In the morning, the pullets were unable to leave, and so they searched out and began to lay in the rows of wooden boxes provided for that purpose.

By early afternoon, the majority of the eggs had been laid and the door was opened. The pullets quickly learned the sound of the snap being undone and would rush out in a frantic disorganized charge, eager to make up for lost time. The last to leave the henhouse was usually Old One-Eye. He would wait somewhat impatiently on the roost till the hens had cleared away. He never quite trusted them, and probably with good reason, since hens carry much of the aggressive nature of roosters, lacking only the overpowering sexual instinct. His lack of ease among the hens meant he spent most of the daylight hours perched on the roost. Release for him meant freedom and a sense of safety.

His second unusual act occurred after the henhouse routine had been established for about two weeks. In the forenoon I would collect the eggs several times. This was largely to prevent the hens from developing the habit of eating eggs. If an egg broke during the laying (a careless hen will sometimes stand while the egg drops), it would immediately be consumed, the pecking starting a chain reaction among the other eggs in the nest, resulting in the loss of some and the fouling of all with yolk.

On the memorable morning, I was searching the lower nests, bent over at the waist, my back to the roosts some ten feet away. A great flapping noise suddenly erupted behind me. I was about to turn and investigate when I was staggered somewhat as the five-pound rooster made a perfect two-point landing on the horizontal plane that my back presented.

Now, to fly ten feet is no particular achievement for a chicken. But to fly ten feet from a standing start on a roost about four feet from the floor, in a chicken house with barely six feet in height inside, and to land exactly on target, negotiating all this guided only by a single eye—that has to be the chicken equivalent of William Tell shooting the apple off his son's head.

His intent was unmistakable. Remaining hunched over, I lurched my way to the door, lifted the hook, and opened it. Old One-Eye never moved. I shuffled outside and, with a sort of a shrug, urged him off my back. He hopped to the ground and, without a backward glance, headed off to patrol his territory.

He did this twice more over the next two weeks, each incident a carbon copy of the first. I will leave you to draw your own conclusions. The actions of Old One-Eye spoke more clearly than any words I could clumsily impart. Trust, loyalty, courage. That mutilated rooster embodied them all.

I finally learned to open the door when I first came in the morning, to stand by it, and wait for a moment or so. While I carefully kept errant hens at bay, Old One-Eye would gracefully hop from the roost and trot over to the door, stealing four or five hours of freedom that the hens never saw.

Eventually, the roosters reached their full-grown size, and it was time to allow them to serve the greater good. My father came from Regina the evening before, and we prepared the truck and the chicken crates for the morning trip to the poultry processing plant at Weyburn.

We rose well before daylight, and with the truck parked by the door to the roosters' house, we began the task of grabbing the unsuspecting birds from their perches and stuffing them in the crates. While my father stayed outside, keeping the door shut and simultaneously holding the lid on the chicken crate, I groped my way along the roosts, clutching scaly legs and flipping the birds upside down. When I had collected four or five birds, I made my way to the door and kicked it lightly to indicate I was ready. When my father opened the door, I handed the birds to him, one at a time, waiting as he pushed each one into the crate. He counted as we did this, until each crate reached its capacity. He then pushed the centre board back on each crate into place and secured it with a single nail.

The job was quickly done, and as my dad began to close the last crate, I stopped him. "Wait a minute, there's one more."

I jogged over to the henhouse and emerged, carrying a tall white rooster. Not in the traditional head-down fashion, suspended by his feet, but upright in my arms. Old One-Eye showed no sign of concern.

"Are you going to take *him?*" my father asked, a touch of surprise in his quiet voice.

"Of course." A trace of indignation crept into my words. "I don't need a chicken for a pet."

My father stood, wordless, for a moment.

"I'll just take him in the front with us," I said. My father nodded silently, his face flooded with sympathy and understanding. He turned and walked around the corner of the truck, heading for the driver's door.

When Dad was out of sight, I gave Old One-Eye a pat. Then I stuffed him into the crate with the last of the roosters, secured it with a single tap on the nail, laid the hammer on the floor of the truck box, and went to join Dad in the cab.

Mad King Grover

Andrew Boden

The miserable years began when we started keeping our grey-black beast, Grover Covington Cat, inside after his third birthday. Grover had fought every cat in our neighbourhood and often appeared on our doorstep with his fur bloodied and his skin torn open on gleaming muscle. I found the penultimate wound on his breast and inside it a marble-sized abscess that oozed stinking pus. We spent the next two weeks flushing saline through the drain in the wound and squirting yellow antibiotic liquid into his mouth. As always, fools that we were, we rewarded Grover's return to health with an open front door. He returned a few hours later, his fur bloodied from a new chest injury.

"The bugger is staying inside," I said to my wife at the vet's office. We'd paid forty dollars for Grover and spent another two thousand on vet bills to repeatedly patch him up. We'd forked out as much on our plebeian puss as we might have outright for an exotic breed renowned for Gandhian non-violence.

"Your cat is the aggressor," the vet said. "See the scratches all over his face and chest? He's not the one running away."

My wife insisted Grover's membership in feline fight club was my fault: like a Marine drill sergeant, I'd trained him to savour violence. I'd wrestled with him since he was a kitten, and our matches always ended with Grover grabbing my gloved hand between his two front paws, chomping on my thumb, and disemboweling my protected wrist with rapid kicks of his hind legs. You couldn't tell he was a bully from his voice, though. Like Mike Tyson's, it was a high-pitched squeak.

"My fault?" I replied. "Perhaps I should have taught him to wave placards and sign petitions?" I couldn't picture Doris Lessing wrestling with her cat, El Magnifico. I pictured her passing peaceful, contemplative moments with her magnificent beast, a dash of satori in each of them. No such moments of awakening for Grover and me—just me. I feared at best I'd heightened Grover's aggression and, at worst, taken a docile kitten and trained him to be the neighbourhood bully. Whatever my role, our only means to stave off early bankruptcy was to make him an inside cat. I'd never done this to a cat before; all the cats of my childhood had gone outside.

When we moved to a new basement suite, Grover was four years old and had so little joie de vivre he didn't even patrol the windows to watch his turf. So, with the approval of our new landlord, we bought him a friend: Jane Austen Kitty, a month-old calico kitten, from the Spay and Neuter Society. We feared bully-boy Grover might beat her up or worse, but to our delight when we introduced them, he began licking her. When he'd finished on one side, he flipped her over and licked her "dirty" side. Grover sometimes beat up "his Jane" as she grew older, but other than his constant desire to steal her food, Grover was content to live inside with his new mate.

Or so we thought.

I'd always feared we'd be forced to move because our cats would pee somewhere they shouldn't and our landlord, on a visit, would smell cat urine. Then would come his ultimatum—the cats go or you go. We found out one early January that one of our cats had no such fears. When my wife picked up the blue plastic sheet that went under the metal stand of our Christmas tree, we discovered that the carpet was sopping wet. At first we thought we'd overfilled the stand's bowl with water or it had leaked. No such

Grover.

luck. I put my nose to the floor, and the stink of urine made me gag. Why hadn't we smelled it earlier? How had the presents remained dry? We scrambled to clean it up. We knew Jane hadn't peed here—she was the most fastidious cat I'd ever met—and neither my wife nor I were offended enough by Christmas to piss on the tree. That left Grover and what we would come to know as his ever-emptying bladder of doom.

We presumed that something about the smell of this Christmas tree had offended Grover. Perhaps a raccoon had sprayed on its lower branches or a Rottweiler had lifted its legs against the trunk and this olfactory insult pissed Grover off. A week later, we found tobacco-yellow spots sprayed against the brilliant white wall near where the Christmas tree had stood. We thought that this was a leftover from the Christmas episode and sponged the wall and carpet and slipped back into pet-owning complacency.

When Grover sprays, it looks as if he is excited to see us. His tail is erect as a ship's mast, his head is up, his body shudders. The only difference is that when excited he meows at volume. Spraying is a silent affair—until he's caught. I can't remember which of us first saw him spraying against the wall we'd recently cleaned, but each time we caught him was as shocking and horrifying as the first. "Grover!" we'd yell, and he always darted away. I thought neutered males couldn't spray, but not so: they can still squirt urine to mark their territory and, while not as stinky as the un-neutered scent, it is just as offensive when done against a wall, sofa, or a shelf of books.

We had to keep our little problem hidden from our landlord. We patrolled that corner in the living room every day. Sometimes Grover wouldn't spray or pee for days or weeks and, just when we'd begin to relax, we would spot streaks of urine running down the wall or a puddle of urine below it. We tried various cleaning products to rid us of the stench and, thank God, we found enzyme cleaners, because they were the only solution that took the smell away. We grew obsessed about keeping the litter box clean lest Grover be offended and show his displeasure by peeing on the carpet. And each time we saw Grover go in his box, we praised him with "Good boy, Lord Groveses!" (after Ramses) and stroked him until he purred.

Upstairs, our landlord kept three cats: Oscar, Cuddles, and Angel. One day he announced that he'd put Oscar and Cuddles to sleep, though they were no more than four or five years old. They'd taken to peeing on his hockey bag after the birth of his son, and the odour so offended him he couldn't take it anymore. Angel lived outside and, soon after the death of her brother and sister, fled my landlord's house to live down the street—a detail my landlord's wife couldn't understand. I was terribly upset to lose Oscar and Cuddles. They were such friendly little cats, and I couldn't understand why our landlords didn't try to find homes for them. Yes, I'd raged about Grover's peeing—"I can't stand being ruled by that cat's bladder!"—and yes, I'd thought about having him put down, but I couldn't bring myself to kill him—not without great effort to find alternatives.

That our landlord had dispatched his cats so casually made us worry even more about Grover's peeing. But we had a clue to solving the great mystery of Grover's bladder: the hockey bag, I learned, had been stored in the downstairs room behind the wall Grover peed on. We didn't usually have access to that area because it was part of our landlord's suite.

But we had a good relationship with him and his wife and, when they went on holiday, they asked us to take care of their upstairs apartment. I went into that little storage room that bordered our living room, and the smell of stale cat urine made me gag. I washed the floors and wood paneling, because with the smell-through-walls superpower of cats, Grover suffered the smelly taunts of his rivals. Problem solved. Only a fool would end that last sentence without a question mark.

The urine-soaked room on the other side of our wall had seemed an obvious environmental cause, but the day after I cleaned it, Grover's MO changed. He started peeing and spraying everywhere. Time for the vet. We had Grover tested for diabetes. No, that wasn't it. The vet suggested Feliway, a concoction that mimicked the odour secreted by the scent glands in Grover's cheeks, to convince him all we owned belonged to King Grover. We sprayed our suite, which only seemed to stimulate Grover's bladder to record volumes of production. The vet suggested Valium.

"For whom?" I asked. "The cat or us?"

"Maybe both," he replied.

The Valium worked for a few weeks, and then, when it didn't anymore, the vet added an antidepressant, Amitryptyline. Success? It seemed that way until the fine summer day when Grover doused the lower shelf of a bookcase that held some books I'd inherited after my father died: several books on residential carpentry, the lost treasures of British Columbia, and a prized copy of *A History of Warfare* by Field-Marshal Montgomery. I now referred to Grover as my wife's cat, and to keep her cat alive, she struggled to clean my books. She wiped them with enzyme cleaner and left them in the sun to dry, whereupon Montgomery's book bloated up like a drowned corpse and burst its beautiful dust jacket. Grover had to go—if not by the needle of our vet, then with a death blow from the now thick and crooked spine of *Build Your Harvest Kitchen*. I tried to convince myself I was doing the right thing. I couldn't live with the smell of cat urine anymore. I couldn't watch helplessly as my books were destroyed. I couldn't live with the constant fear of being evicted. My wife insisted that I would *not* be killing her "Baby Grovey," and I feared we might part over our special-needs beast. But the stars shifted or the Fates changed their minds again, because as mysteriously as Grover's new pissing game had started, it stopped—for two blissful years. We had no idea why. We took Grover off the drugs and marvelled at how his deficiencies had revealed our own.

Grover was nearly ten when we bought our townhouse. We feared that the move would disturb him, and we braced ourselves for punishment by bladder. Nothing. Time for a third cat, *n'est-ce pas?* My wife decided on a purebred Maine Coon—a female, I insisted, because every male mammal I'd ever owned had been a supreme pain. When Isabelle of Wyndabbey arrived, she was six months old and, unlike Jane, refused to let Grover dominate her. Grover grew anxious over Isabelle's failure to cower before him, and we found puddles of urine again. Back to the vet.

"You got a third cat?" the vet said. At least he had the professional grace not to call us idiots to our faces. "Try the Valium again."

"You know the pharmacist laughs at us when we pick up Valium for our cat," I said.

"She should," my wife replied.

Grover's sense that he could no longer control his territory increased his anxiety. He now had three floors to control, a front and a backyard he could only watch other cats parade through, and a new female cat who mocked his rule. He couldn't fight Isabelle into deference, and he couldn't spray and pee everywhere. But, like Nikola Tesla, he pounced upon technological genius. I found him squatting over the heat vents in our living room and heard the tinkle of urine striking the metal ducts and running river-like into the depths of our natural gas furnace. I felt a flash of horror followed by a recognition of his brilliance. I chased him away and, sure enough, the furnace kicked in and Grover's *eau de groin*, his stamp of ownership over everything, filled every room in the house.

It took me two hours to clean the furnace and track the heat ventilation pipes through closets with the fall-on-my-knees hope that Grover's urine hadn't leaked onto two thousand dollars' worth of backpacks and tents.

"What a luxury a cat is," Doris Lessing once wrote. I wanted to write back: "Doris, Grover's medical chart on the vet's computer takes twenty seconds to scroll through from beginning to end. The total tab is over five thousand dollars. My furnace belches cat-urine fumes, and some of my Dad's beloved books can only be read if I wear a gas mask. I envy the cold will of a man I met at a sawmill who told me that he hated his wife's yappy chihuahua so much he shot it off a log with his twelve-gauge shotgun and hid the body in his septic tank."

I have a shotgun, don't I? Upstairs in the closet?

My wife joined me by the furnace. She'd found an article on the Web that advised pet owners that they could reduce a cat's anxiety by shrinking its territory to a size it could easily control.

"Like a pine box?" I asked.

We confined Grover to our master bedroom, which became a kind of retirement facility for elderly cats because Jane joined him soon after Isabelle began terrorizing her. When Grover turned twelve, he slimmed into a rickety thing. I concluded he wasn't long for this world and that I would be free at last of this albatross in cat disguise. But we took him to the vet and learned from a hundred-and-fifty-dollar blood test that he had hyperthyroidism and needed five milligrams of Tapazole a day to restore him to proper weight.

He looked robust again after a few weeks and even played a bit with his stuffed mouse. The vet said that his hyperthyroidism may have caused his pissing jags, but we had to keep him on Valium because as soon as we lowered the dose he peed and sprayed again. He even defied this causal relationship between drug and behaviour, for every couple of weeks we found his spray against the closet doors, or a puddle of urine on the linoleum in the ensuite, or a damp oval beside the nightstand. We placed a plastic tray beneath the closet door with a piece of rigid plastic sheeting propped to catch the spray so it drained onto the tray. We put a second cat box beside the nightstand. We closed the ensuite door during the day. We agonized.

On a cold winter morning this January, Grover snuggled up against me in bed. I stroked him and left my hand on his back to warm his spine. He purred and I scratched his point and he licked his front paw and then my fingers. I told my wife that I don't love Grover anymore and that I only keep him out of duty. One day in my dotage I will be a burden on my caregivers, and I wouldn't want to be euthanized because I howl at the twilit walls and can't control my bladder or my mind. I want to know that there are people for whom personal comfort and convenience are secondary to caring for a pissing, shitting, howling old man or woman or, yes, even a cat. I want to be one of those people.

APPLE-FLAVOURED MOOSE

SANDRA CHERNIAWSKY

Seven years ago, my husband, my daughter, and I unknowingly bought Ellie's home—a wild quarter section of land consisting of muskeg and transitional boreal forest with open field that backed onto four more quarters of bush. Sure, the mortgage papers said that after twenty years of regular payments the land and the trees would be ours, but what we didn't know was that this property had already been claimed.

It appeared empty when we arrived with our furniture and our dogs, but within a week we knew we were not alone. During that first winter, we blazed trails through the muskeg for cross-country skiing and snowmobiling. At the far reaches of our property, we found a network of animal tracks that told us our "uninhabited" land was a veritable Grand Central Station for countless grouse, deer, bobcats, black bears, coyotes, cougars, and many other wild creatures. We realized we had, in fact, taken up residence on land that was teeming with life, a property that was already home to many creatures we knew very little about.

It was during one of those forays that I first met the moose I eventually named Ellie. I was on foot that day with my three dogs and my house cat. The sun was shining warm on the snow, and overhead the ravens tracked our progress. We had just rounded a corner when we came face-to-face with Ellie and her calf. She stood no more than fifteen feet in front of me. I froze. She was at least six feet tall at her shoulders, her long face passive as she stared at us. She was magnificent. We eyed each other for a heartbeat, and then the dogs barked hysterically, and the cat clawed her way up my leg and perched on my shoulder, hissing. As the dogs rushed at Ellie, I did what any rational being would do: I turned and ran into the bushes, leaving the dogs and Ellie to their own devices. I knew better than to come near a mama moose and her baby. I also knew, from that day on, that I was an intruder on this land.

As the snow receded that spring, I made a horrible discovery. I was checking on spring's progress one afternoon when I came across the skeletal remains of a moose calf. It was quite small and was revealed only by the melting snow and the call of the ravens. I assumed the calf met its demise in early fall as most of the skeleton was still intact. It was the warming weather that had alerted the scavengers and informed me of Ellie's loss. I experienced profound sadness for the little animal and for Ellie. I wondered if she mourned as any parent would at the loss of a child. I knew it was the order of nature, but I couldn't help wondering what had happened and how Ellie had taken it.

When I mentioned my encounter with Ellie to the previous owner of our place, I learned that the elderly woman had taken a shine to Ellie and for years had provided her with fresh hay bales and pails of grain. She appreciated Ellie's gentle nature and marvelled anew each year at the privilege of meeting Ellie's calf. She respected this gentle giant and gave her the space she needed to rear her young and live a stress-free existence.

I, on the other hand, did not.

I moved into Ellie's territory and began trying to tame and tailor it to what I envisioned as a perfect acreage getaway. I landscaped the yard and moved earth, unwittingly killing trees and destroying countless habitats and homes along the way. Sure, I boasted to my friends and family that I was protecting the wildlife habitat by not deforesting the land surrounding my yard; meanwhile, I set about creating a pristine landscape free of offending creatures such as insects and ungulates. I planted flowers and vegetables that tantalized the deer, then set up sprinklers to keep them away. I grew berries that tempted the birds, and covered the plants with netting.

That first spring, I began planting trees—thousands of trees—for what I imagined would be a grand shelterbelt. I was ambitious. I lugged water until my arms were sore, and I nurtured each seedling as I would a child. I also planted my first apple tree and was soon rewarded with apple blossoms. I envisioned an orchard. By July, I had eleven small apples on my tree. Each was a perfect globe, growing bigger and sweeter in the summer sun. By September, the apples were a rosy colour, about the size of mandarin oranges. I cupped them in my palms, and my mouth would water at the thought of their crisp flesh. I couldn't wait.

Early that fall, Ellie returned with a new baby—long spindly legs, oversized nose, and soft liquid eyes. He was beautiful. Ellie was proud and protective, but I was able to get within a few metres of her calf for a closer look. By then she knew I wasn't a threat, but when she felt I'd come close enough, she nudged her calf deeper into the bush, and they disappeared.

One evening, Ellie strolled into the yard and ate every last apple. Even the two that had fallen to the ground in the later-summer windstorm. She came back in the dead of winter and ate the young tree down to a stick. There would be no more apple blossoms in the spring, and I would get no apples.

This meant war.

Since then, I have planted dozens of fruit trees—apples, plums, cherries—and since then, Ellie has come to collect her rent every fall. She approaches cautiously. For three or four nights, she scopes the place out, changing her point of entry, marking the differences in light and cover. When she's factored everything in, she waits for the cover of darkness and

Ellie and her calf.

makes her move, skirting the entire yard and coming in from the north, usually aiming for the apple trees first, then the cherries, and the plums for dessert.

The motion-activated light goes on, the dogs raise the alarm, and I come rushing out shouting threats and waving my arms frantically. I've even hurled a few pine cones in her direction. But the damage is already done. She's harvested my fruit.

I've tried dryer sheets, tinfoil, perfume, my own bedding, human urine, everything. Nothing deters her.

When Ellie wanders through the yard at midday, the dogs, Alex, Tia, and Bones, are like a flock of pesky mosquitoes. They bark, growl, dive in, attempt a nip, employ evasive maneuvers, and then dart back to the house for a cookie and a head scratch. Ellie looks at them with indignation and disgust and ignores them for as long as moosely possible, then strikes, stomping her hooves and even charging. She is not easily scared away.

One crisp January afternoon, I was standing outside watching the foray between moose and dogs, even tossing encouragements, when Ellie had had enough. She pawed the ground, lowered her massive head, and charged. I, being the brave soul that I am, ducked into the house, slamming the door. The dogs were on their own.

Through the kitchen window, the drama played. Tia, the brave little mutt she is, threw herself into Bones, bounced off Alex, and tore for the woods as fast as she could. Alex, our arthritic golden lab, tucked his tail firmly between his back legs and hightailed it straight for the back door. Bones, our young border collie, tripped over his front legs, did a three-point roll, found his feet, and ran toward Ellie. I could see realization dawning as all four legs began to backpedal. Clumps of leaves and dirt flew as he realized his mistake and a thin whine tore from his throat. I almost opened the door.

The ground shook under Ellie's hooves as she galloped toward the house, right on Bones's tail. She brought her front hooves up just as he found a burst of speed. He tore around the back of the house and disappeared. Ellie skidded to a halt just a few feet from the door, snorted, then sauntered back to the trees to continue feeding on the young branches of my saskatoon trees.

Since then, the dogs bark from a respectful distance when Ellie comes around. They take chase just for show and only after she decides to head back to the bush.

Just last winter, I was driving to town and I noticed Ellie alongside the road, peering over the fence into the ditch. Her calf lay dead there, probably having been struck by a vehicle on the road and thrown into the ditch by the impact. The body remained there for several days and Ellie stood by the fence throughout, never leaving her baby's side. She kept up her vigil even after Fish and Wildlife officers removed the body. It wasn't until nearly a week later that I noticed she had retreated into the forest to mourn in solitude.

It's been seven years since I first met Ellie, and I still haven't tasted the sweetness of my homegrown apples. I've planted many fruit trees over the years (seventeen, at last count) and put in countless hours of labour tending them, and I have yet to taste a plum or a cherry. Ellie comes like clockwork. She is still met with barking dogs, shouted threats, and fierce arm-waving. We've even resorted to rifle shots aimed at the moon. All to no avail.

Yet when the hunters come knocking, asking for permission to hunt on our land, I turn them away for the thrill of seeing Ellie and her new calf every summer and fall. I can't blame Ellie, after all. I moved into her territory, landscaped her living space, introduced three dogs, and refused to leave. I entice her into my yard every year with the promise of tender shoots and juicy fruit, and then I am offended when she eats them. She tolerates my barking dogs, my frantic arm-waving, my shouts and threats. In return, I tolerate her eating her fill of the fruits of my labour.

My neighbours tease me about my apple-flavoured moose. They laugh as they offer me moose steak with apple reduction. Moose stew, moose jerky, moose burgers.

Let them laugh. I have yet to taste moose meat, and I figure I garden here at my own risk. After all, Ellie was here first.

Wild Teachings: Walking with Bears, Wolves, and Ravens

Vivian Demuth

Like any story or work of art, it started with a mark: a giant footprint, much longer and wider than my own—large enough, in fact, to disturb the forest ranger I was with. "Come look at this," she said, trying to hide her agitation. "It's— It's a grizzly." Like many other people in the Grande Prairie area, she never walked in the woods without a firearm after having heard one too many bear stories, the deadly kind.

I was quite the opposite.

"Wow," I said as I placed my boot beside the bear's footprint. "Those are some toenails! Good to know there's still some old bears around here." I had recently worked as a bear warden in Banff National Park, and I'd had many a bear encounter. I had also worked two previous summers on a remote, fly-in mountain lookout. This was my first day on the job as a fire lookout at my new location, Nose Mountain, in the foothills of northwestern Alberta. To the west I could see the snow-capped peaks of the Rocky Mountain Divide, to the north, an undulating landscape of boreal forest, dusty roads, and industrial development near Grande Prairie.

My job, from May to September, was to watch for forest fires from a glass-windowed, six-foot-wide cupola perched on top of a sixty-foot steel tower. Using maps and a fire-finder's scope, I surveyed the forest in a 360-degree circle with a forty-kilometre radius.

If I saw any unusual smoke, I would send—with lightning speed and pens flying—a report to the local forestry office. In dry weather, when the fire hazard was extreme, I would spend about twelve hours a day in this snug cupola. But on rainy or snowy days, I kept warm in a cozy, propane-heated, one-bedroom cedar cabin equipped with another set of radios, a propane fridge and stove, a solar water bag for taking outdoor showers, and a double bed I shared with a friend's talkative cat who could sense lightning storms long before they hit the tower. I managed to get a couple of rain barrels added to the engine shed that housed a generator, giving me some extra water to haul over to my three-bed vegetable garden, where I grew Swiss chard, broccoli, lettuce, peas, carrots, and various herbs. It was amazing what one could grow on a small dirt patch with a little plastic and a frame. Not far from the garden was a helipad for firefighters' helicopters. There was also a weather station a short walk from the cabin, convenient for half-asleep, early-morning temperature readings to calculate the day's fire-hazard level. Sometimes, the cat and I wouldn't see any other humans for weeks at a time, depending on the condition of the deeply rutted and non-gravelled mountain roads. In the fall, the cat would go home to Grande Prairie, and I would wander, living in different communities in Canada and beyond.

I spent the next eighteen summers on Nose Mountain, and I came to know the many animals who made their homes there. I often saw ravens flying overhead, and I gradually came to recognize that they weren't indistinguishable ravens, but rather particular individuals in a particular flock that spent much of its time in the forest around the tower. They would sometimes fly low over the tower site, spooking the cat, or land on the cabin rooftop in the wee hours of the morning, spooking me. I would often attempt to imitate their caw, hoping to attract their attention, but they never seemed to acknowledge I was speaking to them. Eventually, I resigned myself to the fact that my attempts to communicate were not going to be rewarded.

When I arrived each May, seeing the giant grizzly's tracks wandering through the front yard of the tower site, sometimes in the sparkling snow, became a springtime rite of passage—*his* passage. The only other time I saw his signs was one early July morning when I walked over to check on my vegetable garden. As I approached my budding peas, I wondered why a section of the fishnet fence was sagging halfway down. The answer was in a paw print embedded between my young lettuce and carrot shoots. The elderly grizzly had wandered through one of my garden beds without damaging any plants, without ripping away the plastic solar frames, and without eating a single plant. So much for the myth of big, bad bears! But what exactly was he doing there? I chewed on this for a while until I remembered the female bear scat I had carefully hauled over to the garden for fertilizer the previous fall. Could it be that he danced around my garden carrots and bowed to sniff the sow's scat in the soil bed? That was my gut feeling. This bear's respectful attitude, and the fact that he completely avoided any contact with me, fed my notion that I was privileged to experience and live in the home of a very wise old bear.

I got to know another intelligent and perceptive bear, a female black bear. She and her two cubs hung around the fire tower for a week one summer to feed on fiery red bearberries. I was curious: how close would she allow me? One morning, the sow and her cubs fed within viewing distance of my front porch. I drank tea and watched them. Then I went to my cabin bedroom and retrieved a female grizzly bear skull that was given to me when I worked as a bear warden in Banff National Park. That grizzly bear had died when a tranquilizing dart penetrated her stomach and caused internal bleeding. As I sat back down on the porch with the skull in my lap, a pine tree, one of many trees in the yard, began swooshing and twirling noisily, despite the fact that there was only a faint breeze in the air. I froze, my gaze transfixed on the lone swirling pine tree, while the mother bear took a few steps towards it, then stood tall on her hinds legs to stare at the tree along with me. This seemed to last for about a minute and then the mama bear fell to the ground, again feasting on sweet berries, occasionally sniffing in the direction of my breathlessness.

Shortly after I first arrived at Nose Mountain, I saw what I thought were two people standing along the historic Hinton Trail that runs along the mountain ridge. I was surprised, and being alone, enthusiastically waved and yelled, "Hello!" But they turned and leapt into the bush. That's when I realized they were wolves. I would learn that two was the magic wolf number, that surprise was the name of their game, and that wolves would teach me to howl.

One fall, from the cabin porch, I saw a pair of wolves standing on the tower road. They appeared to be the same light-coloured ones I had seen on the ridge. I half-heartedly tried to call them with a poor imitation of a wolf howl. To my surprise, not only did they start trotting towards me, but four more wolves jumped out of the bush and joined the first two. I had a six-pack of wolves running in my direction, and I could hear the sound of their paws on the ice and their panting: *cha-chung, cha-chung, cha-chaung—ha, ha, ha.* I was ecstatic and quickly ran inside the cabin to grab my camera. As I returned, they stopped, then froze for an instant before leaping towards the side of the road and into the bush. Had they thought that I was one of them for an instant?

One evening, I had a bear *and* wolves at the tower cabin, although I didn't realize it at the time. I was awakened late one night by a strange, whiny howl from right in front of the tower cabin. The cat was standing on top of the bookcase, staring out the window, his eyes fixed on something outside. I wondered if it could be a couple of wolves mating. The strange howling continued. It was such an eerie sound that it frightened me, and I didn't look out. I couldn't have seen much in the darkness anyway. I murmured a few soothing words to the cat while I flicked on the generator switch. The howling sound, and other quieter sounds, slowly moved away from the noise of the engine, and eventually the cat and I went back to bed. The next morning, I found a muddy paw mark smudged on

A family of black bears, from the cabin window.

the screen door and a set of fresh young bear tracks amid a pack of wolf tracks. It had probably been a bear that had been whining at the front porch trying to elude the pack of wolves. I felt bad I hadn't had the courage to look out the front window to see what was going on and perhaps do something else for the bear.

I encountered a threat to the Nose Mountain bears that was meaner than wolves one morning when I went to dump some vegetable scraps at the end of the tower road. As I approached the tower road gate, I noticed a bright blue barrel lying on its side on the main Nose Mountain road. It stunk. When I investigated, I discovered it had slits along its sides and the bottom was carpeted with rotting pigs' feet. Some human animal was illegally baiting bears to make them easy targets for poachers. I kicked the foul barrel into the bush and got the Forestry Department to call Fish and Wildlife, but they were too short-staffed to respond. Eventually, a forest ranger came up to haul the barrel to the town dump, a two-hour drive away.

Later, I had another encounter on the tower road while I was again on my way to dump a bucket of food scraps. When I crested a rise in the road, I walked right into the wolf pack, all six of them. We all froze. I whispered, "Hello." Then the portable radio strapped onto my chest crackled with human voices. The two lead wolves jumped into the bush. I took a few steps forward. The radio crackled again, and two more wolves leapt into the bush. Finally, the last two wolves followed them. I walked cautiously past the spot where all six wolves had been, whispering niceties as I went: "Hello, wolves. Nice wolves. Everything's okay. It's just me." I never felt in danger, although many city people who have never experienced wolves have since told me I could have been killed. A few weeks later, a forest ranger called me on the radio and asked if I had been "taming wolves" because he had just seen the pack, an experience he had never had before.

The most difficult experience I've had at the tower was witnessing a helicopter crash on the slope of Nose Mountain while I was working in the fire tower cupola. I ran down to the scene and attempted to help, but my efforts to revive a Cree firefighter were in vain. I was left saddened and unsettled by this tragic event.

A few days after the crash, when I was feeling particularly lonely, I went for a hike. I was walking along the tower road when I heard a large flock of ravens flying toward me. I had been calling to these ravens for eighteen years without any response from them. This time, when I attempted to caw like a raven, not only did the ravens call back, but all sixteen of them landed in nearby spruce trees. There they sat quietly. I stopped and stood, awestruck. They had responded to me for the first time. I wondered if they had sensed my grief. The ravens' lofty presence in the trees lifted my spirits. I smiled for the first time in quite a while, thanked them, and bowed beneath them before leaving.

I write this sitting in a cramped apartment above a busy street in a city far from Nose Mountain. It's hard to hear myself think over the drone of city traffic, but I think about the bear skull and the pine tree. Placing the skull in the Y of a tree branch has become a fall ritual for me, the last thing I do each year before leaving the mountain for the season. I wonder about the rest of the Nose Mountain community I have come to know. Are the wolves being killed because they are "undesirable," mistakenly perceived as eating human hunters' prey or eliminating threatened species such as caribou? Will the possibility of windmills in this inappropriate mountain location knock out the ravens and other birds? How little healthy wildlife habitat will remain with new logging, oil rigs, and roads? A forest ranger told me she had seen giant grizzly bear tracks in the snow near the tower cabin last spring, a week before I started work there. Perhaps the old grizz I had come to know was still alive and, for some reason, was passing through the tower site earlier than usual. I have never filled out a wildlife-observation form for the Forestry department, like I used to when I worked as a park ranger. While walking on Nose Mountain, I have often had the desire to erase animal tracks to protect them from poachers. These days, I wonder if perhaps the fewer facts we know about animals, the better for them. We know where their habitats are and what their food sources are, and that's all we need to know to protect them. The Nose Mountain community is neither an eco"system" nor a set of "biosemiotic signs." It is made up of living beings, each with its own consciousness. To live with them and enable them to flourish requires political will and wisdom, not more information. Until we can acknowledge and respect the mystery of spirit in all living beings, non-human animals are better off left mostly alone. There are currently national and international efforts underway to give Nature legal rights to exist and thrive. I hope this work succeeds.

I used to think that my sightings of and encounters with animals were the result of luck or chance. I've now come to acknowledge and listen to my sixth sense, my animal sense, which perhaps has been amplified as a result of living alone in a relatively wild place. What gives me comfort from my teachings from animals is that I believe *they* can read *us*, and therein lies some possibility for their survival until humans become wiser and implement alternative ecological economic models.

In the meantime, as I sit in a white room, I imagine a dusting of snow on Nose Mountain as I listen with my heart to the unknown and surprising lessons of that threatened, but very alive, boreal community.

They'll Only Break Your Heart

Ruth Edgett

"**W**hat's the matter, Maggie?"

How can my magnificent dream-come-true horse be in so much pain? A week ago, she was all show-off and long legs, galloping away as usual toward her friends in the pasture. I had turned away laughing and looking forward to a vacation. I figured she knew she was getting a holiday, too. Today I've returned to this.

Maggie gives me only a deep, silent stare and dangles her right front foot, unwilling to take even one step.

I run a hand over each of her legs. The sore one is swollen and warm. I straighten up, stroke her silky black neck, and kiss her velvet nose. Then I hurry to find the stable manager.

"It must have happened yesterday afternoon before they came in for feeding," Chris says. "I had the barn vet out. He thinks it's a bowed tendon."

Take a breath. Okay. A bowed tendon isn't the end of the world. But I can't mess this up. I'll call Blair, my own vet, for a second opinion.

I will happily pay two vet bills; I will pay as many bills as it takes to make Maggie better, because she is not just a horse—she is a gift. Maggie represents my one chance at a late, great do-over. Because of her, my ordinary middle age has transformed into an extraordinary adventure in which crazy horses can be gentled and dreams don't die after all. It cannot end like this.

The year I turned twelve, I fell in love with horses. By the close of that summer, I knew I needed one of my own. I dreamed about it daily, until I could not imagine surviving until the next spring without a horse. When a neighbour asked my father to help him out by keeping one or two of his horses for the winter, my dream was so close to coming true I could taste it. But Dad said no. Like many Prince Edward Island farmers, he could barely afford to feed his own livestock, let alone someone else's.

"I farmed with horses all my life," he explained to me. "I'm done with them now." But he understood how I saw this as a tragically missed opportunity and shook his head sadly. "Don't fall in love with horses, Ruthie," he said. "They'll only break your heart."

He was right, of course, and the first break had already happened.

Broken-hearted or not, I survived the coming winter and many winters after that without a horse. It took twelve years before I was able to revive my dream by enrolling in riding lessons. By the time I had married, moved to Ontario, established a career, and become an experienced rider, I had been offered two chances to have a horse of my own. But there were always other priorities and, though it broke my heart each time, I'd had to turn them down.

Then, at the ripe old age of forty-two, I was given a third opportunity.

"You should think about buying Maggie," said Fay, my riding coach, one day.

"Yeah, right!" I answered, pulling a sweaty saddle from Baron, the dependable old gelding I'd been taking lessons on for years. By this time, I'd talked myself out of believing my childhood dream would ever come true. And even if I were looking to buy a horse, it would have to be something much more sedate than that crazy mare in the stall at the end of the aisle.

Even at twelve years old, Ubetcha Maggie was still marked by her short-lived racing career. She'd left the track at four, but her speed, her drop-of-a-hat explosiveness, and her bushels of attitude had stayed with her into her own middle age. She was a looker, though—I had to admit that. Maggie was as close to black as a thoroughbred can be and tall—sixteen hands—with a glossy coat, long graceful legs, and a full tail that reached all the way to the ground. She held her fine head high.

I'd come off enough horses enough times over the years to be inclined toward safety and security over flash. Yet, every time I came to the barn for lessons, there was Maggie, and there was Fay telling me she thought we'd make a great pair.

"She's really a sweetheart when you get to know her," Fay said. "She has a kind eye."

"Sure," I would think. "When she's not showing me the white of it!"

Finally, I agreed to try her for a month.

"Trust me," said Fay. "I'll coach you. You'll be fine."

Despite Maggie's quick starts and spins, my trembling legs and nervous hands, I began to recognize the kindness in her soft brown eyes. At some point in that first week, I saw past her tooth-gnashing, kick-threatening, darting-off habits and realized that Maggie was just a soul like me, trying to get by in a world that had not always been kind to her.

Our partnership was a challenge, but we came to trust each other. In the years that followed, I put aside my middle-aged caution and took up jumping again because I knew Maggie loved it. Eventually, we left Fay's watchful eye and moved to another stable. Through those years, we had many scares, and I fell off many times, but none of that mattered. I loved Maggie. When I was with her, I was twelve years old again, and dreams really did come true.

"There it is," says Blair, moving aside so I can see the screen of his ThermoScan. "See where the heat is showing? She's got a torn suspensory ligament."

I lean back against the wall with a thump. I've heard about injuries like this. I know the suspensory ligament extends from the back of the knee and wraps around the ankle bones, tying them all together. I've heard recovery can be dicey. If the ligament does not heal properly, a horse's career can be ended—or worse.

And it does get worse. In the following month, we realize that Maggie's injuries are not confined below the knee. She's torn the muscle and damaged the tendons in her upper leg, too. When she fails to improve as she should, an x-ray reveals that she also has two compression fractures in the bones of her knee.

"The only other case I've seen like this," says Blair, "was one where the knee was completely shattered and we had to put the horse down."

I refuse to give it a place to light, but the thought is hovering in the back of my mind that Maggie could die. It's not just the injuries themselves. Shifting her thousand pounds to the other three legs, and standing around in a stall for months while she heals will be hard on her—inside and out. Horses are made to keep moving.

I know next to nothing about what I'm doing, but it is my job to nurse Maggie. Twice a day, I hose her leg with cold water, apply a poultice for the swelling, then wrap it all up. I've watched others wrap injured legs—even tried to learn how—but it takes a special knack to make the bandage just the right tension so it doesn't do more harm than good.

One evening after I've finished bandaging, I enter the riding arena to watch some of my friends laughing and hooting and having fun with their horses. They are doing gymnastics with jumps placed so close together that the horses and riders must focus to get over them cleanly. The horses have to know exactly where their feet are, when and where to pick them up and put them down, and they must do it very quickly. Maggie loves these exercises. She always aces them. She used to.

I turn and re-enter the barn, knowing Maggie will never jump again. As I close the arena door, Josh Groban is singing softly on the radio:

I am strong when I am on your shoulders
You raise me up to more than I can be…

At that moment I realize what's so special about Maggie and me. Together, we can run faster, travel farther, jump higher than either of us could ever do alone.

I go to where she lies in her stall. She is so beautiful—so graceful—with her legs neatly tucked underneath, black velvet ears pointing forward, quiet eyes watching me enter. I kneel down and press my forehead to hers. "Oh, Maggie," I say, and for the first time since she got hurt, I cry. "What will become of you?"

That song is still playing: *You raise me up…*

Maggie is serene and silent, watching me with those bottomless amber-black eyes. They are saying, *I will be all right.*

If Maggie can endure it, so can I. And I keep coming every day.

I've read that love will bring souls back together in life after life, and I have a feeling that Maggie and I may have more history together than we know. Since I bought her, images have come to me—sometimes in dreams, sometimes in quiet contemplation. In one, I see an Egyptian woman, an exile from an ancient tribe, crossing the desert with a horse as her only companion. When a sandstorm rises up, the horse lies down and uses her body to shield the woman from the stinging grit. Another time, a woman in petticoats is galloping a horse at thunderous speed. They reach the top of a hill, the horse stops, and the weary rider slides off into tall, concealing grass. Another vision is of a group of North American Indians pulling an injured rider from her horse and taking her away. The rider doesn't return and, eventually, the horse dies alone, still waiting.

"If this is my debt to you, it is one I will gladly repay," I tell Maggie as I wrap her leg for the fiftieth, or the hundredth, or the two-hundredth time. I vow that, in this life, she will not die alone.

I nurse Maggie all winter: Twice a day for the first three months; once a day after that. We always take a very short walk, just to keep her body moving. I'm getting better at the bandaging. Despite her impatient temperament, Maggie suffers my sad efforts with grace. It is as if she knows she needs help to heal and that I am her only hope.

Through all of this, my best hope is a word, a name for God. "*H-u-u-u-u*," I sing, over and over, making little tunes of it, secretly asking the universe for help. If it accomplishes nothing else, the singing makes me feel better, and I have an idea it helps Maggie stand still for the hosing.

One night I wake up crying. I feel such anguish over Maggie I know I won't get back to sleep until I write something down. So, I get a pen and paper and compose a letter to God. "I'm going to lose Maggie, aren't I?" it begins. By the time I finish writing, the tears are done. I've ended by asking that, if she must go, could it please be in a way that she is not afraid or in a lot of pain. After that I feel better. I've turned her over to the care of a force wiser and more powerful than me.

By this time, Maggie's leg is so swollen it looks like a tree trunk. I've started applying the poultice and bandages all the way to the top. I joke that she looks like a hockey player with all that padding. It's been three months. We could use that help any time now.

I still have the phone number of a massage therapist who works on horses. A friend gave it to me shortly after Maggie hurt herself. "What can massage do for a broken leg?" I said to myself at the time and put the number aside. But now I'm desperate. There is nothing else I, or the vet, can do. There's that letter to God, but I'm not expecting a quick reply. So I call the therapist and say half-heartedly, "Can you do anything to help a horse with an injured leg?" She says, "Yes, I can."

Diane tells me about quantum touch. The term is a misnomer, since she doesn't even need to touch the patient. She simply puts her hands over the part of the body that is hurt and channels energy toward it so that it can heal itself. Perhaps it sounds far-fetched, she says, but she's simply making use of ordinary energy that's out there in the universe. All she does is make herself a conduit. It's no more far-fetched than me singing *Hu* and asking for help from that same universe, so I invite Diane to meet Maggie.

Maggie is a very clear communicator when it comes to things she does not like. She lays her ears back, cocks a hind hoof, grinds her teeth, and snakes her neck from side to side. She can get a look in her eye that says she'd like to swallow you whole. These are the threats Maggie makes when Diane

Maggie and me, Vineland, ON, 2000.

begins exploring her leg to figure out which is the best place to start. At the top? "No!" says Maggie. At the bottom? "No!" At the knee? Maggie lowers her head and starts smacking her lips. "Yes." This is the place.

I wait quietly while Diane cups her hands around Maggie's broken knee. Other people working in the barn stop what they're doing to watch. After about ten minutes—and no one has said a word—Maggie indicates she wants to move. We stand back while Maggie takes one step, then another and another. It's like she's testing the sore leg to see how much weight it can bear. Right before our eyes, she is improving. This goes on—Diane's touch and Maggie's testing—for another fifteen minutes or so. Finally we've reached the turning point. Thank you, God!

By late spring, Maggie is ready for me to get on her back again. Eventually, we work our way up to a canter. Our friends, who have been giving Maggie treats and encouragement all winter long, are happy for us. Since it looks like she's going to be all right, they begin to tell me they didn't think it would happen. "It's because she knew you loved her," says one. "It's because she loves you," says another. Someone else says, "It's because you love each other."

By June, things are looking pretty good. Maggie's in great condition. We've just fitted her with special shoes to make her bad leg work even better.

Of course, she has to show off to her pals in the pasture. That's when she hurts her *other* front leg: another ligament.

Now the old injuries in her right leg start to act up, too. Maggie can't even lie down to rest because both front legs are so weak and sore that she cannot push herself back up to standing. So, it's back to the hosing, the poultices, the bandages—on both legs now—and singing *Hu* every day. We get through this, too, one day at a time. Finally, the vet says the new injury looks as though it has healed. According to him, I should be able to slowly start riding her again.

I try it, but she's not ready. She may never be. Maggie is a senior citizen now, and I'm getting close to being one myself. The month I turn fifty, she turns twenty. I accept that there will be no more galloping through the fields, certainly no more jumping. But that doesn't really matter anymore. I still feel like I'm twelve when I'm with her.

With all of our trials behind us, I have a dream. In this one, Maggie has escaped from her paddock and I am terribly afraid for her. Eventually, from my vantage point way out in the field, I see that Maggie is calmly walking between two men. I know she is in good hands. They are building a stall for her, all in white.

In early January—a month or so after that dream—I return home late from a trip and I'm tired. I notice the message light blinking on the telephone, but I decide to ignore it until morning. Just as I'm ready for bed, the phone rings. I glance at the clock, and I pick up the phone. It's Chris at the stable.

"Why haven't you been answering the phone?" he blurts out. "Blair and I have been here for the last two hours with Maggie. She choked, and we've been trying to clear it."

This is not the first time food pellets have gotten stuck in Maggie's throat. Chris continues, "It was a heck of a job, but she's all right now. Blair says she may have inhaled some pieces of food, and if she did, she'll likely have pneumonia by morning."

I pull on extra winter clothes for this very cold night. I ask my husband to drive to the barn, because I cannot possibly be as calm as I seem right now. As soon as I see Maggie moping in the corner of her stall, head hanging, still half-doped and bloody-nosed from the procedure, I know she is finished.

The only humans in the barn at this late hour are my husband and I, so I cry loudly, "Oh, Maggie!" Over and over. I stroke her gently and try, with a stopped-up nose and wavering voice, to sing that word, *Hu-u-u-u*, but it is not a musical sound. I can feel Maggie saying to me that she's sorry but this is probably the end. I get some old saddle pads and horse blankets together for a makeshift bed and stay the night.

When the vet returns the next morning, he confirms that she has pneumonia. "The first seventy-two hours are critical," he says. "Either she will throw it off by then, or she will not. If she doesn't, we won't be able to save her."

Maggie tries very hard to throw it off. I don't know which one of us she is trying for. Regardless, I am there every day, twice a day, for hours at a time, walking her up and down the aisle, rinsing her frothing mouth, warming her up, cooling her off, listening to her gut, stroking her neck, her face, her ears, saying her name over and over and over. And singing that word, *Hu*.

Near the end, Maggie paces inside her stall. She cannot get comfortable, either lying down or standing. I am peering over the side because she is so unsteady it is not safe to be next to her. She makes the rounds of her favourite places: the corner where she sleeps every night, her feed tub, and the half-wall where I am watching. Again and again, she traces this triangle. All the while I am singing her name and saying *Hu* over and over, like a final lullaby.

Somewhere in the cosmos, a great clock clicks over to hour seventy-two, and Maggie begins her last shuddering steps. She trembles so violently she can barely stand. Her eyes register her final fear, then they find me. She staggers toward me one last time, lurches against the wall and goes down. I know before her head touches the floor that my beautiful friend is gone.

I climb over the side and kneel by Maggie's head. The barn is completely quiet. All of the normal animal noises have ceased. It is as though the other horses are united in silence to observe their friend's passing. I straighten Maggie's forelock, stroke her neck, and try to close her eyes, but I do not cry. My heart is not broken this time. This death is not a tragedy. Maggie's time here was done, and we both knew that. True to my promise, I have seen her out.

EIN GUTES GESPANN

CATHERINE R. FENWICK

The first thing my paternal great-grandparents did when they arrived in Saskatchewan in 1906 was buy *ein gutes Pferde Gespann,* a good team of horses. They bought the horses, a large wagon, and a cultivator before facing the task of building their mud-and-straw soddy. Their worldview was best stated in their motto, *Arbieten und Gebeten*—work and prayer—the spirit of the times.

I was born into this horse-and-wagon world where the primary need was for survival. Dad, like his forefathers, had an uncanny knack for drawing life from the earth. Mine was the fourth generation to grow up on land that was pioneered by our *Arbeiten-und-Gebeten* German Russian ancestors. Horses were key to our survival.

Horses have influenced the evolution of human civilization since they were domesticated around six thousand years ago. The domestication of the horse made travel much easier; great distances between peoples and societies were shortened. People started to explore, bringing about new discoveries and endless possibilities. Horses, with their uncomplaining dependability, have excelled in their service to humanity. Before automobiles, trains, and airplanes, riding a horse was the closest thing to flying.

Horses helped pioneers in travel, policing, road and railway construction, recreation, and agriculture. Prairie historian Grant MacEwan wrote, "If ever there were horse heroes deserving plaudits never bestowed, they were the ones which pulled settlers' wagons and homesteaders' ploughs." In the early 1900s, coinciding with the huge influx of settlers from Europe,

Canada's horse population peaked at more than three million. Nearly one-third of the national herd was in Saskatchewan, and the average prairie farmer owned ten horses. As MacEwan wrote, "Horses on farms were as essential as oars in a rowboat. A farm without them was unthinkable."

My cowboy cousins on Mom's side of the family loved their horses, which became extensions of their bodies when they rounded up cattle, checked fences, or raced one another across open range. I grew up on a hardscrabble dirt farm and admired our horses, but I can't honestly say that I loved them in the same way my cowboy cousins did. Perhaps it was the nature of the work we did on the farm, which always seemed more like drudgery than the romance of ranch work. Dad's German-Catholic work ethic allowed for little play. "*Nutztiere sind für die Arbeit nicht Spielen,*" he said. Farm animals were for work, not play.

Our steadfast hard-slogging team—Pearl, a palomino mare, and Blackie, a sooty buckskin stallion—constantly gave of their power and dependability. My earliest memories are of Dad and his brothers working with our horses. Pulling a stone boat, the horses hauled manure from the barns to the fields and stones from the fields to the stone piles along the fences. Pulling a hay wagon, they hauled hay bales to the haystacks and wheat sheaves to the threshing machine—in the days before we owned a combine—and pulling a grain box, they carried grain from field to granary and later to the Pool elevator in town. They took us to town to buy groceries, to attend school and church, to the post office for mail, and to get the packages of lovely new things we'd ordered from the Eaton's catalogue. Over the years, I came to greatly appreciate these magnificent creatures for their hard labour and uncomplaining dedication.

At harvest time, I drove the team to haul grain home from the field. While Dad circled a quarter section on the combine, I'd lie on my back in the wagon comfortably lounging on an old patch quilt, inhaling harvest smells and—in daylight—reading a book or—at night—looking dreamily up at the star-filled sky. There's a particular smell that comes from a swathed field of wheat in autumn. It's a compound of hot dust on dry straw that comes up from the soil through the hollow stalks of stubble. It's most potent when the crop is thick and rich with abundance; it smells like earth and the promise of new clothes.

Pearl and Blackie, my only companions, stood at ease in their traces, waiting for the call. *"Katie, kommen!"* I'd jump up, start the team with a slap of the reins, and we'd be off in the direction of Dad's call. We'd hustle to get the wagon in position under the combine spout to receive the load of wheat into the wagon. After the first dump of grain, I'd have something softer to lie on and dream away the time until the next call. When the wagon box was filled, I'd drive the team into the yard and unload the wheat into the auger, which carried it up into a hole in the roof of the wooden granary. The best load was the last haul of the day when Dad would get off the combine and ride home with me. Dad unloaded the wagon while I led the team to the water trough next to the well, then into the barn for a rubdown and a much-needed rest. There'd be more long hard-working days until all of the grain was in the bin.

Sometimes our horses were called upon to expend nearly every ounce of energy to get one of us to the hospital in the next town. They did so one stormy winter night, in late March of 1956, near the end of the worst winter since weather records had been kept in Saskatchewan. Ten years old and sleeping hard, I couldn't figure out why Dad was shaking my shoulders, lifting me out of bed, standing me on the cold hard floor in the middle of the night. He was trying to get me to understand something: *"Katerina, sie müssen aufwachen. Ich nehme Mutter ins Krankenhaus."*

Mom has to go to the hospital? I shook myself awake.

The baby! The baby was coming! "Yeah. Okay." I got up, and followed Dad to the front door.

Dad went out to hitch up the horses. Outside, a blizzard was raging. It had been snowing and blowing for three days, and deep, wind-packed snowdrifts had blocked the roads. The hospital was ten miles away.

Dad soon returned from the barn. *"Hören mir zu, Katerina,"* he urged. "Listen! Phone Donauers and Uncle Pete. Tell them I'm taking *Mutter* to the hospital in Montmartre. Tell them to turn on their yard lights, so I can find my way. Phone Schmidts and tell Mr. Schmidt to get his team ready. My horses are going to be worn out by then. I'm going to drive them hard." He shook his head. *"Och, die armen Pferde.* Tell Mrs. Schmidt to phone ahead to the rest

Dad with his team and wagon, circa 1940.

of the neighbours along the way and ask them to turn on their lights. Otherwise, I won't find my way.

"Those poor horses," he said again, and he hurried out the door.

Dad would not follow the roads, which were buried anyway, but instead would shorten the trip and avoid the worst of the snowdrifts by travelling cross-country. The Schmidt farm was halfway between our farm and the hospital.

I was walking toward the phone when Mom came out of the bedroom wearing her warmest winter clothes, carrying a small suitcase. She kissed my cheek and said, "Thanks, Cathy." She looked worried about leaving me in charge at such a young age, but what else could she do?

"We'll be fine. I can take care of things." My voiced quivered with poorly disguised fear.

Dad came in. *"Kommen, meine Liebe, der Schlitten ist fertig."* He grabbed the blankets piled by the stove and helped my mother out the door. She hunched forward, holding her belly, carefully making her way down the snowy steps. They crawled into the sled. Mom wrapped herself in the pile of warm blankets and huddled in the back corner. Dad leaned forward— arms outstretched, casting his energy toward our harnessed team—and shouted, "Go Pearl, *aufdrehen!* Hey up there, Blackie! Hup! Hup!" He slapped the leather reins hard across their backs. Clouds of thick mist bubbled from their flared nostrils. Steam rose from their quivering bodies as they took off in a spray of snow and ice crystals. When they got to the treeline at the end of the yard, I saw them struggle to get some speed while sinking into snowdrifts up to their bellies. In a few moments, they reached the stubble field where the windblown snow was only knee deep. They ran hard and soon faded into the whiteout. I waved helplessly at their invisible backs, then rushed to the phone to call the people along the route who would help them all get safely to where they were going.

The next morning, the smell of food cooking woke me. *Is Mom back home?* I jumped out of bed and stumbled into the kitchen. Caroline, who was nine, had stoked the cookstove and was making porridge and scrambled eggs. Mom and Dad weren't home. We six little girls were holding down the fort. Looking out the window, I saw that the day was calm and sunny, probably cold enough to freeze your eyeballs if you were outdoors. Eventually, I joined my sisters at the table and tried to eat.

When I next looked out the window, I saw our team coming slowly across the sun-sparkled field. The reins were loosely wrapped around the railing that stretched across the front of the sled. There was no need to drive the team—Pearl and Blackie could find their way home. Dad's face was almost entirely wrapped in a red scarf I had knitted for him. The brim of his sheepskin cap covered his eyes, sheltering them from the burning cold. I loved the way Pearl and Blackie pranced across the wind-smoothed stretches of snow. Pearl had an air of pride about her and Blackie held high his handsome head as they entered our yard. It was as if they knew they had done something very special.

I watched Dad unhitch our team and lead them into the barn, where I knew he would later rub them down and give them water, oats, and a much-deserved rest. In the porch, he peeled off layers of clothing.

"Mommy's fine. *Sie hatten ein kleiner Junge.*" We girls laughed and cheered, relieved to know that Mom was all right and happy to have a little brother. After six daughters, Dad had his boy, someone to carry on his name and take over the farm some day.

Three more brothers and two more horses eventually joined our family. Dad mellowed over the years, and we were permitted to ride the horses, adding more *Spielen* to the *Arbeiten und Gebeten.*

A couple of years ago, I drove my car through the Coteau Hills heading toward the southwest corner of Saskatchewan. Rufus Wainwright was singing "King of the Road" on CBC Radio. I sang along: *"Boomp, boomp, Queen of the Road!"* A few streaks of wistful clouds meandered across the sun's face in the hazy September afternoon. In the wind was the sweet smell of hay and a trace of frost. The curvaceous bitumen highway wound its way in and out of the Coteau.

I know this smell, this rancher's landscape. It's the place where Gramma Irene filled her hope chest; where my mother dreamed of better things; where we came to play with cousins, marvel at their riding skills, cutting young bulls from the herd, roping, branding, castrating. Later we roasted prairie oysters over an open fire. I once rode with my cousins out to what is now Grasslands National Park to see a rattlesnake pit. Travelling west on Highway 13, I passed familiar places—Kincaid, Hazenmore, Ponteix—and came upon a herd of market-ready steers and heifers. Orangey-pink light pressed down on a noisy river of moving brown backs crossing the road, herded toward a shit-drenched corral.

Two cowboys on quads held back the highway traffic on both sides of the streaming braying cattle.

When did ranchers give up their four-legged live mounts for these 250-horsepower gasoline-guzzling contraptions? I wondered what my rancher uncles and my farmer father would think of this. On our farm, horses helped with the work until the early 1970s, when Pearl and Blackie, our old and feeble team, *ein gutes Gespann*, were retired to the pasture.

I arrived at my cousin's ranch in time for a late supper. "Say, if you're not too busy tomorrow morning, could we ride out to Grasslands?" I asked.

Now that machinery has taken over farm work, Canada's horse population is about one million. Although they are rarely used in the fields these days, horses are being recognized for their abilities to help us humans in new ways. People with a wide range of physical, mental, and behavioural difficulties gain self-esteem and strength by interacting with horses. Horseback riding provides another form of mobility for people who use a wheelchair. According to the American Psychological Association, equine therapy has proven to be helpful for people who have experienced trauma, depression, and anxiety. Interacting with horses is a great benefit in assisting people with behavioural concerns such as attention deficit disorder, substance abuse, eating disorders, as well as relationship and communication problems. Therapeutic horse ranches are springing up, like prairie crocuses in springtime, across the landscape of North America.

I'm not surprised. Horses have been humans' partners for six thousand years, and our relationship with them will continue to evolve.

THE ONLY TIME

PENNY L. FERGUSON

I'm no expert, but I'd say he's in bad shape," Dad said, looking away from the downed horse and into the face of the frail, gnarled man beside him.

Magnus's jaw tightened and he nodded. His forefinger flicked the end of his nose as he snuffed. In the narrow stall, Fred, the old chestnut gelding, lay on his side on the floor. His breath came in short snorts. Steam rose from his lathered coat, his heavy scent mingling with the smell of hay. I looked at the two men standing side by side: Magnus, short and bony; Dad, tall and brawny. I had the faith of a seven-year-old that between Magnus's stubbornness and my dad's ability to make everything right, they would make Fred okay. I knew he'd be up whinnying as usual to be let out of his stall every time he heard footsteps approaching the weathered old barn.

Dad stepped around the horse. His leg brushed Fred's flank as he looked at the ceiling. Usually friendly and looking for a pat, Fred paid him no mind.

"If we pull off a couple of floorboards by that beam," Dad said, pointing upward, "We can sling ropes over it and use them to hoist him up. I don't know but he might do better if we could get him on his feet."

"Yeah, that would work!" Magnus agreed, anxious to seize any filament of hope.

"We'll need some help. Penny?" Dad turned toward me.

"Yeah," I said, coming forward eagerly, willing to do anything I could to participate in Fred's resurrection.

"You to go to Nana and Grampy's. Get Grampy and Nelson, and bring them back here. Tell Nana to phone Pearly Munn and ask him to come look at Fred right away. And Penny—" Dad's big hand caught my shoulder as I turned to go, "don't stop to play along the way. Go straight there!"

"I will, Dad," I assured him earnestly, annoyed that he thought I didn't grasp the gravity of the situation.

I ran to Nana's as fast as I could, praying for Fred all the way, just like I'd been taught in Sunday school, hoping for something miraculous, some form of divine intervention. I delivered the message to Nana and Grampy. Nana went for the phone while Grampy, Uncle Nelson, and I started back toward Magnus's barn. As the men strode along, talking about how attached Magnus was to that old horse, I jogged beside them on the dirt road, trying to keep up.

Magnus had lived alone on the farm with only his old horse and a few chickens for company for as many years as I could remember. His mother had passed away the year I was born, and Magnus had never married. As his neighbours, we were the closest thing he had to family. He'd come over most evenings to play crib with Mom and Dad or to keep an eye on me when they went out. We'd play crazy eights till it was time for me to go to bed. He never read me bedtime stories like Mom did, and he got mad the first time I insisted that he should. Later, Mom explained to me that he couldn't read, and she told me just to ask him to *tell* me a story the next time. Magnus gave me a quarter each month when his pension came, after he hired a car to take him to town to buy groceries and booze. He would stay on a bender until the alcohol was gone. We always kept an eye out for him to make sure he didn't pass out in a snowbank and freeze to death.

When Grampy, Uncle Nelson, and I entered the barn, Dad was in the loft with a crowbar. Dust sifted softly into the air below him as he moved about upstairs. I could hear him grunting, and nails screeched unnervingly as he forced the last three floorboards off the beam. Bits of chaff and dust rained down to settle on Fred's coat. I waited for the customary flick of his tail, but the horse didn't seem to notice the dust. After sneezing, Magnus stepped forward and knelt, trying to brush the dust away, but it stuck to the horse's damp body.

Unfurling two grizzled ropes, Dad fed the ends over the beam and down through the hole he'd made in the floor. Catching hold of the descending ends, Magnus tugged, and the ropes whirred over the beam. I watched Dad's back as he descended the ladder from the loft, and the men discussed the best way to get the ropes under the horse. While they were talking, a truck barrelled in the yard, rocks flying beneath its tires.

I announced, "It's Pearly." It felt like the old barn sighed with relief. Everyone around these parts knew Pearly knew everything about sick horses. I guess he just knew everything about horses, sick or well, because it was always his team that won the horse haul at the annual fair. I'd sat with Dad each year for as long as I could remember, flinching as the leather reins stung Pearly's dapple greys into action at just the right moment, dragging the weighted sledge yards beyond what the other teams achieved. Pearly would fix Fred right up. He didn't have all of the fancy gizmos the expensive vets from town used, but he could whomp up potions that put most horses back in action.

"Good day, boys," Pearly said as he strolled nonchalantly into the barn like he owned the place, or at least knowing that the knowledge he brought to the situation afforded him some sort of sense of entitlement. He was a thick little man, much shorter than my Dad, with curly, fiercely red hair and a splattering of freckles. Wasting no time, he walked over to Fred, bent down, and took the horse's huge head gently in his hands. Fred's dull eyes looked at him but didn't seem to focus. Pulling back an eyelid, Pearly began his examination of the horse.

"Uh huh. Feeling kind of lousy, are you, old fellow?" He patted Fred's brown neck with a tenderness that was surprising considering the cocksure deportment of the man. He looked up the nostrils, then forced the mouth open, moving the thick tongue from one side to the other between the yellowed teeth. Pearly's hands ran slowly down Fred's neck and along his ribs and spine. We watched in silence as Pearly performed his rites, as silent as when we pray in church. It seemed like we'd been holding our breath the entire time.

He thrust his hand along the horse's rounded belly. Fred's eyes rolled back. He whinnied in pain, foam spraying from his mouth.

"Sorry about that, old boy," Pearly said, slapping Fred's neck affectionately. He moved his hands back and forth, feeling a section of the horse's underbelly. Fred's breath came faster, and he moaned. Moving around to Fred's rear, the man lifted the horse's tail and took a long look. Standing up, Pearly slapped the dust and hay from his worn clothes. He looked around the floor of the stall. "Any road apples this morning, Magnus?"

"No. He ain't had any for a couple of days," Magnus said, rubbing his gnarly hand across his stubbled chin.

"What you feeding him?"

"Just standard fare—hay, oats, water," Magnus said, shrugging his gaunt shoulders.

"Let's have a look," Pearly suggested.

"They're all fine," Magnus said testily. He spat on the floor to emphasize his irritation. The barn was silent for a moment. Pearly took off his red and white baseball cap, which read "1966 Horse Haul Champion," scratched his head and replaced the cap before speaking again.

"Now, I know you wouldn't intentionally feed him anything that'd hurt him, Magnus, but sometimes things happen. Better to check and be safe than sorry."

"Oats is there." Magnus grudgingly nodded his grey head toward three sacks slumping dejectedly like old drunks against the wall. "Hay's my own. Up there." He motioned toward the loft. "Water's fresh every feeding. The same as I drink, and I'm still up walking around!"

Pearly reached into the bag of oats and drew out a handful of the grain. He fingered the golden kernels in his palm then sniffed the oats. Putting a few grains in his mouth, he ground them between his teeth then spat them onto the floor. "Oats is fine." He tossed the rest of the oats into the trough. Picking up some hay from the morning feeding, he looked at and smelled it. "Hay's fine too."

Me with Fred and his owner, Priceville, NB.

Pearly took off his hat again and fingered it respectfully, hesitantly. "Well, boys, looks like a torsion," he said in the same voice I'd heard people using when offering condolences after someone's relative had died.

I saw Magnus wince as if he'd been struck. Whatever a torsion was, I knew it had to be bad.

"What's a tor—," I began to ask, but I was silenced by a withering look from Dad.

"Only one cure for a torsion," Dad commented shoving his hands deep into his pockets and rolling his lips in upon themselves.

"Most merciful thing's to do it right away," Pearly said. "Sorry, Magnus. Darn shame. Fred was a fine old horse." He coughed, scuffed his heavy boot through the chaff on the barn floor. "Well, nothing more I can do for you here. The wife's expecting me back," he said apologetically.

The men mumbled their thanks as Pearly headed for his truck. We listened for the engine and the sound of tires on the driveway. Pearly was good with horses, but it was also well known that when one had to be put down, he cleared out faster than men when there's a dirty diaper to be changed. Feeling my bottom lip begin to tremble, I fought against it, but it shook like it wasn't even part of me.

"Well..." Grampy began with a nervous cough.

"Not yet," Magnus said defiantly. His little blue eyes were hard like marbles, his jaw rigid with determination.

"No, you can't! You can't shoot Fred!" I blurted, knowing I should be silent but speaking anyway. Tears slid down my cheek.

"Penny!" Dad shot me a look.

"But...."

His glare silenced me. I sucked in my bottom lip and stared at the wall. I couldn't look at the men or at Fred. I felt like they were betraying me somehow. This couldn't really be happening. Images of all of the times Magnus had hoisted me up onto the horse's back and led me around the daisy-filled pasture; of all the juicy apples I'd saved from my lunch to take to Fred after school; of how he'd give that welcoming whinny he saved just for me; of how he'd nudge me until I gave up the apple I held behind my back; of all the rides on the rickety grey wagon back to the woodlot that supplied our winter's wood, watching Fred's tail snap over his twitching rump to swat away flies; and of Fred trudging along with the plough turning up the rich earth as we followed along behind making rows and planting.

"If it's a torsion, he's got to be put down," Dad explained.

"Not yet!" Magnus insisted. "I could get a vet...."

"Nearest vet's in Fredericton. Hundred miles round trip. 'Sides, it would cost too much. And on Sunday..." Grampy said, "all that money wasted for nothing. Better to get over with." I looked him straight in the face, into the shadows beneath the bill of his cap, briefly hating him for his common sense. I thought of the forty-three cents I had saved up at home in the fancy little bottle Mom got jam in last year for Christmas. I thought of offering it, but I knew it wouldn't be nearly enough. Vets from town were expensive, and we all knew that Magnus lived on only a meagre pension from the government. We were all too poor to have anything to contribute.

Magnus looked at the other men. He looked as helpless as I felt.

"He's your horse, Magnus. What do you want to do?" Uncle Nelson asked gently.

"Maybe if we can get him on his feet, like we was going to...."

"If it's a torsion," said Grampy, "that won't help. Pearly is usually right about these things."

Magnus stooped, stroking Fred's sweat-soaked face. "I need more than 'if' and 'usually' before putting a bullet in this old horse," he said tenderly.

"Well, let's get at it then," Dad said with resignation. It wasn't usual for Dad to relent on any point, especially if it meant wasting a Sunday doing something he clearly felt was hopeless. At that moment I loved him for giving in, and I knew he'd help save Fred.

With a great deal of tugging, grunting, and cursing from the men and groans and snorts of pain from Fred, they finally managed to tie one rope around the horse behind his front legs. The other went ahead of his hind legs. Stopping to get their wind, the four men mopped sweat from their red faces with coat sleeves.

"OK, boys. Time to do it," Dad instructed. Dad and Magnus seized the free end of the front rope dangling from the hayloft, Grampy and Uncle Nelson, the back rope. The men pulled downward, straining with muscles taut, veins bulging, and sweat beading their foreheads like little rhinestones. The beam creaked, and Fred exhaled loudly. I squeezed in to help, straining for all I was worth. Slowly Fred was dragged to his feet.

He laboured for breath and his legs would not lock beneath him. Every time the rope was allowed to go slack, he sagged. The men reached out to snap his knobbly legs into place, but they continued to buckle.

Magnus kept talking to the old horse. "Come on Fred, old boy. Lock those legs. You can do it!" He coaxed Fred as we held the horse in place, our muscles aching. The old man's strength and patience were nearing an end. "Stand up, Fred!" Magnus bellowed. He slapped Fred on the shoulder. The horse's flesh twitched under the sting. "You useless, mangy old bag of bones!" he cursed. "You've got to do something to help yourself. We can't do it all!"

"It's no use, Magnus," Dad gasped, veins standing out on his neck, his arms starting to tremble under the strain of holding the horse upright. Eyes closed, Magnus nodded and the men tied off the ropes. Fred hung like a sack of wet cement. We watched and coaxed the rest of the afternoon, but Fred only grew weaker. Many times I raised my hand to Fred's sagging head, wishing I could will him some of my young strength. I was looking at Magnus, thinking how, in the shadows deepening in the barn, his old face looked tired and wrinkled.

Magnus finally shook his head. "There's nothing more we can do. Get your gun, Hartley," he said flatly.

"No," I pleaded. "You can't let them, Magnus!" My fingers clutched the dirty blue corduroy of his coat sleeve, and I shook the old man's arm. "You can't just give up! I thought you loved Fred—"

"It's got to be done." He yanked his arm away from me.

"You don't love Fred! If you did, you wouldn't let them do this! I hate you! I hate you!" I screamed at the old man, tears running down my face, stamping my foot.

"Penny, be quiet!" Dad snapped. I slumped against the barn wall and bit my lip until it hurt.

"Sorry, Magnus," Dad said, resting his hand briefly on the old man's shoulder. I wasn't sure if he was apologizing for my behaviour or for not being able to help Fred. Maybe it was both. "You can get another horse younger and stronger than Old Fred was."

"Don't want another darned horse. They're too much trouble to look after. I'm getting too old for it." Magnus was expressionless.

"Come back to the house, Penny," Dad said quietly. I followed at a distance, not jogging like I usually did to keep up to my dad's long stride. Once home, I went to my bedroom and flopped onto the cot, burrowing my face into the pillow, straining my ears to hear Dad talking to Mom as he took the rifle from the rack. There was click as he shoved the clip into the breech and left the house.

Mom tapped softly on my door.

"Penny? Penny, are you okay?"

"Leave me alone." I didn't want to hear any more about how it had to be done.

"Penny, dear?"

I didn't say anything. Eventually, she went away. I lay on the bed tensed, waiting, thinking about all of the times I'd patted Fred and felt his hairy lip tickle my hand as I fed him sugar.

After a long time, the crack of the gun came, reverberating through to my soul. I flinched at the sound and pressed my face deeper into the pillow until I could hardly breathe, hoping Mom wouldn't hear me sobbing.

When I heard Dad come back, I stifled my crying and slipped out of the house. I had to get away from them, to go someplace where I could cry and not have to hear lectures about getting used to the cruelty of life. I ran across our yard and into Magnus's. Going around the barn, I stopped short. Magnus was sitting in Fred's wagon, bent over with his hands covering his face. I could hear him sobbing. He hadn't seen me, so I stepped back around the corner, peering around to gaze at him. Seeing him like that, I felt remorse for the things I had said. I waited until he seemed to be quietening down. I walked up to the wagon Magnus and I had ridden on so many times behind Fred. "Hi," I said.

Magnus didn't answer. He just sat with his face buried in his hands and didn't offer me a hand or look up as I pulled myself up into the wagon. I sat on the far edge of the seat running my fingers along the greyed seat and still he did nothing. As I slid toward him, I could feel the rough splintery wood catching at the fabric of my slacks. Wrapping my arms around his waist, I felt the old man stiffen slightly, then his arms went around me. Magnus didn't say anything, but I felt a sob-stifling shudder run through him. We sat in this strange silence until Mom yelled for me to come home. When I pulled away from him, neither of us said a word. I had seen the old man laying dead drunk under the maples in his front yard. When we kids raided his apple tree, I saw him so mad that I thought he'd have a stroke. I even saw him write his name in a snowbank once. But this was the only time I'd ever seen him cry.

DAISY

DONNA FIRBY GAMACHE

During my childhood years, my family lived on a southern Manitoba farm northwest of Minnedosa beside the Little Saskatchewan River, a river prone to springtime floods due to the runoff from melting snow or heavy downpours. Our cattle herd averaged about thirty to forty cows, with an equal number of calves each summer, and a somewhat smaller number of yearlings kept each fall to fatten and sell the next winter. Because much of our farm was hilly, cropland was limited, and the cattle were our major source of income. The cattle spent their summers grazing on the hills and along the river, with many miles of fences needed to keep them off the flats, where wheat and oats were planted.

Winters, the livestock spent close to the farmstead, days in a low-lying sheltered area west of the barns that my father kept full of hay, and nights in one of the two barns. The new barn was a loose-housing building, while the old barn had stalls and pens where particular cows, and steers that were being fattened for sale, spent their nights. The cattle kept there soon learned where they were to go, and around four or five each afternoon—earlier if it was stormy—they wandered up from the daytime shelter and lined up in front of the correct door.

Most of the cattle were Herefords, handsome red-brown animals with white faces and perhaps white throats or napes as well. Some were registered purebreds, some not, but because the herd was small, each was given a name, and my father, my younger brother, Bruce, and I could easily recognize each individual. We didn't need numbered ear tags to keep them straight. Some of the cattle had human names, like Alice or Mary or Harry, while others were named for something unique in their appearance or background—such as Snowbank, who was named for the location where she was born. Others were named for some identifying behaviour, such as the heifer we named Puller because of her habit of chewing and pulling on the sticks we carried to guide the cattle into the barn.

Mother and my older sister, Joyce, didn't help with the barn chores as often as Bruce and I did, though they sometimes did the nightly milking of our one milk cow, who was kept to provide milk for our own family, since we were some distance from town and couldn't easily buy fresh milk. I preferred outdoor chores to indoor ones, so I eventually took over the milking.

For many years, our milk cow was Daisy, a Shorthorn—not a purebred, but a fine milker and a dandy mother to her yearly calf. She was a dark red-brown with a blotched brown-and-white face, not as handsome a cow as some of the others, but that wasn't why we kept her. She produced a good calf each year, and she stood patiently to be milked, even by an inexperienced child—which I certainly was in the beginning. Unlike some of our previous milk cows, Daisy wasn't a kicker, though I did have to watch out for an occasional tail switch. I hitched the milking stool closer to the cow, so my short arms could reach to do the job and—once I had learned the technique—rested my forehead against Daisy's warm flank. The milk struck the bottom of the milk pail rhythmically, and the smell of warm milk mingled with the other barn smells. Occasionally, I would squirt milk from the cow's teat to the nearby barn cats and kittens that waited, *not* so patiently, for me to finish and pour them a pan full of frothy, warm milk. In their eagerness, they'd sometimes stand up on their hind feet to beg for a squirt of milk.

Once the milking was finished and the cats were fed, it was time to pail-feed Daisy's calf, which was, of course, kept locked away from her so it couldn't drink the milk we wanted.

Daisy crossing the flooding Little Saskatchewan River.

Besides her patience, Daisy possessed another virtue. Unlike some of the other cattle, Daisy *always* came when we called her. I suppose, looking back on it, that she knew she would be rewarded with a measure of grain. Probably she was also uncomfortable and eager to have the milk out of her heavy bag. Whatever the reason, Daisy was somewhat like the proverbial mailman—she was not stopped by wind, nor rain, nor sleet, nor storm, nor flood.

Flood! That's the one I particularly remember, for our farmstead was situated in the basin of the Little Saskatchewan River, which brought springtime runoff from the southern flanks of Riding Mountain National Park. Two streams—the Little Saskatchewan, which meandered in slow-moving, wide curves, and the Rolling River, faster and narrower—flowed across our land and converged at a fork that we called "the joining" about half a kilometre upstream from our farm buildings. If both tributaries happened to be in flood at the same time—which occurred occasionally—the river rose and spread through the maples and willows that edged the banks, and out onto the nearby pastures and fields. Fortunately, all our buildings were safely set high enough to escape such floods. In summer, the water might run only a foot or two deep just below our barns, and we often waded and splashed in it. But in spring after a winter of heavy snowfall, or after a particularly heavy rain, we were always warned to stay far away from the riverbanks—a warning we always heeded, for we had seen how quickly the river could rise, how it eroded banks and flooded over low-lying areas.

Daisy, however, didn't understand such warnings. She was accustomed to crossing the river often, for the greenest grass always seemed to grow on the other side! High water didn't deter her, and she was a good swimmer. She was also smart enough to realize that when the current was fast and the water high, she needed to start farther upstream in order to prevent being washed too far downstream.

Daisy was well known for swimming the river whenever she took the notion to do so, but she was also known for coming home promptly whenever she was called by a loud, "Come boss, come boss, come boss." "Come boss!" would always bring Daisy to the barn at a brisk pace, sometimes almost a run. And if the river was in the way and had to be crossed, that was a minor detail to her.

Some days Daisy might cross to the far side after the morning's milking, and during the day the river might rise considerably. No problem! Daisy *always* came home. The water might be just above freezing, even with small ice chunks floating in it. The current might be fast, threatening to sweep her downstream. But Daisy willingly braved it when she heard our, "Come boss, come boss" calling her home for the evening's milking.

I think of Daisy sometimes—of her eagerness to do the job she was assigned, of her determination, and of the clever way she assessed the swollen river in front of her before launching herself into the water. Perhaps people could learn a thing or two from our old milk cow.

Heart the Size of a Small Car

Mark Ambrose Harris

for Jazz

The ocean is honest and unapologetic in its certainty: regardless of how it is treated, it will ebb and flow long after we become a mere memory on this rock. The boundless quality of this vast body of water is at once reassuring and terrifying. Because of this, I was looking forward to visiting the west coast. My summer had been a sour one. I bore witness to a painful drawn-out breakup, saw friends dealing with illness in their families, offered a shoulder to cry on when pets died, and meditated on those left behind as another loved one dealt with the effects of a suicide. However, the weight and sorrow of death came closer as summer ended.

In mid-September, a reckless driver struck and killed a dear friend of mine named Jazz. She was someone I went to high school with. Someone I had known for nearly two decades. Jazz was the person with whom I shared my first kiss, and we toiled together through the confusion and metamorphosis of adolescence. Then suddenly, gone. Obliterated in such a violent and senseless death. As autumn arrived, I was looking forward to leaving my life behind for a couple of weeks. I would be visiting friends in Vancouver, Victoria, and San Francisco, and I found comfort in the prospect of just sitting by the water and thinking about what had been lost. Little did I know what the ocean would provide.

About halfway through my trip, I was sitting in the back seat of a car rolling along Route 1. My partner and I had just been treated to a visit to the Monterey Aquarium, and our host was driving us back to San Francisco. It was late in the afternoon, and the sun splintered into diamonds on the water, the ocean outside my window providing an endless kinetic horizon. We stopped in at a roadside café for coffee and dessert. As I munched on my brownie, a young woman was walking about, clearing tables, and chatting with customers. She reminded me of Pat Benatar, her hair short and spiky, retro earrings dangling in an asymmetrical fashion.

Our friend asked her if there was a spot nearby where the road would lead down to the shore, or if there was a public beach in the vicinity. Smiling and charming, she took a moment to think and then inquired, "Oh, are you going to see the whale?"

Seeing our surprise, she explained that a blue whale had beached itself nearby and died. The waitress gave us detailed directions, so we finished our snacks and got back into the car. While I thought it might be sad to see the deceased animal, I could not pass up the chance to see a blue whale, such an elusive creature in the wild, up close.

We turned off the highway and pulled into a small parking lot. Walking down to the beach, I felt a pang of disappointment. There was nothing there. Just sand dunes and seagulls. Then, to our right, we noticed something that looked like a little wooden sandwich board crossed with a hazard sign, obstructing a path that led to another segment of the beach. Moving towards the sign, I began to smell something pungent, and it was clear the whale was indeed nearby. On the plywood was a printout from some official source warning not to touch the carcass or to remove any samples of the whale's tissue. It also explained the grim circumstances of the animal's demise. A boat had struck the blue whale, who then succumbed to her injuries. The whale had been pregnant, and so both mother and calf met their end on the shore.

We moved past the sign and walked through a passage nestled between dunes and rock face. Again, it was the smell that met my senses first, a blend of sea salt, damp sand, and rot. We continued onwards into the cove towards the cawing of gulls, and there, right in front of us at the water's edge, was the enormous, lifeless body of a blue whale. The animal was resting on her back, belly-up, partially submerged in the churning water.

A grey silence descended on us, all colour evacuating from the scene. The falling sun was now behind an endless wall of cloud. The waves were liquid pewter as they crashed into the mammal's sides, and despite its size, the carcass swayed back and forth with the push and pull of the waves. Because the whale had already been there for a week, her skin was beginning to peel and flake away. The bright hues of her hide were burned and bleached by the elements: the unforgiving sun and the corrosive bite of brine. The midnight blue of her underside was deteriorating to reveal pale blubber, blanched and sterilized.

Fully aware that blue whales are immense animals, I was nonetheless in awe of her size. Here was the leviathan of myth and lore, the behemoth of the deep. As a child, the first book I learned to read on my own was a story about migrating whales. When I was a bit older, I read other nature books, counting the number of bus-lengths that would equal the measurements of a grown blue whale, and imagined gentle giants doing slow but graceful ballets, their dark shadows moving just below the surface of the water. Now, I felt an acute sense of sadness in seeing such a majestic entity left to disintegrate and spoil. A buffet for gulls, parasites, and microbes.

A large chunk of her tail was missing. It was clear that one end of the wound had occurred when marine biologists removed a piece of the whale in order to perform a necropsy, as the cut was clean and precise. The other half of the gouge was ragged and tattered, as though sharks and other fish had fed on the body as it travelled towards land. The birds pecked and plucked from the open skin, undiscerning palates devouring carrion.

Hearing more squawking to my left, I turned to see a group of gulls moving about on the beach. The birds were congregating around something, though I could not focus on what it was. Then I realized I was looking at the shape of small tail fins beneath a light dusting of sand. It was the dead calf, lying a few feet from its mother's body. It is not clear to me how the unborn calf ended up exposed to the elements, but both animals were now food for the birds. The tail, however, is all that I can remember of the baby. Overcome by sorrow, I had to look away. Our companion walked away from the scene as tears welled up in his eyes. My partner and I stood there, holding one another, crying.

There was irony in the fact that I had boarded a plane with the hope of moving away from death, and yet here I was, standing face to face with this mortal coil. Moreover, while I fear creating meaning out of pure chance, I could not help but think of my deceased friend as I stood on the shore. My dear friend Jazz, a few months shy of her thirtieth birthday and already with years of humanitarian work in Uganda and Mongolia under her belt, had just landed an incredible new job working for the United Nations' Food and Agriculture Organization in Haiti. While she was walking on a sidewalk in Santo Domingo, a car driven by a man who shouldn't have been behind the wheel jumped the curb and ended Jazz's existence. To think of all the light, love, and potential extinguished in that fatal visceral moment is maddening. Because Jazz had been abroad in the recent past, I do not face a constant sense of absence or loss. Yet, there are moments when the realization erupts, piercing and painful: I will never see her again. That sense of finality is tough to reconcile.

The blue whale is not only the largest animal on earth, it is the largest animal to have ever existed. With a life expectancy of eighty to ninety years, it takes nearly ten years to reach sexual maturity. It is also the loudest animal on earth, its song approximately eighty decibels louder than a plane taking off. Removed from the buoyancy of water, a blue whale would be crushed to death by its own weight. Perhaps that was why the whale looked deflated, as though her final breath had caused an irreversible collapse. So much promise for astounding feats, cancelled. The unborn calf, decades of life ahead of it, annulled. These thoughts passed through my heart as I cried quietly, standing between the whale and her stillborn.

Perhaps heightening the morose atmosphere was the fact that we had just come from the Monterey Aquarium's seahorse exhibition. There, tiny creatures entwined their tails together in a miniature embrace and swayed gently in the water. Surreal animals with leaf-like appendages dazzled with brilliant colours, hovering as if suspended in mid-air. This seahorse dance was so delicate, their very existence minutia in the immeasurable unknown that is the ocean. The seahorses instilled a sense of peace, their aquatic serenity the marrow of utopic dreams. In contrast, the whale was even more goliath, the chaos of the natural world omnipresent. The sadness of the scene was palpable and the sights, sounds, and scents of mortality were difficult to escape. The presence of the dead whale and her deceased calf proclaimed something that was impossible to ignore: you too will face death. One day, you will die.

Everything ends, this is certain. I am not sure if it helps to think about what comes after death, as we rarely think about where we were before birth. Though I am a staunch atheist, I cannot help but be affected by the dreams I have—the dreams in which my friend is still alive, and the dreams of the whale with her fading blue skin. The visions of my friend make me pine for just one more moment with her, to make her proud of who I have become. When a loved one's life ends, I engage in an irrational thought process that if I just had enough to give, they might return. I suppose this is a common twist on denial, though I know that there is no bargaining with death, no barter or bet grand enough to ward off the great beyond. The spectre of the whale makes me long for a time and place where the annihilation of the natural world was not such a distinct possibility. In my dreams, Jazz speaks to me in reassuring tones. In my dreams, the whale is silent and motionless. Therefore, I continue this process of reconciliation. I try to make peace with the fact that what is gone is not coming back, and that the ocean will always give and take. We are all animals on this land, and in one way or another, we are all just waiting for the birds.

HOME INVASION

MELODY HESSING

Wood rats are of no agricultural significance because of their rocky habitat and foliage diet. Their attraction to deserted buildings, however, makes them a nuisance of some economic importance. Given sufficient time they can wreck the interior of a cabin and render it almost uninhabitable.
—*MAMMALS OF CANADA*

I'm home alone at our cabin in the Okanagan, tucked in my favourite chair, looking out the window. The lake spreads before me beneath a sunset of clamshell pink and blue-grey clouds. The tap drips, the fridge hums, and I swoon to a symphony of soft sounds. I exhale and stars sprinkle the heavens.

My husband and I built this log house thirty-five years ago. We were smitten by the unique, if endangered, biodiversity of the valley. We already knew that this steep, rugged plot of ponderosa-and-bunchgrass terrain belonged to others, because we saw them firsthand: species as varied as rattlesnakes, blue-tailed skinks, white-headed woodpeckers, and canyon wrens. To preserve this habitat, we tucked our prefab log house uphill and out of sight of the road and installed a composting toilet. We built the place by hand, without a road, trying to be unobtrusive, to be at home in the wild.

Years later, we moved back to the city for jobs, kids, and economic survival. But we hung on to this place, our touchstone to the land. These days, I'm in the early stages of retirement and living intermittently at the cabin. Jay is still working in the city, driving up when he can on weekends. With no neighbours in sight and no road access to the house, I'm sometimes uneasy there alone, but the landscape sustains me. Today, in the first week of October, bright red flame-thrower branches of sumac banner the hillside. Just outside the window, aspen leaves spatter the ground, yellow and burnt. There is solace in the dregs of summer, the first breath of autumn and winter.

As I survey the sage and gold-tipped rabbitbrush just outside, branches and logs clatter from the woodpile. I jump to my feet and run to turn on the porch light, trying to see more clearly. Nothing is out of place, so I sit back down, leaving the light on. Soon there is another scatter of sound, as if a poltergeist is rearranging the firewood. Then silence.

For the next hour, a frantic but erratic force scuttles around the house. The sounds are sudden and unpredictable. Tiny feet skedaddle. Then nothing. Gnawing, nudging sounds, a crash, and more scampering of feet. Smaller than a bear, more chaotic than mice, spunkier than a raccoon. It sounds like a pack rat. Sometimes at night pack rats gallop around the outside skirting board, like runaway horses. But when I look outside on the porch, I don't see a thing.

I phone Jay for advice and consolation. While I'm on the phone, a tiny nose and whiskers, then paws, and finally the whole grey body and puffy tail of a pack rat appear, then parade back and forth on the window sill on the front porch, just two feet away on the other side of the glass, sniffing for a way to get in.

I drop the phone and lurch across the room, open the front door, and scream at the rat, grabbing and sweeping the broom in a frenzy of motion. Racing back indoors, I slam and lock the door and return to the phone.

"You'd better set the trap," Jay advises before we hang up.

I bait the Havahart with peanut butter on a cracker, and place the trap on the side porch. Once in bed, I jam in my earplugs, read about France, and listen for hours until I hear the metallic clunk of the trap. The rest of the night I listen to the rat clinking around the cage. The next morning, enclosed in the grillwork, the soft grey fur, whiskers, beady little black eyes, and long furry tail of the pack rat await liberation.

Above the Kettle Valley Railway tracks, I open the trap under a clump of pines. *Petit raton* sniffs cautiously at the open-door policy, then scuttles into the pine needle duff. Relocation doesn't work for bears! Who knows about the success rate with rats? Hmm. Maybe I could seek funding under the Attorney General's office, a grant for the rehabilitation of rodent offenders, an attempt to mitigate woodrat recidivism. I could paint fingernail polish on rodent digits to identify them. Then I could identify repeat offenders.

Back at the house, I attack the porch with a broom, as if cleanliness and order will ward off rodents. The old apple box that we store kindling in is lined with rat shit and cactus spines. I should be wearing a respirator. Holding my breath against hantavirus, I sweep the porch, restack the firewood, and settle down. The sun sets, the fridge purrs, the wind whistles outside.

That evening, I am reading in bed, waiting for the new moon to scythe the night.

Suddenly, the sound of hind feet, like a baby Thumper, drum rolls in the attic just above my head.

Oh no! Does this happen in Provence?

A week later, it's late afternoon when a gnawing sound scrapes from just above the Clivus toilet vent, maybe on the roof. A pack rat is trying to get into the attic, and then it is only a matter of time before it will eat its way into the main floor of the house. It's happened before.

The wobbly aluminum ladder clatters as I set it up beneath the hatch, armed with my tools: flashlight, work gloves, steel wool. Beneath the attic's trusses floats an ocean of billowing pink fiberglass insulation, peppered with old mouse and rat shit. I pull myself up, grabbing the rafters, and step only on the edge of the trusses, to avoid springing the traps (the Have-No-Heart kind) or stepping on the ceiling (because I'd go right through). Like Curious George, I swing my way over to the fan. It's hopeless: I can't deconstruct my way out of here. I'm here to be "in nature," but the ceiling is pinpricked with light, where shingles are loose or have shifted. These are all possible entries for mice. Or bats. Rats? Yuck!

After stuffing more steel wool around the vent stack, I monkey-swing back to the trap door. In the corner, I spot a deer mouse, dead in a sprung trap. I hold the trap between my thumb and index finger and take it down the ladder. Outside the house, I cross the crusty rock plateau, then lift the spring to roll the body into a small crevice. Wee mousie is a soft, supple taupe-grey; its tail hangs limply and its whiskers catch the sun—clear, like tiny bits of cropped fishing line. Nestled in the rock, its tiny toes articulate like those of a newborn baby.

This is a problem for the lover of nature. After thirty-five years, my opposition to capital punishment has become theoretical.

Later that day I am in line at Walmart, buying a rat trap, when the woman behind me leans over and says, "Too bad my dad's not around any longer." I raise my eyebrows. What does she mean?

"He'd come out and shoot 'em for you."

Two days later, Brent Mountain above Summerland is illuminated by snow. Kinglets, juncos, chickadees, and one pesky Steller's jay bustle about the feeder. Night comes early. At eight o'clock, a necklace of light rings the lakeshore, but the new moon hides in an inkjet sky. A ravine of darkness surrounds the house. The stars forget to shine.

I'm settled in my favourite chair when I hear it: the percussion of little feet, stumbling on the porch.

In nature, you're never alone.

BESSIE AND THE YOUNG VET

BUD INGS

It was one of those baffling cases they don't tell you about in veterinary school: a Holstein cow that simply refused to get up. As I knelt by the motionless animal sprawled in the stall, the owner, a gruff old farmer with fifty years' experience with livestock, stared at me with one eye closed. "Me dad would have me cow on her feet if he was alive," he said in a booming voice. "Two things me dad always did for downed cows. Pour water in their ears and cut a piece off their tails to let the poison out. You never did that."

True. I had not tried either remedy.

I was an inexperienced veterinarian, less than a year out of vet school, and still trying to prove myself. The patient was a black-and-white cow named Bessie, and she was lying on her side in a stable in northeastern Prince Edward Island, apparently almost unconscious. Her owner, Pius MacDonald, was becoming impatient. He was not the kind of person who would wait long for results, and from the start I could tell he was not impressed with me. No wonder. I was in my mid-twenties, slight and boyish-looking. Moreover, unlike the local amateur vets he was used to dealing with, I was a college graduate—grounds for suspicion right there—and came from a community thirty miles away. He had never heard of me.

To me, Bessie's problem looked like a classic case of "milk fever," an illness that sometimes afflicts high-producing dairy cows after calving. The name of the ailment is misleading. The animal doesn't really have a fever, but, in many cases, it has a below-normal temperature due to a sudden loss of calcium in the blood. If the cow is not treated quickly, she probably will die. On my first visit, I injected the standard dose of calcium and waited for the best part of an hour for Bessie to rise. No results. Finally I told the owner that if she was still not on her feet by morning, he should call me.

Sure enough, the call came the next morning. Bessie was still down. Would I please come and see what I could do? At vet school, I had been told that one of the cases that could really get under a vet's skin was a cow that refused to get up. It was as hard to diagnose as a mysterious itch. Apparently, my day had arrived. Worse, I knew it would be difficult for a young doctor to convince a seasoned farmer like this one that any number of problems might be to blame.

In the course of four visits to the farm, I tried everything I could think of that might stimulate that black-and-white beast. Nothing worked. I was beginning to think Bessie was enjoying the whole thing. She was eating like a horse and seemed pleased with all the attention she was getting. But she would not attempt to move.

On my fifth visit, I was greeted by five or six experts from neighbouring farms. Each of the animal specialists had his own opinion. One remedy that was "never known to fail" involved sprinkling a downed cow with holy water from the church.

After a half-hour of these consultations, I thought I heard a snap in Bessie's pelvic region. I decided to do a rectal examination, and asked my consultants to move the cow back and forth. Sure enough, there was movement in the pelvis that indicated a fracture. Finally, I had uncovered the reason for Bessie's immobility. "Your cow has a broken pelvis, Mr. MacDonald," I announced, "and she'll never get to her feet."

I felt as though I were in front of a firing squad. Mr. MacDonald raised a finger and boomed, "I just wish me dad was alive. A smart man, he was. He'd have that cow back in the pasture by now. You can't get the old bugger up, but he could have."

"I'm sorry, sir," I said, "but you might as well call the packers. I can't do anything more for your cow." I could see the disappointment in the old man's eyes. As I turned to go, he shouted, "You never even got me dog to bark at her head!"

I thought perhaps there would be no harm in the dog therapy, and, to please everyone present, I invited the resident collie to put on his show. He danced from side to side, barking, but Bessie paid little attention to him other than looking as if she actually enjoyed the serenade. When I left the farm, I was sure of one thing: nature was on my side. A fracture is a fracture is a fracture.

Four days later, Mr. MacDonald phoned again. "Me cow made her feet, Doc! I shouted in her ear just like me dad used to do. A smart man was me dad. And she just leaped up, and now she's eating grass!"

I wasn't prepared for this news. I had felt the pelvic movement as plain as day. How in heaven's name could she get up? Still, I replied in my most professional tone: "Well, that's great. Let me know if she goes down again, will you?"

In an attempt to solve the mystery, I phoned one of the older veterinarians in the province, Dr. George Fisher, the provincial director of Veterinary Service. He laughed. "You got the case that tried to make a fool of you, eh? Well, it happens to all of us sooner or later. It does feel like a fracture, but what happens is that the pelvic ligaments don't tighten up for four or five days after calving. They gradually heal, and then they manage to get up."

When I hung up the phone, I felt like a bit of a fool. Had all my injections and vet school skills let me down? As the days went by I tried to forget the whole incident, but the case kept coming back to haunt me. A few months later, I happened to be in Mr. MacDonald's neighbourhood. Glancing at the pasture as I drove by his farm I spotted Bessie, happily grazing. The cow I said would never get up! I imagined I saw her wink at me as I drove by. In return, I gave her a little salute. She had taught me a

few good lessons—about the limitations of book-learning, about the resil-
ience of cows, and, most of all, about the importance of keeping a humble
attitude and an open mind when dealing with patients. They were lessons
that would stand me in good stead for the next fifty years.

As for that gruff old farmer, well, I suppose he learned something,
too: you just never know what might happen if you trying shouting in a
cow's ear.

LEARNING TO LOVE COYOTE

MARCUS JACKSON

My partner and I rounded up our menagerie of thirteen cats, six dogs, and two birds and moved to a small bungalow on 128 acres of land in the Columbia Valley in the southeast corner of British Columbia. The property had been a mink farm at one time, but the most recent owners had used it as a summer getaway. The land had been left to grow naturally for thirty or more years, and except for one small cultivated garden plot near an old chicken coop, most of it was open meadow and trees. Past the bushy edges of the forest, a wonderful cathedral opened up, and I spent hours wandering well-worn paths among the trees. The forest was perfect cover for many of the creatures inhabiting the area. Owls, ravens, songbirds, mice, voles, rabbits, squirrels, flickers, woodpeckers, grouse, bears, and coyotes all made a home in that forest. The Columbia River marked the western edge of the property at the bottom of a gentle sloping field. In the winter, eagles, coyotes, wolves, and elk picked their way along the marshy banks of the wetlands searching for food.

I had lived there just a few months when I lost my beloved little cat Lucky, so named because he had survived being hit by a train (yes, really!). He'd strayed a little too far from the safety of the yard and met his demise. All I found of him was his collar, some tufts of black and white fur, and wet pink stains on the snow. Losing that cat made me hate coyotes. I was constantly scanning the property from the back porch, and if I saw one too close to the house or looking a little too comfortable in the fields, I'd pull the .22 out of the closet and take aim. Although I fired many warning shots at their backsides, I never actually hit one. Killing wasn't my idea of wildlife management, but I wanted to create a hostile environment in the hope they would find another place far away to get their meals. My persecution lasted through the spring into early summer, but my urge for revenge began to wane after a month of driving to and from work.

Despite being a university graduate and a working artist, I'd taken one of the only summer jobs I could get: cutting grass for twelve dollars an hour at one of the many local golf resorts. Even though I had to get up at four in the morning to make it to work on time, it was one of the best jobs I've ever had. Being up early wasn't so bad after the first cup of coffee, and the forty-minute drive to the resort at that time of day meant I had a lot of time alone. Over the summer, I learned where to watch for animals who might be crossing the road and a few of my early morning animal encounters included a moose cow crossing a fence with her brand new calf, a pair of mule deer with their fawns in tow, a couple of bighorn sheep cracking heads during the rut, eagles perched on the ribs of roadkill, and coyotes scavenging for food. The first month I drove that stretch of road, I counted, on average, three new dead animals every day: twenty-one animals were killed every week that month along just twenty-seven kilometres of highway. Deer, elk, ravens, squirrels, and coyotes all fell victim to the metal monsters on the blacktop.

The first coyote I ever picked up off the road had been struck and killed by a vehicle on the highway right in front of the house. My partner had seen it lying there when she was returning to the house from the little general store just a few hundred metres up the highway. She was angry at the sight of another senseless animal death and suggested I go and take a look at it. I drove up the hill to the highway, creeping along the shoulder until I reached the coyote. At first glance, she looked as though she might have just been lying there taking a nap. She wasn't in an awkward broken position, and I couldn't see any blood. As I approached her, I had a horrified feeling that she might not be quite dead and half-anticipated some type of movement—a gasp, a twitch, a growl.

I suppose the impulse to pick her up arose from the fact that she was completely intact and could therefore be mounted and somehow memorialized. She was still warm when I picked her up—she'd probably been dead less than an hour. She weighed more than I expected, and I moved as quickly as I could, not wanting to be struck by a vehicle myself, but also hoping I wouldn't be spotted by a neighbour. I placed her on a tarp in the back of the truck, made a U-turn at the general store, and drove her back down to the house. I moved the tarp to the ground and uncovered the dead animal. After the dogs had sniffed and inspected her body, I got my first real intimate look at a coyote.

The smell of wet dog was overwhelming. Blood and brain matter had oozed from her ear since I'd moved her; a clot had formed in her nostril. Her nose and mouth reminded me of those of my own dogs. I looked at her eyes, still right and wet—they could have been the eyes of any dog, except her pupils were fixed and dilated, staring dreamily ahead at nothing. I grabbed my camera from my studio and began taking pictures because I needed to hold onto that moment of sadness and anger and awe. I photographed her whole body, her head, her feet, and her ears; her blood stained my leather work-mitts as I examined every part of her. I tried to find the evil predator, the worthless scavenger, the deadly dirty varmint, but I couldn't find her.

I didn't realize this coyote would be the first of many, nor did I know she would become the key to unlocking the puzzle of my own identity, as well as the inspiration for my current art practice.

I started to see coyotes everywhere: one or two at a time, minding their own business, they wandered the edge of the highway at dawn and crossed the north field at dusk. I heard them sing to each other across the Columbia River. While lying awake one night, I heard a mother teach her pups to sing. She started barking, and then about six or seven smaller voices started *kai-yai*-ing in response. Then one sharp bark from her, and everyone was quiet. I saw seven young coyotes chasing each other through an empty pasture during an early winter snowstorm. I watched a coyote sniff out and dig up a dead bird from a snowbank. It seemed as though I couldn't go anywhere without seeing a coyote, and I started to wonder if maybe they were trying to tell me something.

In order to figure out what a coyote might be saying to me, I needed to learn more about them. That fall, when I returned to the city for art school, I began doing research: fact, fable, myth, legend, lecture, essay, academic papers, scientific studies, newspaper clippings, anatomical drawings, photographs, and paintings. I learned about a coyote's habitat, life expectancy, diet, behaviours, den preference, mating cycle, gestation period, litter size, and the sad truth about puppy mortality. I read up on taxidermy, hunting regulations, trapping, skinning, mounting—everything I could get my hands on in the library or access via Google—but it wasn't until I read the Aboriginal myths of Coyote as fool, trickster, sex-maniac, demigod, saviour, magician, and culture hero, that I realized Coyote had been trying to tell me something after all.

In Aboriginal stories, Coyote only *appears* to be a selfish, greedy fool. Coyote plays the trickster in order to teach cultural lessons about values, ethics, sociology, tradition, and family. A cunning and devious mother, he brings about a sense of order and community through his actions. In Aboriginal myth, Coyote is not a varmint but a great spirit, a deity capable of transformation and acts of heroism. He is able to take the form of either human or animal. He is also able to transform himself between the sexes—to be male or female or both.

The Coyote figure is essential to understanding the cultures from which his stories originate, and Coyote has also become essential to understanding my own identity. As a transgendered person, I know what it's like to be misunderstood. It is difficult to be both male and female, to be cast in the role of teacher by the very nature of your own existence. I have to explain, justify, and facilitate understanding of my gender/body conflict to friends, family, community, and government. Coyote, embodying both animal and human, both male and female, has taught me what it means to be a teacher. And Coyote has something I desire: gestalt.

Through my research and artwork, I learned how to describe my identity positively. However, I am not a member of a First Nation and therefore feel unable to access the cultural and linguistic affirmations in the same way a First Nation person might. How, then, do I talk about my gender identity or my artwork, which references my identity through my relationship with Coyote, without appropriating or misunderstanding a culture of which I am not a member? I use actual coyotes. Most of the time by scraping them off the road.

In my art, Coyote is fragmented. She is dead, dismembered, dissected, skinned, deboned. I'm used to the strange looks, the "eews" and the "yucks," when people see my work. I photograph the animals where I find them on the roadside. I either take the dead animals home or dismember the corpses right there, taking body parts to make my art. Sometimes, like a forensic investigator, I make

Coyote and me.

impressions of their pawprints. Back at home, I take more pictures, photographs that are more intimate. I use these images as inspiration and reference when making prints or mixed-media drawings. In the objects I make—books, prints, and sculptures—I mix Coyote's fur, feet, bones, skull with manmade objects: gears from an old clock or tarnished silver teaspoons or weathered barbed wire. Each piece of art suggests a story, a myth, a legend, or a half-remembered dream. I am trying to explore what it means to be human and/or animal, male and/or female. I am trying to make something sacred. My work is greeted sometimes with reverence and sometimes with disdain, but never with apathy.

I have stopped my car time after time and picked up one coyote after another, each creature a loss, each its own spirit, each one a brother or sister in my newfound pack. We are not done with each other, Coyote and I—we have lessons still to learn and time yet to play the fool.

DISCOVERY

LINDA JOHNS

When I first saw her, she was an eight- or nine-day-old robin fledgling crouched at the side of the road, and too young to be on her own. Putting her up on the branch of a nearby apple tree, I withdrew and waited to see if one of the parents would appear. Predators, however, have a way of dividing families. An hour later I carried her into the house with the intention of launching her in a couple of weeks; something I'd done numerous times before with other separated youngsters.

Except that she never did leave, and that was a turning point in both our lives.

Her efforts to satisfy her own particular needs within the whirl of a busy human environment led to her rather unusual name. Calling insistently when she was hungry, only to be overlooked, would provoke her finally to hurl herself straight into the core of the prevailing activity, her beak gaping determinedly, and personifying in every indignant feather the rural expression, "another county heard from." So County she came to be called.

Our home is a rambling ground-level building with a loft and high cathedral ceiling at one end. It is beautifully surrounded by acres of woodland and meadows. Trees close to the house bring wild bird activities continually into close range and provide frequent sightings of other wild creatures as well. County was never caged; the entire house was always at her disposal, and the daily unfolding of her life within its precincts was an illumination and a rare privilege.

Within a week of her arrival County developed an insistent chronic cough which persisted for many months before finally ceasing. I decided against her leaving, feeling that she'd never migrate successfully with a breathing handicap. Anyway, by that time she was reigning supreme over the establishment and leaving didn't seem to be on her mind.

I fed her a variety of foods for which she gaped readily: currants, worms, bugs, fresh fruit, canned dog food, cheese, lean ground beef, and cooked egg yolk. I would dip the occasional tidbit in water, shaking off the excess, since she hadn't learned to drink yet. She needed food, in quantities of two or three caterpillars' worth, roughly every half-hour, from dawn to dusk, and would call repeatedly when hungry. This call was not to be confused with her steady "location" note between feedings, a sort of radio contact between fledglings and foraging parents to which I tried to respond verbally for reassurance.

Not distinguishing between these two calls has led many well-intentioned people to overfeed stray nestlings. This often results in death. I found that a good way to regulate County's feeding schedule was to put myself in a parent bird's position faced with three or four hungry youngsters. I would imagine myself flying off and hunting patiently through the foliage, returning finally with about two fat caterpillars (a beak-size serving) which would quickly disappear down the throat of nestling number one. Then I'd remove the fecal sac produced invariably at this time, drop it well away from the nest, and go off to find two or three more wrigglies for nestling number two, and so on. By the time I'd get the last one fed, it would be time to feed the first one again—about twenty minutes later. Imagining the process in this way helped to prevent me from overfeeding County.

For the first week County slept on towels in a little draped box in a warm area near a lamp. When she objected to being bedded in it each night so strongly as to bounce up against the cover over and over again like a stubborn little feathered frog, I let her choose her own roosts. Sometimes she'd select the shower-curtain rod, the upstairs closet, the back porch, the horn of a wall-hung cowskull, or the drying pegs protruding from a hand-hewn beam in the living room. She always changed the chosen spot every two or three days, leading me to speculate if that were a necessary safety maneuver in the wild, because of scent buildup, or perhaps because of accumulated droppings below (although she did very few at night).

Gradually County became more and more mobile, ever on the go, bursting with curiosity about everything, and endowed with a lively teasing nature. Two frequent victims of her devilishness were Desmond and Molly, a pair of young domestic pigeons who had arrived a couple of months previously when they were about ten days old—winsome but woebegone. Desmond had been battered and defeathered by a flock of grown pigeons and Molly was suffering from an impacted crop. Mild disinfectant and warmth for Des, a mineral-oil tonic and crop massage for Molly, and a softened nourishing diet for both had worked wonders so that by County's arrival they were feathered, flying, and bright-eyed. They were never caged either and had more flying room indoors than I could have afforded outdoors with the costs of weasel-proof wire caging. A few shelves on the wall for feed dishes and roosts gave them a secure base from which they pattered about the floors with timid curiosity, always keeping near each other with rounded eyes of wonder. Gradually their confidence grew and they would bask daily in a warm patch of sunlight on the floor, getting up again and again to follow it as it glided through the house. But their innately gentle nature collided frequently with County's exuberant cockiness, setting the stage for endless entertainment. Their idea of quiet amusement was to play with a heap of buttons I'd given them toying with them, and tossing them up to fall. County's idea of amusement was to snatch the buttons out of their mouths in passing and drop them onto their heads from above. There were moments when she teased them mercilessly—like swooping over Desmond from behind and thumping him on the head with her feet en route. She continually desecrated the clean drinking water in their bowl by bathing in it, dropping buttons-or-worse into it, and periodically indulged in scattering their food pellets and grit over a surprisingly wide range. If they were dozing, nothing delighted Country more than swooping them repeatedly into ruffled annoyance and then scampering ahead of them as they bore sedately down on her, cooing irritably in the dignified majestic anger of pigeons.

Her greater speed and maneuverability made her almost invulnerable but her overconfidence was her downfall. Hovering over Molly one day and paddling her feet on her head, County suddenly found herself seized by a leg in an unprecedented turning of tables and shaken thoroughly by an irate Molly, who turned a deaf ear to County's plaintive squeaks of pain and remorse. And on more than one occasion, hearing a disturbance, I'd enter a room just as County was streaking out and see mild Desmond dropping a mouthful of robin feathers with evident satisfaction.

To County, *everything* was to be explored. Through her eyes I began to view the house in an altogether different way. What had appeared to be an aesthetically—pleasing whitened cowskull hanging on the wall, was in reality a pair of perches ideal for preening and napping. Lampshades offered electrically warmed roosts particularly cozy for drying wet feathers after a bath, and the woodbox was a prolific hunting ground for insects. A mundane broom impassively sweeping the floor was actually for challenging and chasing, and the scattered sweepings a positive triumph.

But not every added dimension was so benign. A tall roomy boot, an open crock of honey, or a half-full coffee mug were innocent preludes to disaster for a curious, inexperienced fledgling. Because young robins examine everything by jabbing with their beaks, I became one of the tidiest, if not one of the most paranoid, of mortals, perpetually unplugging appliances and hiding knives and scissors, often to my own personal inconvenience. Moths weren't the only creatures to be attracted to the open flames of candles, and the electric stove at mealtimes contained such a wealth of nightmarish possibilities that I doubted if I'd ever be free of the burden of owning one. Even a sink full of soaking dishes and sharp utensils would loom menacingly with hazards. Spilled spices had to be cornered instantly, and hot baked goods locked in the bathroom to cool, it being the only room with a door—and without mice. Dangling mobiles had to be removed from high-speed flyways, and I developed an intense fixation about pins, thumbtacks, and staples on floors which I found myself indulging even in other peoples' houses. The consequences of neglecting even a stray elastic band was brought suddenly to my attention one morning when County, after playfully toying with one as though it were a worm, swallowed it. Fortunately it caught around her lower mandible and I was able to snatch her up and gently pull the remainder out of her throat in spite of her indignant struggles.

The horrendous possibilities involving thread she thoroughly explored one day when I was out. When I arrived home, the living room looked as though it had been systematically gift-wrapped by a gigantic spider. There was thread joining every visible object. County had discovered an antique spoolholder holding several spools which allowed threads to be pulled our easily. One thing had led to another and, getting several entangled around her feet, she'd flown all over the house and even up into the loft attempting to free herself, while the unwinding threads behind her wrapped themselves liberally around every projection she passed. She'd finally managed to tie herself quite tightly to a large piece of driftwood and was still struggling and terrified when I came in. It was a lesson on thread neither of us ever forgot.

County's enjoyment enriched even the most minute and common occurrences. It became so infectious that I found myself quite sharing her delight as she chased drops of water falling from freshly misted plants or soared astoundingly straight up to the peak of the cathedral ceiling to return triumphantly grasping a tiny spider in her beak—or better yet, one of those shudderingly huge ones I visualized dropping down on my head some night. Or into my tea. Even the sprinkling of rain on the roof moved her to song in rippling warbles and trills, transmitting to me, through the sudden beauty of music, unnoticed changes in the weather outside. The gentle rise and fall of a robin's rain song harmonizes so exquisitely with the fluctuations of pattering raindrops that they will always remain interwoven melodies in my mind.

Even the daily arrival of morning County saluted with jubilant songs and flights more truly worthy of the "renewal of light" than our usual reception of "just another day." She'd start with high-speed flights and loud "barking" while swooping back and forth through the house at grey dawn, and then land on my head to waken me, pulling my hair and eyelashes impatiently and resorting, when all else failed, to thrusting her bill right down into my ear. This *never* failed. Then she'd flit from windowsill to windowsill, wing- and tail-flicking with bursts of singing, glorying in sun or rain, and taking in the bustling activities of the outdoor birds as though seeing it all for the first time—an enviable freshness of mind she retained year after year. And her enthusiasm was decidedly contagious. Once I'd finally been roused, I'd often stand beside her trying (usually in vain) to see just what *she* was seeing—what was provoking that excited bark and terse, cocked head with every feather upright in participation? But if after all that time I was still somnolent in a tumble of blankets, County would often nestle down on my head, or nose, or chin—whatever was available—and preen companionably or sing softly.

Even her silence spoke. One still afternoon poised reluctantly on the brink of winter, when only a few scattered yellow leaves were lingering on the trees, and the infinite mingling of summer birdsongs had dwindled to the winter feeder calls of jays, juncos, and grosbeaks, I suddenly missed County. A short search revealed her sitting silently on a windowsill looking out on the late golden light. Sensing the fullness of feeling permeating and surrounding her, I knelt quietly down beside her as she gazed out unblinkingly into the sky.

With eyes huge and dark and far-seeing, she turned her head and, as in a vision, I saw in her eye centuries of migrations crossing the vastness of her inner skies from the eternal springs of memory.

Flights criss-crossing in unending streams, lives upon lives evolving through the ages, and all encompassed in the eye of a single bird, an eloquent Eye that loomed as large momentarily as the universe itself....

With County, even common household tasks became Events. When I sat down with huge bowls of fresh chanterelle mushrooms resigned to a couple of hours shredding and debugging, she perched on the bowl rim delighting in any bugs I found and often carried off pieces of mushroom to pound smaller and eat. When I baked, she was usually feet-first into the mixing bowl sampling the batter and extracting raisins, her special favourites. She would stalk impatiently up and down the counter while muffins, another favourite, were baking, peering through the glass door of the oven at them. Frequently I baked just for the fun of doing it with her. If I washed my hands under the kitchen tap, she'd edge down my arm into my cupped hands to enjoy her own shower under the dribble, drenching me to the waist with spray. And her "raised eyebrows" look from atop the shower-curtain rod could convulse me with laughter while I showered.

But proper bathing for County was not just a hasty cleansing process fitted into the most convenient time of day as it has become for most of us. The moment was *selected*—which in itself I found worthy of consideration. And there was a particular ritual to be followed that enhanced and prolonged the intense enjoyment birds always have when bathing. Fresh water, of course, was essential. Stepping into her water dish, stepping out again, and fixing me with her eye immediately galvanized me into bringing fresh water. Then she'd hop about in the dish doing speculative beak-flicks to test depth, shooting water out in all directions. Choosing the deepest area (due to the tilting dish), she'd indulge in a few tentative wing-flicks, gradually accelerate to a watery blur and then suddenly stop, hop out, and coyly feign a brief interest in probing under the dish. Hopping back in, she'd do one or two more wing-flicks before really churning up a turmoil of spray by vibrating each wing alternately, as an ever-advancing tidal ring glistened around the dish. At this point, she usually hopped out for a few shakes before returning for more splashing, interrupted by several moments of perfect stillness when she remained motionless with all her feathers puffed out, emitting a tiny high-pitched whistle while the water lapped gently around her. Finally, with another resounding flurry, thoroughly saturated and satisfied, she'd fly heavily to a warm roost to preen, pulling the feathers dry through her beak. Then she'd oil her feathers by taking oil from a special preening gland at the base of her tail and distributing it all over her feet and feathers. The final result was a beautifully groomed appearance and a prodigious appetite, the satisfaction of which was invariably followed by a prolonged nap. One of her favourite drying roosts was on the gentle curve of an overturned deer antler which was strategically placed under a feather-warming hanging lamp. For me, the shedding process inherent in a cast-off horn is a reminder in the wider sense of the progressive sheddings marking our inner growth. This image was movingly emphasized by the artless charm of this young fledgling, poised awkwardly between nestlinghood and adulthood, and edged in light descending from above.

A Bird in the Hand

Shannon Kernaghan

As the weather shows its fall shades and the leaves decide they can't hang on any longer, my autumnal reflection is interrupted by the cooing of two pigeons on my balcony. They preen themselves for several minutes and then, with twigs, mark out a secluded area behind the folded lawn furniture: the perfect spot for a nest. One fans its tail and bows to the other.

I shove open the patio door and rush towards the pair, pulling off one of my slippers and waving it, calling out, "Shoo! Shoo!" I chase them off, but they must sense my lack of sincerity because they're back moments later. Again and again they return.

After several days of this ritual, I realize they have become permanent dwellers. Every day I am able to move closer to them before they flee from my waving slipper. I'm not exactly a lethal weapon.

One Christmas Eve, when I was eight, my dad was coming home from work, and when he stopped to fill up at a gas station he noticed a pigeon shivering on a window sill. My father could never resist a furred or featured creature, especially one in distress. The pigeon didn't move when Dad approached and carefully picked it up. Dad tucked it inside his jacket, where he kept it warm during the ride home.

"Leon, a pigeon?" my mother said when Dad presented us with the bird. "We're having thirty people for Christmas dinner tomorrow and

Me, age eight, with Patrick.

you bring home a stray pigeon?" I'm surprised she didn't throw the bird *and* my dad into the nearest snowbank.

"But Mom," I pleaded, "it's freezing outside, and he must be someone's pet." I went to Dad and took the bird from his hands. "Look how he snuggles in my arm."

"If he's someone's pet," Mom said, "then someone will be missing him. You two make a phone call to the Humane Society and find out if there were any inquiries." She gently ruffled the shimmering blue-green feathers on the pigeon's neck. "Make sure you keep him in the laundry room."

"Okay, Mom." I wasn't about to attempt any more negotiating for one day. My dad had already headed to the basement where I heard him pouring seed we kept for the backyard feeders.

We had no success in finding an owner—not with calls to the animal shelter and radio stations, not with the "Found Pigeon" signs I tacked up reluctantly on the bulletin boards of stores in our neighbourhood. My attempts were half-hearted because I wanted him to stay with us. Despite an array of store-bought gifts, the bird was my favourite Christmas present.

The holiday festivities ended, although not before the pigeon became a member of the family. He didn't stay in the laundry room for long. Every morning, Patrick—the name I chose for the bird—hopped onto my dad's knee where he helped himself to toast crumbs and dry cereal. For bathing, he appropriated a decorative fountain in the front-hall planter. To shake off the water, Patrick flapped his two-tone grey wings and always seemed puzzled to find himself airborne.

"Sometimes I wish he'd fly away," muttered my mom, surveying the hallway runner that had become worse for wear. Unfortunately, a free-flying pigeon and wall-to-wall carpeting don't mix. Since Patrick had the advantage of high flight, no heads or shoulders were safe.

When spring arrived, Patrick surprised us by laying an egg in a colourful nest of Monopoly money on April Fool's Day. She was no bird-brain: she knew the importance of feathering her nest. Overnight, Patrick became a "Pat" and a "she." The catalyst for her egg-laying remained a mystery because she hadn't been with other pigeons. Years later, I discovered all she needed was the sight of another bird. That's when I remembered how she would admire her reflection in the mirror over the fireplace mantle.

In addition to being an agreeable playmate and constant companion, Pat landed me a half-page spread in the local newspaper. A reporter heard about our unconventional pet and came to our home for pictures and an interview. We were neighbourhood celebrities, at least the day our story appeared.

Pat was intelligent and made her demands known. Although we let the bird outside as soon as the weather warmed, she never went far.

When she wanted to go out, she'd flap her wings noisily against the door. And if no one let her in quickly enough, she'd fly to the kitchen window and flutter against the glass. This bird always found her way home.

Although *we* were accustomed to a pigeon soaring overhead, not all of our guests were comfortable. When we had company, I'd put Pat in my room and close the door. However, she was a social bird, and she didn't like being left alone. By balancing on the knob and flapping her wings, she figured out how to build enough momentum to open the door and join the party.

Summer vacation? If the family dog could join us at the lake cabin, why couldn't Pat? I put her in an unused hamster cage for her inaugural ride. We learned a few important things during that trip: although pigeons fly with speed and endurance, they don't travel well in the back seat of a station wagon. Pat bobbed her head nervously when I held up the cage to show her the highway traffic. In hopes of comforting her, I let her out of the cage and set her on my shoulder. She settled for a few moments, until she opened her beak and peppered the back of my parents' heads with bird seed.

"Holy cow!" I shouted, trying to slow the spray with my open hand.

"Leon, watch out for that truck!" my mother yelled at my father, who was distracted by my hollering and the shower of seeds. "You nearly cut him off! Shannon, put that bird back in her cage!" We had ourselves one carsick pigeon.

By the following autumn, Mom's patience had lessened. Pat's downfall was her inability to understand the concept of acceptable bathroom habits. Mom heard about a Montessori school eager for live-in pets. Resourceful as ever, she made her sales pitch by referring to Pat as a rock dove, and soon found the bird a new perch. Although I realized Pat wasn't designed to be an indoor pet, that logic didn't stop my tears from flowing when I introduced her to a new home. There, though, she was free to venture outdoors while having the safety of a warm pen to spend her nights.

I cried a second time when Pat—a homing pigeon—made her way back to us, across the city and through blinding rain. When we returned her to the school, she didn't stay long. According to the teacher, Pat failed to reappear one night.

Although pleased by the news of her chosen freedom, I felt sorry for myself. "If I could only see her one more time, to know she's all right and that she doesn't hate me for giving her away." That became my childhood dream, my unfinished business.

My dream unfolded one year later when Pat appeared on our roof. And this time, she didn't come alone. Another pigeon, making a series of throaty coos, hovered nearby. I spotted them from the living room window and ran outside to the patio. Pat quickly landed on my shoulder and then fluttered away, perhaps listening to her mate's nervous *oorhh oorhh* warning. The two birds stayed in our backyard for most of the afternoon until finally disappearing as suddenly as they'd arrived. I remember smiling and giggling for the rest of the day, knowing Pat was doing fine in the wild and that she had a mate. Even better, she remembered me. I could stop pining for a freezing bird rescued on a cold Christmas Eve. Our special bond would last forever.

Since then, I've always felt fondly towards these birds considered a messy menace to the neighbourhood. I also comprehend how kind-hearted my parents have been to all the furry paws and feathered wings that have landed and perched on their doorstep over the years.

But that doesn't help with the problem of my present-day pair who've already surveyed and staked their winter home on my balcony. From my window, I watch them fan their tails, strutting around my storage containers. Maybe I'll throw in the slipper and head to the nearest hardware store for one of those plastic owls. I refuse to put out the welcome mat. After all, I just installed new carpets.

THE HUNTER

JOANNA LILLEY

"**A** huge tree fell down in the wind here the other day," said our English friend Sue on the phone from Vancouver Island.

I was sitting on the couch at home in Scotland. My husband and I had submitted our emigration applications to Canada House in London two months before. Sue had emigrated a few years earlier, so we considered her our unofficial emigration advisor. I took a sip of tea and listened.

"The tree was known for having an eagle's nest in it, and of course the nest came down too," Sue told me. I tutted with sympathy for the eagle. "Guess what was in the nest when they had a look?"

"Oh no," I said. "Not baby eagles, I hope!"

"Nope. Collars," said Sue. "Pet collars. Over thirty of them. Cat collars. Small dog collars."

I didn't say anything. I never have been any good on the phone.

Sue, on the other hand, is very good on the phone. She always gets to the point, and this was a point she made often: "People aren't letting their little dogs off the lead any more on the beach. Bald eagles sweep down and carry them off. If they can grab dogs, cats are no problem. No way should you bring your cat to this country."

"Those poor dogs," I said. "And cats." I didn't know what else to say because there was no way I could consider leaving Snapdragon behind.

Snapdragon on the woodpile, Marsh Lake, Yukon.

I knew all about the food chain. I learnt it at primary school. I didn't like looking at pictures of food chains, though, because human beings were always at the top, which was where I most certainly didn't want to be. I wanted to look after animals, not eat them. In Scotland, Snapdragon was almost at the top of his food chain. All that was above him were foxes, slug pellets, and cars. He went hunting every day, dragging squirrels, pigeons, and rabbits through the cat-flap to crunch them up in the darkness under the bed.

Despite Sue's repeated advice, when my husband and I finally moved to Canada, Snapdragon came with us. I had raised him since he was five weeks old. Thirty-something and childless, I was like a dog who's been given a kitten to raise and thinks it's her baby. I loved my orange companion with his stripey tail, his rusty purr, and the dark stain in his amber right eye that was the same shape as the birthmark on my thigh.

In Canada, Snapdragon didn't know there were now several species above him on the chain: coyotes, wolves, wolverines, lynx, bears. And eagles. Creatures he'd never seen or smelt. There were unfamiliar species below him on the food chain too. Not that this fazed him. He munched up chipmunks as if they were cousins of the rabbit family.

Herbivores, like me, shouldn't really have carnivores as pets, even a carnivore who purrs when he smells toothpaste, stretches out for tummy rubs, and lies on the rug ready to be pulled along the wooden floor. In Scotland, when Snapdragon brought his prey into the house at night, I would lie in bed with my fingers in my ears so I couldn't hear him snapping skeletons and chewing organs. Yet I fed him cat food. Occasionally, someone else would make the same connection I made every day: wasn't it hypocritical for a vegetarian to buy meat for her pet? I had done a little research, and while dogs could be fed a vegetarian diet, it was much harder with cats. I'd need to source synthetic versions of essential nutrients—taurine and arachidonic acid, among others—that were otherwise only found in meat. So I never made this effort; I carried on buying cat food from the supermarket each week.

Herbivores probably shouldn't live in the Yukon, either. To survive in the north, all my food except some vegetables has to be trucked or flown in. It isn't easy to live entirely on local food, but at least omnivores could either buy local elk, bison, and caribou or go hunting for such creatures themselves.

Seeking space, wildlife, and wilderness, my husband and I had moved to the mecca of hunting, where Aboriginal people carry out their indigenous practices, where incomers arrive in response, perhaps, to some atavistic urge to stalk, kill, dismember, and eat, and where humans, from time to time, are attacked by bears and coyotes. I had removed my hunter companion from Britain's weary ecosystem and inserted him into the Yukon's vigorous one. There was no way for me to warn him he was playing with the big boys now.

While Snapdragon got busy killing chipmunks, mice, voles, dark-eyed juncos, red polls, and squirrels, I carried on wishing I could find a pair of bolt cutters big enough to cut myself right out of the food chain. I tried to ensure Snapdragon remained the hunter, not the hunted. I played with him and drugged him with catnip to distract him from wanting to go out. When his meows became too heart-rending, I let him go out during the day but made sure he was in at night. When I relaxed the rules and let him out early in the mornings, I stood on the back porch and clapped my hands to scare off predators, at least until my husband told me to stop making such a racket.

Four years after our move to the Yukon, Snapdragon didn't come in for breakfast one morning. It was June, a week after the summer solstice, the time of year when Snapdragon meowed and pawed at me all night to let him out because it was as bright as midday. Sometimes I gave in so I could get some sleep.

That morning, after CBC Radio clicked on, I didn't follow my usual routine because my husband and I telephoned our niece in England to wish her a happy thirteenth birthday. I was aware that Snapdragon hadn't come in for his breakfast and that this had never happened before, but I went to work anyway, hoping it was because I had been on the phone and hadn't called him in, not because he wasn't there to be called.

That evening he still hadn't come home. In the rain that fell all that night, I delivered posters to every house on the surrounding streets in case he was trapped in a shed or a garage, although I knew he wasn't. The next day, I put on my wellington boots and waded through the flooded creek behind our house in case he was wounded or stranded on a miniature island, although I knew he wasn't.

I went looking and calling for him every morning and every evening for ten days. Once a day, I brought home a stone and placed it along the edge of the back porch. Sometimes I picked a stripey stone in honour of his markings, sometimes a plain, smooth one that was calming to hold.

I stopped collecting stones when a neighbour down the street left a phone message saying that a couple of weeks earlier, another neighbour had gone to the airport early one morning and had seen a coyote crossing the highway with a ginger cat in its jaws. It took a couple more days to establish this wasn't Snapdragon because it had happened before he went missing, but I didn't go out looking for him any more. Nor did I ever did find out whose cat that had been.

A month later, we had a gathering at our house for the faculty and friends of the music camp my husband had helped to organize. I kept myself busy all evening doing the dishes so I didn't have to keep lying when our guests asked how my summer was going. While some people might have understood that I was going through the same bereavement process as I would for a human friend, I still wasn't physically able to say the words: that Snapdragon had died. Email had saved me from several impossible conversations.

My neighbour Linda came into the kitchen while I was up to my elbows in dishwater.

"I'm so sorry," she said. She was one of the guests who knew about Snapdragon's disappearance, seeing as I'd gone round asking her to check her basement, her closets, every closed door.

I exhaled slowly and flicked the water off my hands before I turned. She gave me a strong hug.

"I think my dog found something," she said. "He kept going back to this place every time I took him for a walk. Behind our houses, just off the trail."

"What did he find?" I asked.

"Some fur, you know, the right colour."

I nodded and said nothing.

"It was a family of coyotes, I'm sure," she said. "There's no way just one coyote would have managed to corner him on its own. He was too quick." She paused. Her eyes were shining.

"I didn't know whether to tell you."

"No," I said, "I'm glad you did. Really."

I meant it. Having the certainty helped a little. None of us is free of the food chain, after all.

I still haven't asked Linda to take me to the spot. I don't know if I ever will.

And I still haven't told my friend Sue that Snapdragon is dead, not even by email. Every time we speak on the phone, I pray she won't ask me how he's doing. So far she hasn't. It's one thing to realize someone was right, it's another thing to have to tell them so.

Now, when I remember the dark stain in Snapdragon's amber eye, it takes the shape of the silhouette of a coyote trotting towards him, just at the moment he turns to see it.

COUNTERPARTS

ROSE-MARIE LOHNES

"This cat is freaking me out!" I said to my husband.

I had been lying on the couch relaxing with a good book when Raven, normally a standoffish animal, had jumped up on my chest and stared at me. Without so much as a blink of her narrowed eyes, she continued to hold my attention for a long minute. This was unusual! What did she want? Was her buddy Tinker locked in a closet somewhere? Nope, Tinker was asleep on the mat by the door.

As abruptly as she had arrived, Raven gave up staring at me and walked the length of my leg, slowing as she padded across my shin, blowing out and then sniffing all the way from my knee to my ankle.

Unnerved, I gently pushed her off, then got up and walked about. When I returned to the couch and picked up my book, though, Raven repeated the same strange process.

The incident was so unusual I thought about it all day. That night, I wrote in my journal, "Raven has me baffled. What would possess her to smell my leg to the point of being a nuisance?"

After our elderly cat Moggie had died, Corwin and I had wanted to add a pet to the household again. We visited the local Shelter for Homeless Animals in Distress (SHAID). The shelter was actually a house, and in each room there were cats, cat trees, feeding dishes, litter boxes, and the overwhelming odours of both ammonia and disinfectant. We had already decided we wanted a mature cat, not a kitten, so we asked the volunteer on duty to point out older cats.

We stood in the middle of the room, eyeing up a dozen or so handsome animals. I prefer a cat with a lively, loveable personality, while Corwin prefers a cuddly lap cat. A huge Maine Coon, obviously the alpha cat of the group, growled at us from atop a cat tree. We crossed him off our list of possibilities. I had to fight the urge to turn to the kittens.

Corwin immediately eyed Tinker, an obese, short-legged female tabby. "She reminds me of Moggie," he said, as he picked up the cat that had already deposited fur on the legs of his jeans. "Look at her. She's got a handsome necklace, eyes that look rimmed with mascara, and a luxurious coat. How could you resist?" Tinker snuggled into his neck and purred.

"Ha!" I said. "You wanted a snuggly cat! Remember Moggie? He pulled that same snuggly bit at first, and then he never allowed anyone to pick him up again." Corwin just smiled. How could I say no?

While Corwin snuggled unabashedly with Tinker, I walked over to tell the volunteer we had found our cat. Just then, I felt something winding around my legs. I looked down to see a tall, regal, ebony-coloured feline with large, round, emerald eyes. To my surprise, she rolled over to expose a white G-string.

"That's amazing!" the volunteer said. "Raven has never approached anyone before!" She stared, open-mouthed.

"Hi, Raven," I cajoled, squatting down and reaching to let her smell my hand. Before I could touch her, she disappeared like a wisp of smoke, retreating to an otherwise deserted corner of the room.

From her safe place, Raven gazed at me from half-lidded, anxious eyes. She was gorgeous—I was smitten.

The worker, seeing that I might be interested, told me Raven had been a feral kitten that was captured in a live trap when her mother was killed. A woman who already had too many cats rescued her, but Raven was the only one of the litter who could not be socialized. At the shelter, she hid in the corners, too terrified to interact with anyone, feline or human. Her reluctance to socialize—and the fact that black cats are less likely to be adopted—made her future seem bleak.

"Would you consider choosing Raven?" she asked. "Her chances of being adopted, after eight months here, aren't great. And you can guess the alternative."

"Corwin," I called. "I think we might have a problem. I can't leave Raven here."

"We came for *one* cat, not two!" Corwin protested feebly, hugging Tinker close to his chest.

But when I told him Raven's story, he sighed heavily and then nodded his head.

Corwin chose Tinker. I did not need to choose a cat. Raven had chosen me! Corwin and I had each gotten the type of cat we wanted—or so we thought.

We went to the desk to fill out the paperwork and pay our adoption fees while a worker put Raven in a cardboard carrier. The cat was obviously terrified. As she cowered in the box, her hair was standing on end, ears in a pagoda stance, eyes narrowed to slits, claws extended.

When we put the cats in the car, Tinker lay down in our cat carrier and purred. Raven cowered in the makeshift carrier, her eyes wide and wary. As we drove off, we heard Raven vomit. Corwin wondered aloud if he should turn the vehicle around. I said I would clean Raven up once we got home.

By the time we got home, the car reeked of cat feces. We carried the cat carrier and cardboard box into the house. Once let out, Tinker strolled around the house, surveying and marking her new territory. Corwin put on leather gloves, took the cardboard box to the bathroom, and put it in the tub. I filled a pan with warm water, found an old cloth, and prepared for the onerous task ahead. I opened the cardboard box, but Raven, obviously terrified, did not move. I sat back and waited. And waited.

She stared at me. I waited some more. Finally Raven stepped gingerly over a puddle of vomit and into the tub. Her carrier was full of feces and vomit, but she was perfectly clean and glossy.

I stood back and opened the bathroom door. Raven leapt from the tub, spun around the corner, bolted for the open door to the basement, and disappeared. Apparently her original interest in me had not lasted!

I gave her a few hours to settle down, but then curiosity got the better of me. I went downstairs to investigate, and after searching every nook and cranny, I looked under the bed to see two round eyes staring at me from the furthest corner.

We left food, water, and a litter box near the bed, and although Raven clearly used them when we weren't there, we didn't see her for three days. Corwin declared that once she finally came out, we would catch her and take her back to the shelter. Fat chance I was about to allow that to happen!

When she finally appeared at the top of the stairs on the fourth day, I waited for her to make the first move. Back arched, eyes like saucers, her fear was palpable. Tinker charged at Raven, sending her racing downstairs once again. A few days later, Raven crept up the stairs again. This time, she jumped over Tinker and landed in the living room. Her back was arched, her fur on end, her tail a fluffy black flag. Every claw was extended, her pupils dilated and wild.

I held my breath, knowing that Raven had taken the first step toward becoming part of our household.

My husband suggested again that we return her to SHAID. I simply said, "She's my cat. She chose me and I'm keeping her."

Corwin shrugged his shoulders as if to say, "She's your problem."

Three weeks after the strange incident when Raven sniffed my leg, I was talking to my sister, Sandra, who had just been diagnosed with sarcoma.

She advised me to check for three colours on any of the suspicious moles I had checked on a yearly basis.

"Pink? Really?" I asked. I had only been looking for changes in shades of brown.

"Definitely."

"I didn't know that. I have one on my shin that might fit that criterion. It's got a pink edge, but I don't think it looks much different from most of my other freckles."

"You'd better get it checked."

I waited until my next regular checkup. When I showed the doctor the mole, he was concerned enough to send me to a plastic surgeon for a biopsy.

It was melanoma. I needed to have the mole and the surrounding tissue removed. The surgeon removed the lump from my shin as well as a lymph node from my groin. The malignancy was confirmed, but the lymph node was benign. As a precautionary measure, I was advised to see the oncologist every six months.

I made an appointment with our veterinarian to have both cats vaccinated as per our adoption agreement. A few days before the appointment date, I placed the carrier in the living room, door open, hoping to familiarize the cats with it. Tinker slept in the carrier. Raven sniffed and marked it. I put treats inside, but Raven couldn't be enticed to go far enough into the cage to risk being captured.

Finally, the morning of the appointment, Raven sneaked warily into the confined space pursuing a treat. When all but one leg was inside the carrier, I said, "I've got her!"

Ha! Raven's two front paws hit the end of the cage, which then ricocheted off the wall. Her sudden movement sent me, the cage, and a nearby chair flying. Raven disappeared down the stairs. I called the vet's office and told them we'd be bringing one cat, not two.

While Tinker was getting her shots, I asked if short legs and a stout body were characteristics of the Munchkin breed I had read about. The vet said, "Well, you can think what you like, but I think Tinker's parents were just a little too close in the gene pool."

Every day Raven became a bit braver, but she disappeared whenever company arrived, whenever Corwin or I moved unexpectedly, or when I turned a page in a book. She exhibited an irrational fear of enclosed spaces, likely a result of her experiences in the trap. She couldn't bear to be in a room with a closed door.

Friends of ours, Ruth and Warren, came over one afternoon to meet our new cats. Raven hid in the basement while Tinker made nice with everyone. Warren just smiled. "You wait and see. In the end, Raven will be the lap cat and Tinker will be more standoffish."

One day, Raven finally walked over to me and nudged my leg with her forehead. I gently petted her head. She disappeared again. Months passed. Day by day, as Corwin watched us tentatively bond, he began to talk less about returning Raven to the shelter. It eventually became apparent from her sultry-eyed gaze that she had fallen in love with me. My heart swelled the first time she allowed me to stroke her glossy fur, the first time she purred, and finally, the first time she jumped up on my lap.

Four months after she had sniffed my shin, Raven crawled up my chest and began investigating my cheek. I had an *aha* moment as I recognized her behaviour: *This has happened before!* I leafed back through my journal and, sure enough, it had been three weeks before the doctor suspected melanoma that Raven had smelled something amiss.

I looked in the mirror, but I could see nothing significant on my face. However, since the melanoma diagnosis, I wanted to be prudent. Off I went to the oncologist. I did not tell him about Raven, but I did ask him to examine my face. Sure enough, I needed some treatment on my cheek with the doctor's nasty smoking stick.

He asked me to come back in four months rather than six.

Raven is not unique in her ability to sense things we humans miss. There are a number of documented cases of cats detecting ill-

Raven and Tinker at the door.

ness. There was Fozzy, who sensed Crohn's disease flare-ups, Blue, who detected recurring lymph node cancer, and Zeuss, who predicted grand mal seizures.

A cat named Oscar came to public attention in July of 2007 when David Dosa, a geriatrician and assistant professor at Brown University, featured him in an article. According to Dr. Dosa, Oscar predicted the impending deaths of more than twenty-five terminally ill patients. Dosa suspects that dying is accompanied by odours that the cat can detect. Oscar was right too many times for it to be considered chance.

What I found most interesting in my reading about cats with super-sensory powers was that all of the cats mentioned, including Oscar, were strays or had been adopted from shelters. They appeared to develop a special psychic relationship with whomever they saw as their rescuers. Or, as some people have hinted, these cats and their caregivers may all be a bit fey. No one knows of any particular cat that can sense illness in visitors or strangers, and there is, so far, no evidence that *any* cat could be trained to do so.

Although Tinker is the alpha cat, Raven has developed a very proprietary air toward her. When Tinker shows any sign of discomfort, Raven lavishes attention on her by cleaning her face. Once, when Tinker was inadvertently shut into the workroom downstairs, Raven paced and meowed until I followed her. This resulted in some playful cuffing between the two cats once Raven ascertained that Tinker was okay.

These days, Tinker is aloof. She will often hop onto the arm of Corwin's chair or sit on the couch beside me, allowing me to massage her belly—if it's *her* idea—but she's not a lap cat. Neither cat likes having her nails trimmed, but Tinker, now the not-so-snuggly cat (Warren was proven right!) is more difficult to deal with, once caught. She scratches and occasionally attempts to bite the hand that restrains her—usually mine.

Raven continued to sniff out things I did not see. Twice more she identified spots that required attention, and I began to trust her diagnoses.

Six months ago, when I was having laser surgery on my eye, the surgeon spotted a small lesion on my eyelid.

"Given your history of melanoma, we should get your oncologist to look at this," he said.

"I don't think that spot is malignant," I responded. "My cat hasn't sniffed it."

"Pardon?"

"I have a cat who has diagnosed cancer for me three times, and she has never been wrong."

The doctor just smiled, clearly skeptical.

I made it clear I did not think it was necessary, but that I would go to the oncologist anyway.

A few days before I went to have the eyelid looked at, Raven crawled up by my neck and sniffed my collarbone. I could feel nothing amiss. I checked in the mirror. Nothing.

"Look, Corwin, Raven is freaking me out again, and I can't see or feel anything."

"I'd pay attention if I were you!"

During my appointment, I told the oncologist I thought the eyelid issue was probably a fool's errand.

"Hey. Coming here is never a fool's trip. Don't ever think that! Let's have a look."

After he examined the lesion, he said, "You were right. It's a small cyst, not a melanoma. Nothing to worry about."

"Would you humour me and check out something my cat thinks is a problem?

"Your cat?"

"My cat. She thinks there is something on my collarbone that needs attention."

"How, exactly, does she tell you that?" he asked good-naturedly.

"First, she stares me right in the eye for an inordinately long period of time and then sniffs the area over and over."

"This I have to verify," he smiled, checking my collarbone where I indicated that Raven had showed some concern.

"I wonder if my cat or the surgeon is the best doctor!" I challenged.

Finishing his examination, he laughed. "Kudos to the cat! Your surgeon loses that one. Let's burn that sucker off."

After he'd treated the diseased tissue he said, "You never told me about the cat."

"I wasn't sure whether it was just a coincidence. Besides, most people wouldn't believe me. Raven is just an ordinary cat, but so far she's been right four times out of four."

"That's one hundred percent accuracy! You keep that cat, okay?"

There's no question that I am keeping Raven—you see, I love her as much as she loves me.

Although she will never be the kind of cat I can scoop up and cuddle, nowadays she follows me around as if she's a small dog. She begs for treats, will eat anything from corn to potato chips to cottage cheese, and plays fetch with a ball of tinfoil. She's a southpaw: she uses her left paw to catch objects as well as to retrieve a bit of food from her dish, licking it from her paw as we would lick our fingers when eating finger food.

Raven refuses to be ignored—much like an impatient two-year-old—jumping up from all four feet at once and landing with a thump when I don't respond quickly enough to her invitations to play. I swear that she can *smell* a book or a newspaper. She can be sleeping peacefully on our bed, but within minutes of me picking up reading material in the living room, she is nudging the pages, asking to sit on my lap. She gazes at me and cocks her head to one side, emitting a winsome "please," then pats my knee until I make lap space for her. Occasionally she holds my finger, much as a human would, between her two paws.

Raven is so black that she appears indigo blue, with silver highlights, in the sunlight. She sometimes sits, statue-like, in a pose that is often captured in cat figurines. When she lashes her tail, she reminds me of a black ceramic cat clock—tail whipping rhythmically to show her emotions. If Raven could talk, I believe it would be with a royal British accent.

Raven has an extensive vocabulary: her responses to certain commands show an understanding that often amazes me. My "Mommy wants a hug" usually results in Raven jumping on the bed for an affectionate head-butt. We have "conversations" in which my comments and queries are acknowledged with a variety of vocalizations and body language that involves her ears, tail, eyes, and even hair, indicating that she has understood me. She has me convinced that *she believes* she is talking to me. I can't explain the elation I feel each time I hear her rare purr, her eyes narrowing to languid slits as she physically projects her contentment. With me, she is home.

Raven has provided me with years of unconditional love, loyalty, enjoyment, and affection. She adores me, and the feeling is mutual. I do not own her, and she is not a pet. She is a friend. I saved her life, and now I am convinced she has saved mine—more than once.

LIVING LIGHT

CHRISTINE LOWTHER

"What on Earth is that noise?"

"More accurate to ask what in the ocean."

"Well, what in the ocean, then?"

"That's my resident harbour seal."

"You're kidding!"

This is a conversation I had all last summer, whenever visitors came to my floating home in Clayoquot Sound on the west coast of Vancouver Island. A young seal would often rest on one of the flotation logs under my greenhouse and snore. Sometimes it would blow bubbles in the lapping water, which could sound alternately peaceful, humorous, or rude depending on the seal's whim.

The animal had not yet learned to be shy of humans; this much was evident in its relaxed, unafraid behaviour. Earlier in the season, I had heard it crying for its mother over on the rocks beside the island flanking my neighbour's oyster farm. It was a plaintive sound, but I knew not to intervene. This was nature: the mother went fishing, and the pup missed her. The baby was not abandoned. Many times I had heard of people picking up what they thought was an orphaned seal and taking it to a rescue centre—causing the permanent separation between parent and offspring that they mistakenly believed had already occurred. On the other hand, I also knew the odd sharp-eyed local who had rescued young seals at death's door.

I frequently got in my kayak and floated close enough to the rocks to spy on the pup through binoculars, making sure it was not at that door.

But as long as it continued calling loudly like that, there was a good bet nothing was amiss. It still had strength. It wanted food.

Later, as the seal grew, it seemed to gain some independence, and took my little bay for its own. It would surface to inspect whatever humans happened to be paddling around. In general, harbour seals like to follow me, always with a peaceful slow-breathing presence, patiently watching through those large, liquid eyes. One seal, two, sometimes even three will tag along. They won't come as far as the main channel of Lemmens Inlet, where I venture to look for porpoises; other seals are already there. I am not expert enough to tell them apart. But I did get to know the one that took to swimming near my houseboat. He, or she, was smaller and more lightly coloured than the other seals, and came closer. Much closer.

"No. I'm not kidding. Come see for yourself. You have to tiptoe."

The seal would be resting on a log a mere couple of inches from the floorboards of the greenhouse, between which are wide gaps. A person could quietly lie down and place her eye to a gap—and have to hold her breath or the seal might feel it. I'd look down on the back of its grey head, and watch the long whiskers around its nose and study the mottled pattern of its fur. I could hear every nuance of breath, and a sudden snort could be startling.

There are, of course, many other animals in my world. I am anchored at an apex of freshwater stream, salt sea, and ancient temperate rainforest. This coming together of habitats teems with wildlife. Black bears wander the shoreline, turning over rocks, munching on small crabs, and grazing on shore grass. Minks emerge from the ocean, shake their gorgeous fur, and scamper up the rocks into the forest. Raccoons dig in the early morning low-tide mud. The odd snake swims over to my dock to bask in the sun. Bald eagles teach their young to fish. Families of river otters help themselves to my decks, climbing aboard to roll on the warm wood and deposit their droppings. The babies unabashedly run over my solar panels. Otters have growled up at me from between the floorboards. They eat lustily and noisily, crunching on shells and crabs. They are wild. Last summer's seal, I liked to tell myself, was not so wild. I pretended it was mine.

It might be closer to the mark to say I was the seal's pet human. I waited for him, looked for him—or her. I thrilled with each sighting, every encounter, marvelled over the seal's graceful skill in the water, felt goosebumps and knew I was being watched. I would look up to meet those huge eyes, calmly fixed on me from a position next to one of the landlines anchoring a corner of my home to the shore. For a moment, we would both just look.

"Hello there."

The seal would nonchalantly tip backwards to return to its submarine realm. I often saw it gliding close to the bottom, upside down, ignoring fishes which appeared to tolerate the predator in their midst. A spidery, slender kelp crab creeping along the submerged rope might catch my attention, and when my eyes flickered back, the seal would be gone.

Other times, at a distance, a telltale broadcast splash could be heard. It wasn't seals playing, or courting, or arguing. It was seals surrounding schools of fish and scaring hundreds out of the water at once, causing the sound of many small bodies slapping the surface as they fell back down to their doom, or their escape, as the case may be. This feeding technique could be a group effort or carried out by only one seal. Although it must have been terrifying for the fish, I always liked the sound—found it relaxing, even. I knew that seals, perhaps including my favourite one, were feasting. Splash after splash would fill the bay, sometimes with an echo off the side of Lone Cone Mountain. A skilled seal could keep the school in one spot. Less work. More eating.

I never got into the water when the seal was around. I had no wish to frighten this creature in its own habitat, its only home, and risk destroying our comfortable, convenient, and (to me) deeply satisfying companionship. I had tried swimming with other seals in the past. They had come near enough to ascertain that I was something from which to flee, leaving me

Me, looking for seals in Clayquot Sound, BC.

disappointed and alone in the cold briny water. No. I was determined not to scare my young friend. Yet for all I knew it was observing me the times I did take to the water. I cannot pretend to have known its whereabouts at all times.

Near the end of September, it was time to make the most of the bioluminescence before the autumn storms began, darkening the water and forcing me indoors. Bioluminescence is, quite literally, living light. Dinoflagellates, single-celled plant-like organisms, produce flashes and submarine sparks through a chemical reaction when agitated. These light effects are pure magic, whether streaming from my paddle with every stroke or making the faster-swimming fish glow.

My friend Maryjka arrived for a sleepover one night. She came to kayak around the house under the stars—and to create galaxies of her own. While she paddled around the bay, I enjoyed the hot tub, as I did on many summer nights. That may sound opulent, but the tub is funky rather than classy. A friend made it from salvaged cedar. It is heated by a solar collector, which means only clear days allow for a nice, hot soak. So hot, in fact, that I take breaks by diving into the ocean, enveloping my body with white-green light.

"Do you think this totem animal of yours will make an appearance?" called Maryjka from the kayak.

"If so, you'll hear breathing close by," I answered from the tub.

The air was still, trillions of stars dominating the world. The Milky Way was huge, a swath of "biolume" curtaining the wide sky that spanned the houseboat.

Soaking away the weariness of peak-tourist-season servitude that bound me to the nearby town of Tofino, I became aware that Maryjka was speaking again. She sounded like she was talking to a baby. I sat up straight and listened more closely.

"Hel-*lo* sweetie, how *are* you? Oh, so *nice* to hear you and to *see* your pretty, *pretty* lightshow!"

"Uh, Maryjka?"

"Oh, hello, *hello* sweetie!"

"Is it—?"

"It's the seal, look! It's surrounded by bioluminescence! It's a darting white cloud circling the kayak!"

I had never heard her so excited.

"Come in closer," I demanded. She paddled gently up to the float. There. Something like Casper the Ghost, or a seal in photographic negative. A frisky aura scooting around her boat. Then the lights faded: it had surfaced. We could hear it breathing between us. That close.

"I'm getting in," I said.

"*What?*"

As soon as the seal had submerged again, I clambered out of the tub, but instead of diving into the dark sea, I slowly lowered myself in, gripping the deck. The water was heart-stopping, as usual: a great contrast to the temperature of the hot tub. But I was used to going back and forth. I found it invigorating and even a little bit dangerous. And now I was going in with a seal.

Over the years, I have had eyebrows raised at my approach to wild animals. I swim with moon jellyfish. Why not? They don't sting. Once, onto a deck packed with gawking visitors, every swimming guest quickly vacated the ocean when a fourteen-legged, green, antennaed isopod torpedoed through the water. Me? I jumped in to check it out. Another time, I pursued a young cougar, just to make sure I hadn't imagined it.

I know there are scores of people who travel vast distances and undergo various kinds of suffering to get close to wildlife. I'm not special. I have read about scientists falling in love with their research animals, ignoring extreme weather just to be near them, no longer collecting data. I don't suspect anthropomorphism. I think it is rather akin to fierce love, a longing that makes us reach from our limited, tame, human selves. We want to belong to a place in the way they do, to join their ranks like the missing fishermen of legend. We yearn to slip out of our skins and into theirs, or, failing that, at least secure their blessing.

I did not have to wait long for the seal to come to me. Its streamlined form circled and swished directly beneath me, just out of reach of my stretching toes. Maryjka sat speechless. I gasped with excitement. After a few moments, I felt contact. A quick, careful flipper grazed my heel. That was all, and that was enough.

This waterborne creature was not my totem. It was not my pet. Our worlds could only intersect temporarily, with my forays into the ocean or the seal's onto the floats of my houseboat. Nevertheless, I considered it a guardian. When conjured, this sprite would appear—silvery, ethereal, wrapped in a veil of living light.

DISCOURSE WITH A
MOUNTAIN LION

MICHAEL LUKAS

The trail to Trout Lake climbs fifteen hundred feet directly up a ridge. The difficulty of climbing this ridge—not to mention the fact that the campsite below is still closed from the fatal bear-mauling in the 1980s known as "The Night of the Grizzlies"—discourages many hikers from entering this drainage of Glacier National Park. I was headed up the valley on the nine-mile trail to Arrow Lake, planning to go from there on to Lake Evangeline. After I crested the ridge, the trail switchbacked down through fir, aspen, and huckleberry bushes ripe with fresh berries I snatched as I hiked by. Continuing on up the trail past the logjammed foot of Trout Lake, I strolled along the east side under the punctuated shade of broken cliff faces and dense stands of Douglas fir. I watched the surface of the lake for trout rising, to see if I might want to wet a line there on my way back.

Habitually, I couldn't help tracking. I picked apart an owl pellet, freeing the skeleton of a ground squirrel from its hair-knotted cocoon. Weasel tracks, maybe marten or even fisher, crossed the muddied depression in the trail, not to mention several deer. Half a mile from the head of the lake, a large corded scat curled a crescent in the middle of the trail. Cat or canine, squatting to take a shit? Two deeply set, clawless strained prints confirmed it had been the former. I brought my hand close and felt warmth emanating from the scat, soft with digested flesh and hair. Looking up to the fir-pocked cliffs above, I saw the place revealed for what it was.

I took a short break at the head of the lake and ate my lunch of crackers and GORP. Beyond the lake to the north, the trail kept tight to the cliff face. The tall grasses and tangled alders of the streambed gave way to steep sub-alpine forest slopes and crumbling, rocky outcroppings. As the trail hugged the bench, twisting in and out of sunlight, the steady hum of silence awakened my senses. There was *something* somewhere above. All the animals knew it.

I stopped and looked up at the crags and boulders above, listening intently, watching. I backtracked, a proven strategy for catching a cat on the prowl or deer following the salty musk of sweat. After a minute or so of sitting and waiting, I continued my hike toward Arrow Lake, each step a conscious effort carrying me up the trail. But once more, compelled by the sensory swell, I turned back down the trail to check, despite having heard nor seen a thing. I went farther back this time—a hundred yards, two hundred—searching, scanning the falling slope below, looking up between the cracks and fissures of rock, around distant boulders. I waited. Nothing. I turned up the trail, moving cautiously in step, more certain than ever.

At the top of a slight rise in the trail, I halted: hair raised, ears pricked, nostrils flared, every inch of skin knowing. I spun around to face it.

With his right front paw raised in mid-step, the mountain lion froze. Only twenty feet separated us. The face was tawny and white-whiskered. The tail danced in a swaying rhythm. I gazed into the steady amber eyes, which inquired back, waiting for an answer.

I made myself big: raised my arms, beat my chest, huffed, growled, and cursed in a primal, necessary display of false confidence in the face of the unknown. The lion cowered, dipped his shoulders, and shrunk back like a house cat squirted with water. Farther down the trail he slunk, keeping his eyes on my flailing arms. Near a bend in the trail below, the lion composed himself and leapt out of sight downslope in a single bound. I listened. Not a leaf stirred.

I'd long envied people who had encountered lions, having never myself seen more than a wisp of a tail. But this lion was stalking me.

I'd spent free time in previous years near Boulder, Colorado, searching for signs of mountain lion, or cougar, in a volunteer predator-tracking program to establish lynx and mountain lion numbers in Eldorado Canyon State Park. Establishing local cat populations not only aided in preserving habitat in the area, but would help prevent the development of a copper-mining claim in a valley adjacent to the park's western boundary.

I saw the violence of a cougar kill once atop a ridge above that canyon. Unlike the occasional mule deer eviscerated by the local free-roaming dog packs, this fawn's ribs were rent back from the sternum, as if parted with steel surgical spreaders. She was thoroughly devoured, picked clean by a host of local scavengers. My cheeks were flushed from snowshoeing up the slope. I could feel them pulsing in the cold air as I realized the cat's precision, its certainty.

Attacks on both domestic pets and people were up in the nineties in Colorado, as they were elsewhere across the West. The environmentally conscious locals of Boulder County were torn: they wanted to protect the cats, but were fearful of what was beginning to seem like an invasion. It just didn't seem normal for mountain lions to be coming down into their yards.

However, with people filling the tight canyons west of town, with young lions pushed out of the shrinking territory by their elders, with locals happy to let deer forage on apples in their backyards….

"If they want deer," a local sheriff, who spent more time than he liked cleaning up after the results, once told me, "they're gonna get lions too."

In the 1950s, in a cave in South Africa, anatomy professor Raymond Dart uncovered what he believed to be a stockpile of early hominid weapons: a variety of weathered, broken animal bones. Among them were crushed and punctured Australopithecine skulls and skeletal remains. Dart believed these pre-hominid ancestors cached the bones as weapons, declaring this "cache" the first hominid arsenal. His explanation for the punctured skulls? Trophies of warfare, murder, or even cannibalism.

After years reviewing specimens, anthropologist Bob Brain was skeptical; he doubted Dart's assumptions and looked to the animals and land to piece the story back together. At Swartkrans, he uncovered numerous bones, some of which came from Australopithecines. As he excavated the site and several similar cave sites, he noticed a correlation still typical in South Africa: open cave mouth, roots growing up from the saturated soil, a tree above a cave, a pile of bones accumulating below. He discovered an ancestral hominid skull with two prominent punctures in the back. Brain noted: "Interestingly enough, the spacing of those two holes is matched almost exactly by the spacing of the lower canines of a fossil leopard from the same part of the cave."

Whatever predator we might imagine ourselves to be, sometimes humans are food.

A quarter of a mile later along the trail, I was bodily certain the lion was still behind me. Sweat trickled from my armpits over my ribs, and my head and neck tingled like I was about to be tapped on the shoulder from afar.

"Okay!" I yelled, turning abruptly.

The lion paced to a stop a hundred feet down the trail, his long black-tipped tail swaying to a rest.

"Enough! You can't follow me like this all day!"

He shrunk back a bit, regained his composure, then settled and cocked his head.

"Look! I wanted to see you, but this has got to stop!" He sat down on his haunches, a broad swath of white cresting up his elongated chest. His big tail swept the ground and twitched. His dark amber eyes blinked.

I was talking to a mountain lion.

On the morning of January 2, 2001, thirty-year-old Frances Frost left her home in Lake Louise for the cross-country trail loop around Lake Minnewanka. She skied down the Cascade Fire Road in solitude, gliding off into the wild environs close to her hometown of Banff. Around one o'clock that afternoon, she took her last breaths in the jaws of a cougar. From the puncture wounds in her neck and shattered vertebrae, she could not have suffered much. She likely didn't even realize what was happening to her.

Wildlife officers determined the mountain lion had stalked her for almost two miles down the trail before finally closing the distance, covering much of the final ten yards with a leap, landing his crushing weight square on her back. The bite could not have come much farther behind. Despite her fitness, Frances was slight of build, alone, her senses drowned in the demands of physical strain.

It was the first mountain lion attack resulting in death in one hundred years of records in British Columbia. The Banff police chief echoed public concern: "Normally wary cougars are abandoning their natural fear of people. They're moving further into the townsite to get at their food source—elk." Displaced cougars wreaking havoc! Predatory lions with a taste for human blood! From California to Colorado, Arizona to Alberta, this perception solidified—something had changed in cougar behaviour.

Frances Frost's body was recovered late the next day, a healthy male mountain lion still guarding her body. Attempting to drag his kill from the blood-encrusted, freeze-hardened snow, the lion was shot dead. As an environmental activist, Frances, her father said, would have wanted the lion to live.

At a turn in the trail, the slope rose slightly up to a large chalky boulder bending the track above. I leaned over my hips, strode heel-to-toe up the rise. I could feel him. I knew he was coming. I stepped off the trail and slid behind the rock, slipping out of my pack. Fumbling nervously, I retrieved my camera and waited. Peeking an eye around the boulder, I watched as the lion emerged and stepped casually around the turn with his whiskered chin turned up to the cliffs above. As he rounded the bend, I stepped out and revealed myself. He slowed to rest in the middle of the trail and looked up at me as I snapped the shutter. The sun on his back illuminated the caramel sheen of his coat.

"Hi again," I said softly. "I just wanted your picture."

There seemed to be no threat in him, just interest, and a demand for recognition, as if we were partners in a conversation left unfinished. I continued to speak, to communicate my gratitude, my wonder, my confusion. He sat on his haunches and cocked his head once more, listening to the warble of sounds coming from my lips. He settled in the middle of the trail, curling up in a patch of sunlight, his raised neck and head framed by wisping blades of grass and an impossible crown of golden-petalled flowers. The thick, long cord of tail thumped twice as he stretched into a more comfortable position. *You are a* cat, I thought, *some sort of feline we name cougar, pantera, catamount, mountain lion, but who exists in all his particularity before me, with me.*

The moment was broken by twigs snapping above. I caught a glimpse of brown fur moving through the trees, then stillness: a deer?

The lion reared up abruptly. I clicked the shutter and caught a last glimpse as he bounded up the slope into the woods above.

A few months later, I related the story of my encounter with the mountain lion to Ed, a self-consciously Montanan rancher and family friend. Ed chuckled as he jostled the ice in his bourbon. "You were a heartbeat away from being a meal."

"I don't know, Ed," I said. "It wasn't that simple. Maybe I could've been food, but something else was going on there."

I fixed a couple more cocktails and followed Ed as he ambled on sore joints out to the deck to watch the moonlight on the west slope of the Mission Mountains. Ed broke the silence with a deadpan tease: "It'd a been a shame if he'd got ya."

Janie, my free-spirited, New Age neighbour awaiting the inevitable inversion of the magnetic poles and the resulting shift in human consciousness, disagreed. She instructed me that the lion was my spirit animal, my totem. "He is your brother," she asserted succinctly. "He wanted you to understand this, so he appeared to you."

I wanted to believe her, wanted to believe that my desire to help these lions, to protect their habitat, had somehow manifested in this encounter. I couldn't, though; I didn't even understand where to begin. What's more, I knew it wasn't true in any comprehensible way for me. Mountain lions are generalized predators, near kin of our friend the leopard, taking advantage of whatever easy targets come along.

The idea of kinship weighs on me, though: that I've opened myself to a relationship that acknowledges thousands of years of coexistence, that somehow humans and lions have learned to respect each other, that long ago, somewhere, an understanding developed to minimize conflict. Attention is the key. I want to believe I'm tapping into that link once more, upholding my end of the bargain. This lion seemed evidence of the complexity of this relationship of vague tolerance. Maybe the lion was not my brother, but I was certainly not "just a meal," as Ed so confidently insisted.

Here was a relationship I was obligated to negotiate in the moment, a relationship we have with lions that is never of our choosing, not our right to define alone. It is here that the already "we" is revealed, undermining the encounter as a confrontation between man and animal. Here, a lion and a human meet, acknowledging a shared world we have never left, a world we are constantly renegotiating.

THE OLD DOG

B. A. MARKUS

My mother is on the phone making plans again. She's decided that Blackie won't be getting a family funeral. He won't be buried in the backyard under the crabapple tree. "I'm looking for the least expensive option," she explains to the person on the other end of the line. "He's just an old dog."

I look up from where I'm sitting at the kitchen table and watch her repeat the instructions: "A cardboard box," she says. She scribbles on a scrap piece of paper. "Remove collar and tags." She scribbles again. Then she puts down the pencil and straightens up. "Of course. I understand." She says she will call again during office hours when the time comes. She hangs up the phone and says, *"Bon. C'est fait,"* to herself in the way that means she feels good because she's solved another problem.

I don't talk about what's happening because I'm not supposed to know. There's no one for me to tell anyway. Of the four of us girls, I am the only one left at home. I am the only one around to watch Blackie dying.

This is all wrong. Blackie doesn't really belong to me at all. He never sleeps in my room and doesn't automatically obey me like he always does the others. But I know I'll miss him when he's gone, especially now that my older sisters are all off being adults in other places.

Blackie is a good dog. He still stands at the big picture window and sees me off to school every morning. And he always barks twice to greet me when I return at the end of the day. I don't like the sound of his back legs dragging across the floor outside my room at night, but it's nice to know that someone remembers to check and make sure I'm in bed. Even if it is just an old dog.

These days, Blackie is the only one in the house when I get home after school because my parents are always coming back late from appointments and meetings I'm not supposed to know about.

One day in November I come home after school as usual. It is just past four and the streetlights are already on. I'm happy because I find my key right away. It's in the front pocket of my knapsack exactly where it's supposed to be. Tonight I won't be stuck outside waiting for my parents to get home and let me in. Tonight I won't have to sit through another lecture.

Blackie doesn't bark like he usually does when I get in.

"Hi, Blackie!" I've gotten into the habit of talking to the dog when my parents aren't around. "I'm home after another thrilling day at school."

Blackie is in the kitchen. He doesn't raise his head when he sees me, but whimpers and tries to wag his tail. There is a puddle of pee beside him.

"Oh," I say. "I see."

I use a big wad of paper towel to mop up the mess. I lift up his back end to get at all of the pee he's lying in. Blackie looks up at me with his sad brown eyes and tries to wag his tail again. He knows I'm trying to help, trying to make it all better. I wet another bunch of paper towel to wipe away the smell and then throw the wad in the garbage can under the sink. Blackie's breathing is raspy. His chest sucks way in and then pushes out again with each breath.

I kneel beside him, pat his head, and run my fingers down the length of each of his long floppy ears. "You're a good dog," I say, and I turn over one ear and look at the soft black hairs and the pink skin on the underside. Here, at least, there is no sign that anything is wrong. Here, at least, he looks the way he always has.

"You're a very good dog."

Blackie whimpers. He shivers. I go into the living room and turn up the heat to twenty degrees. My mother keeps it at ten degrees during the day when they are out, and I am only allowed to turn it up to fifteen when I get home. She says with the way things are now we can't afford to waste money on heating bills. I'll have to remember to turn it down again when I hear the car in the driveway.

I sit in the kitchen with Blackie
and do my homework for a while.
At first he is restless, but then he
settles right down. The hum of the
refrigerator and the warm whoosh
of the furnace fill the room. It's cozy
in the kitchen. It feels safe, peaceful.

My parents are fighting when
they walk in the door.

"Don't do that," my father
yells. "I hate it when you do that."

My mom, me, and Blackie.

"Now, now." My mother is
using her careful voice. "It'll just take one little second."

"I said *no!*"

The flimsy plywood closet doors squawk, and I know he's pushed her
into them again. I look out in time to see my father waving a wire hanger
in front of my mother's face.

Then he turns and glares at me. "What's this?" he's still holding the
wire hanger. "What's this for?"

I don't say anything because it's no good answering when he gets
like that. You just have to let it pass and pretend it never happened. After a
while, my father stops yelling and hands the hanger to my mother. He walks
into the kitchen, still wearing his coat and boots, and sits down on one of
the kitchen stools. He stares at his hands like he's never seen them before,
first the palms, then the backs, then the palms, and then the backs again.

My mother hangs her coat on the hanger, removes her boots, lines
them up perfectly in the tray like she always does, and puts on the embroi-
dered Chinese slippers she keeps in a basket by the door. In the kitchen,
she sees Blackie on the floor.

"He had an accident," I explain. "He can't get up." My mother leans
over and touches her fingers to the dog's quiet chest.

I know I should just keep quiet, but I start to say it anyway, "I think—"

My mother straightens up and cuts me off right away. "It's normal," she says. She quickly washes her hands and begins pulling leftovers from the refrigerator. "There's nothing to talk about."

My father is still staring at his hands, the palms, the backs, then the palms, and then the backs again.

My mother inspects the lettuce, peels off some rotting leaves, and drops them in the garbage. She notices the two big wads of paper towel. "What's this?"

"I told you," I say. "He had an accident."

"You wasted a whole roll of paper towel." The way she says it, I can tell that she hates me. "Are you insane?"

I snap my binder shut and think about the girls at school and how most of them would have just left the dog pee there for their mothers to mop up. But I know better than to argue with her.

"I need a drink," my father says.

"I'll get it." I am grateful for an excuse to stop talking about paper towel. I pull over my stool to reach the liquor cabinet high above the stove.

My mother doesn't look up from her place at the sink. "Not tonight. He's not allowed."

"I said," my father's voice is louder now, "I need a drink."

"Why can't he?" I ask, still up on the stool. "He likes it. It calms him down."

My mother removes the tinfoil from last night's leftovers. "Get down off the stool," she says, her voice as cold as ice. "You're blocking the oven."

My father notices Blackie on the floor. He leans closer to the dog's body. "Wanna go for a walk, boy?" he asks. "Wanna go?"

My mother stops working. She's forgotten about me. She's watching my father and the old dog.

"Hey, boy." My father reaches down and jiggles Blackie's collar like he always does. "How about the men of the house get some air?"

I try to keep my eyes on the linoleum so I won't have to watch what's happening in front of me, but I can't keep myself from looking my father and the dog. My father has his fingers under Blackie's collar now and is starting to pull. The dog's fuzzy head flops to the side, his black tongue lolling out of his mouth.

"Come on boy, time for a walk."

"Please, Frank," my mother finally says in her careful voice. "Let him go."

I watch my father getting mad again. I see it coming at us like a tornado, and this time I can't take it, not with all of us trapped together in the kitchen like that.

"Dad," I say. But no sound comes out because there is a giant lump taking up all the space in my throat.

I try again. "Dad." This time it's loud enough for him to hear. "Blackie can't get up."

My father doesn't get it. He can't figure out why the dog isn't moving. He can't stop pulling on Blackie's collar.

"*Dad*." I reach out and touch my father's cheek with one finger to get his attention, to get him to look at me. "Blackie's dead."

My father finally turns his head. "Bevvie," he says. He looks up at me like he just noticed I was there, and then he starts to cry. He cries like a little kid, his breath coming out in big gasping sobs, like his heart is going to break in two. Big fat tears pour out at the corners of his eyes, roll down his face behind his glasses, and make tiny puddles on the linoleum. I want to stay beside him. I want to wrap my arms around him and hold him tight the way he used to hold me when he could still make me believe that everything would be all right. But my mother doesn't want that. She gets between us right away and pushes me to the side. She thinks she knows what to do. She thinks she can clean up the mess he's made with the old dishtowel she's holding in her hands.

I'm only fourteen, but even I know it's too late for that.

THE LIGHT OF RAVENS

CATHERINE MCLAUGHLIN

held the raven. His black feathers shone like obsidian against my blood-red suede gloves. My left hand supported his head as wind ruffled the short feathers on his neck and shoulders. I felt the heat that remained in his full breast. But his eyes were closed and a wing was askew. Standing in that empty parking lot, in the minus-thirty chill of the last morning of the year, I held light. From that fallen raven came the shimmer, the buzz, the golden glow of light.

On my drive to the west end of town to pick up a gallon of paint that icy morning, I'd watched for ravens, enjoyed the couple who played in the thermals above 214 Place, our downtown high-rise, the small flock that hovered over the curving brick of Grande Prairie Regional College, then plunged down, soared up. The ravens' quest for fun always inspires me.

As I pulled into the large parking lot surrounded by the big-box stores that were my destination, I spotted a small flock of the dark birds playing in the ice fog near the fast food diner's grease dumpster. As my car approached, they rose up till there were only two black birds by the roadside, then one. All but one had lifted up, hovered, then flown to safety.

I got out of my car and looked around, then made a quick decision. The fallen bird had to be moved from the road. My boots crunched in the cold as I walked towards him. I bent and gently picked him up, then walked across the road to lay him on fresh snow by a nearby light pole. Reluctantly I returned to my car and headed for the paint store. A friend's

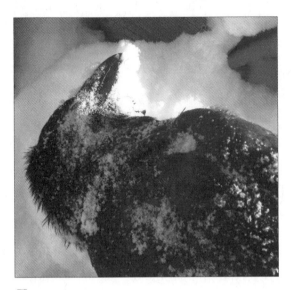

The raven.

son was helping me with some house painting, and I was the gofer, out to pick up more supplies.

My shopping completed, I sat in my parked car and tossed around questions. What if I'd been mistaken and the raven was still alive? What if he became lunch for his famished flock? Ingesting sufficient calories to survive in this northern winter was a daily chase for all outdoor creatures. Do ravens consume their own dead? Is carrion ever just carrion?

The small flock had disappeared, but the dark body remained where I had placed it. I imagined an employee of the nearby ladies' wear finding him, then returning with hands gloved in plastic to dispose of him in a dumpster. She would mistake him for garbage.

I drove home with the raven in the back of my small car.

On my return home, I stood at the door and called to Kelly, interrupting his painting. I held out the raven in my arms: look what I found. Kelly's face illustrated the process of his thoughts, then he exclaimed over the handsome bird. Once, he told me, he had rescued a litter of foxes. Animals trusted him.

I placed the raven on top of a snow-covered box behind my fence, then returned to my work. For the next few days I checked on him, noted the accumulation of new-fallen snow that was gradually concealing him. Dealing with this death confused me. What does one do with a dead raven? The people at bylaw would pick him up and take him to an incinerator.

Digging in the earth wouldn't be possible for several months yet. And should a raven be buried, anyway? Impossible to imagine that high-flying bird beneath the depths of the earth. Could I leave him out in the country somewhere? But I couldn't just go on someone's land and leave a raven. Crown land was probably out of the question, too.

Then a friend came to mind. Trish lived on an acreage west of the city. Trish would understand. After making the call, I headed out, the raven once more in the back of my car. The brilliance of the January sun blessed the strange journey.

Trish pointed out the burial ground reserved for family pets; then she waved towards the north edge of their land and explained that wild creatures are placed on the earth there, beneath the trees on the ridge. Cradling the raven in my arms, I tramped a path over branches and deadfall into the trees. A light wind disturbed snow that had fallen on the branches and it floated softly down. I examined him one more time before placing that dark and shining bird at the foot of an aspen. I brushed up some snow to conceal his body, left his head, his face, uncovered. I wanted to be sure he could be seen from the sky. In the chilly grove of aspen and spruce, it seemed that a light switch had been flipped: in the sun's beams, prisms of snow crystals magnified the light to a bright glow.

These were troubled days for me. It had been less than a month since my elderly mother had died. My sleek, muscular black cat named Raven had chosen to leave me the very same day, showing me he was done. Memories of cats with big personalities and the void of deep and permanent loss still suffused me.

A few weeks later, I was walking through my neighbourhood—originally a farm, its perimeter now bordered a rail yard. In my search for beauty while walking here I often looked to the sky. A raven couple flew above me, headed northeast over the city where I knew they had a roost. A third dark flyer joined them. Ravens can regularly be observed winging their way across the city just before dusk, heading for the shelter of the bush some miles out. While at their night roost, the birds teach their young, socialize, and share news about the location of food.

Prruk! Prruk! I heard from above me. I looked up. I had caught the attention of the third raven as he flew overhead. *Cr-r-ruk,* he called.

I stopped and called to him: "I see you!" He turned away from the others and flew south again, just ahead of me. As he spoke once more, this raven flipped in mid-air, gave a slow sweep of his wide wings while inverted, then righted himself, stroking the air again. I watched as he lazily flipped back and forth three times, calling loudly with each move. Then he flew off.

I stared as he disappeared in the dusky sky. What had I just seen? Shaking my head with astonishment at this gift, I headed home where I keyed in a search on my computer: "Can ravens fly upside down?" Turns out they can. While they soar and play and scrap with each other in the air, ravens perform all sorts of acrobatics. That includes remaining in full flight while upside down. But what I saw was different. This dark bird flew solo. He chose to give me a gift. A raven gave me the light of my own smile.

A westcoast Haida legend tells of a time on earth when there was only darkness. It was Raven who brought light to Mother Earth. He tricked Grandfather into giving him the three boxes that held the light from the stars, the light from the moon, and the light from the sun.

I suspect Raven kept a portion of the light just for himself.

My Summer with Russell Crow

Karin Melberg Schwier

It's my husband's fault, really, since he was the first to feed the crow. He flew in one evening (the crow, not my husband) and stood on the sunroom deck, looking at us as though whatever we were about to barbeque would certainly be shared. Perhaps he felt he had found some sympathetic souls. Turns out, my husband says, he found his soul mate.

The crow eyed us up and down with what could only be described as delight at the prospect of an impending snack. It was my husband who went inside to the fridge; as the screen door rattled shut, the crow danced on the Plexiglas roof, his toenails clicking like tap shoes. Rick came out with a tiny piece of pork loin, and he held it up. The crow locked his tracker beam on it, cocking his head one way, then the other, his eyes as black and shiny as watermelon seeds.

Caw!

My husband tossed the bit of pork. The crow picked it off the roof, threw his head back, and downed it. With a look that clearly suggested seconds, he hopped from one beam of the pergola to the next, like a child jumping rocks across a creek. He—we assumed it was a "he" for some reason—settled just over the barbeque. His tail feathers vibrated and dipped; a greasy white-and-grey splat landed on the barbeque lid. Rick said, "Okay, that's it," and waved the crow off with the broom. That was that: our brief Marlin Perkins wildlife encounter was over. Or so we thought.

When the crow was still hanging around the next morning, I said we should name him.

"That's asking for trouble," my husband said. "With a name comes familial responsibility."

On the walk to the farmers' market, I suggested "Russell."

"Obviously."

That evening, when we brought our glasses of wine out on the back deck, the black kite swooped down from the elm in the back alley and glided over the back fence. He landed on the back of the patio chair next to mine.

"Hi, Russell."

Gackle, he said.

"Do you think he's someone's pet?" I wondered. Russell stared at me as though I had suggested something inappropriate.

"Maybe he's got rabies," my husband suggested.

I sipped my wine as Russell jumped to the tabletop and eyed me sideways. He picked at some old bits of hamburger bun left from lunch.

Caw.

A quick Google search for "crow gender" on the laptop revealed that our choice of name hadn't been as clever as we thought. Apparently it's a bit of a cliché. Females, apparently in keeping with the pop culture theme, are Sheryl. Without blood testing, it's nearly impossible to tell a male from a female, so we decided to stick with Russell.

Our Russell was impatient as we sat enjoying the evening. He jumped from one chair-back to the next. Over my shoulder, he pecked at my silver earrings and then noticed the tag on the back of my collar, digging into my shirt and pulling at it.

He hopped on the table and showed me how empty his mouth was.

Caw.

I stood and pushed back my chair. There was a bit of boiled potato in the fridge from last night; maybe he'd like a little of that. As I turned to go inside, Russell lifted off and followed overhead. He waited on the sunroom roof, following until he lost sight of me, tap-tapping his nails. As soon as I reappeared, he opened his beak like a chick in a nest would, and jumped along the sunroom Plexiglas to keep up with me. He hooked his claws around the arched metal beam, slid down like he was going over a waterfall, bungeed out, and sailed over to the patio table, cawing, beak gaping. I set the potato in front of him. His mouth—do you call the inside of a beak a mouth?—was a furious shade of pink. I picked up a small bit of potato and dropped it down his gullet. He wagged his tail.

"I didn't know crows did that," my husband said.

"He looks like he's smiling."

"I think this is the beginning of a Stephen King novel," my husband said, going to refill his glass. "Or that Alfred Hitchcock movie."

I fed Russell a few more pieces, each one cutting off his begging mid-croak as he gulped each bit down. When he was finished, he neatly wiped his beak back and forth on the edge of the table as if he were cleaning a pocketknife. Then he jumped on my head, and I felt him lifting bits of my hair. He was cooing, raspy, like a dove with a very bad sore throat.

My husband went to get the camera.

Early the next week, as I got out of the car after a trip to the grocery store, I told my husband, "If we're going to be gone for two weeks, I'd better weed the flower beds."

"I'll mow," he said, "so the house-sitter just has to worry about feeding the cats."

"And Russell," I said, hoisting a ten-pound bag of Yukon Gold potatoes out of the trunk.

My husband stood at the door with a bag of groceries and a look on his face.

"Are you kidding me? You are actually buying potatoes for him for while we're gone? Russell is a wild crow," he went on, "and he's going to be too fat to fly. Doesn't he go somewhere for the winter? And besides, he won't learn how to eat what he's supposed to eat."

"Like pork loin?"

"Mmmmm."

I could already hear Russell kicking up a fuss in the backyard. I went into the house and put on a pot of water.

It was a hot afternoon, so I put on my bathing suit, grabbed my gardening gloves, and pulled the hoe out of the garden shed. On my hands and knees, I picked a point in the perennial flower bed and began to hack at the weeds.

Caw.

With a swoosh of wings, Russell landed beside me and inspected the job I was doing. He stepped up on the blade of the hoe and looked at me. I poked a finger into his chest and he hopped off.

Caw, gackle, he said, a little annoyed. As I churned up the earth, he tilted his head sideways.

"Watch your toes, Russell." He backed up as I dug in the dirt. A fat earthworm twisted in the freshly turned earth, and I pointed at it. "Russell, look!" I said with great gusto. "That's what you're supposed to eat. Quick! Grab it!" The worm was trying to corkscrew itself back into the dirt.

Caw?

"Oh for heaven's sake, look. You'll like this." I picked up the worm and held it in front of him. He grabbed it and gulped. I swear a smile spread across his face.

Gackle, glurk, glurk!

So began a very noisy seek-and-destroy buffet that lasted over an hour, punctuated with my exclamations—"There's one!"—and much squawking and wing-flapping. Soon Russell was pulling worms out himself, but I had to keep pushing him out of the way, so great was his enthusiasm for hopping around on top of each dig I made with the hoe's edge.

Occasionally, he was distracted by a butterfly or a bug and wandered off after it, but as soon as I called his name he ran back to see what new delicacy I had uncovered. At one point, he actually opened his beak and rudely showed me a mouthful.

Later that day, Russell sat on top of the sunroom and made sad gurgling sounds and chattered, monkey-like.

Gargluck gackle gackle gluck gluck cleep.

"He's probably got heartburn," my husband said.

His visits were regular now, and he would stop by four or five times a day. Sometimes it was clear he'd come to play. He'd pick up twigs and drop them over the side of the sunroom, or he'd stagger around on the lawn after dragonflies like a deranged penguin. He played with the sponge I left in a bowl of water that I used to wipe down his, uh, deposits. His glee over the sponge was clear: he'd perch on the edge of the bowl, stab at it to make it bob up and down, or grab a corner and try to flip it over, cackling over the splashed water. On some visits, he just wanted a snack and a scratch. Then off he'd fly with more pressing business elsewhere.

In mid-July as I packed for our trip to a conference in Indiana, I felt an odd maternal tug. What would Russell think when I simply didn't appear in my bathrobe with my cup of coffee on Monday morning? We would be leaving the house before sunrise, and, presumably, since crows do not see well in the dark, he would still be fluffed up, asleep, high in the boughs of one of the big neighbourhood spruce. How disappointed he would be to arrive on the sunroom roof, only to be met by silence.

With us away and the house-sitter not arriving until that night after ball practice, Russell might spend the day with no one to visit and no bit of cooked potato to be had. I left out his sponge. Would Russell be confused?

"My mother thinks you've lost your marbles," the house-sitter emailed in reply to my last-minute instructions. To her credit, Kelsey

Russell Crow, sharing our BBQ.

agreed to visit with Russell when he came around and to give him a little potato if he asked for it. But would he take what she offered when he saw that it wasn't me?

We were gone for two weeks, and Kelsey reported only a couple of intermittent sightings. Maybe Russell had found a girlfriend, or at least remembered he was a crow.

The afternoon we returned, I went out to the garden to pick Swiss chard.

Within minutes, I heard the *woosh woosh* of wings. A crow landed on the fence at the other end of the garden. Was it Russell? I straightened up. As familiar as we'd become, one crow, frankly, looks like any other.

"Russell, is that you?"

Caw! Wings wide, Russell flapped and *ran* down the top of the fence toward me, hopping off at the last second to land on my shoulder in a very piratey way. He pecked at my hair and earring and ran his beak through my hair, now and then punctuating a steady stream of caws, clicks, and gurgles with sharp pecks, and a tone that demanded, "Where have you *been*?"

The back door opened and my husband, from behind the camera, said, "I heard Russell." After a moment of shooting photos, he added, "He is actually wagging his tail."

Russell rode on my shoulder, hopping from one to the other, tapping at my earrings as I filled the bowl with Swiss chard for supper. He jumped up and flew ahead of me as I walked back to the deck. He hopped to the patio table and squatted while I gave him a good scratch on his head. He closed his eyes and cooed.

I introduced myself to Candace Savage, a crow aficionado who wrote *Crows: Encounters with the Wise Guys of the Avian World*, and who lives just a few blocks away. I wanted to understand our fledgling yard guest better.

She told me that the cooing and carrying on are signs of recognition and affection. "The coos are associated with bonding and appeasement, so you are right to find them cozy," she said. "Crows also engage in a lot of mutual preening—allopreening—in family groups, so you are definitely offering your friend some pleasure and comfort."

Russell seemed to grow taller and thinner as the summer went on. One particularly wet day, he arrived looking like the proverbial drowned rat and sat long enough to have a neck scratch. His feet were muddy, and he kept wiping his beak on my sleeve and the backs of the patio chairs. Before he flew off, presumably to a dry roost in the spruce trees, he tilted his head back and caught raindrops running off the patio-table umbrella. With a reproachful looked that suggested we should let him in where it was warm and dry, he said, *Cack gackle,* and flew away.

Russell learned about levered windows and quickly understood that an opening window meant one of us was on the other side. Russell would hop from the bedroom window to the bathroom window, following the travels of people inside. My husband said it was disconcerting to step out of the shower and see Russell leering at him.

Russell found the ledge outside my office window and, though it was quite narrow, he perched there and watched me work. There was much fluffing of feathers, throaty gurgles, gargles, and tail-wagging when he caught sight of me. It began to remind me of a junior high crush, or perhaps a stalker.

He liked to study me up close. With the intense scrutiny of a dermatologist, he would examine my skin, and any flaw he found was fair game for a good peck. Depending on his mood, it could be a light tap or a good jab. He was also fascinated by my teeth, and if he was close I had to be careful about showing enough enamel for him to investigate.

"You *do* know crows carry West Nile," a nurse friend said, wrinkling her nose.

Most earrings I wore generated some interest, but a particular pair of silver ones with light blue moonstone drops just drove him bonkers. I had to hold my hands over my ears so he wouldn't snatch them; even then, he knew they were there, tantalizingly out of reach. He'd try to pry my fingers open with his beak.

Crows are collectors, and Russell must surely have had an interesting assortment of souvenirs stashed somewhere: a ball of cat hair, seized after I brushed the cats on the back deck one afternoon, a fishing license, a ball of tinfoil, a Canadian Tire receipt, a scrap of paper with an important phone number on it, and an orange bottle cap. He even tried to make off with a fork once while I ate lunch on the deck, but as a result of my shrieking and grabbing, he made off with a dill pickle instead.

One afternoon, Russell came to stand on my foot while I was deadheading lilies. I reached to pet him on the back, and instead of hopping away he flopped down on his side and rolled over on his back, toes curled. He stared up at me.

"Are you having a stroke, Russell? Do crows have strokes? Don't tell me you've got the avian flu or something."

He didn't pull away when I touched his toes; in fact, he seized my finger in his claw. I put my other finger down and he grabbed that one with his other claw.

"Now what, Russell?"

Gargle.

I lifted and he held on, hanging upside down, one claw tightly clasping each finger, and eyeing me. I lifted him up about a foot off the ground, then put him back down. There was no letting go. I lifted him again and swung him gently, like a tree branch in the breeze. Still he held on. We did this for about five minutes until I eventually had to carefully pry his claws open enough to release my fingers. He lay there, feet up, looking much like an expired crow. I picked him up, righted him, and he hopped away to play in the sprinkler.

No one I talked to had ever seen a crow do this. Candace suggested I contact Dr. John Marzluff, a professor the University of Washington in Seattle whom Candace affectionately called "Dr. Crow." So, as Russell peered at me through my office window and amused himself by peeling the paint off the window frame, I called Dr. Crow and described the game. The professor was stumped.

"That's weird is what that is," Dr. Marzluff said. "Normally, when you touch a bird's feet, they'll contract and grip, so that's not surprising. He obviously doesn't want to get away or he'd let go and fly off. But I don't know what being stiff is all about. He's controlling it, so it does seem like he's playing and getting something positive out of it."

We weren't sure how far Russell's territory extended. We knew he spent time in a neighbour's yard. She had something in a cage in her backyard, rabbits maybe, so that may have been of interest. One afternoon while

our street was being paved, I had to park about a block away. As I got out
of the car, I saw a crow on foot, drunkenly chasing a moth.

"Russell, what are you doing?" I wasn't sure if it was Russell, but I
figured if it wasn't, the crow would ignore me.

The bird skidded to a halt, moth forgotten, and opened his wings.
Beak agape, he turned and ran toward me until he was about five feet
away, then lifted up and landed on the roof of the car.

"You shouldn't be running on the street," I said, locking the car.
"You're going to get run over not paying attention like that."

Gackle, glurk, glurk, gackle. He jumped off the car roof and landed on
my shoulder. We started to walk home, when I noticed a woman, keys
poised at her car door, mouth agape.

I remembered something Dr. Crow said: Russell's lack of fear and
his assumption that all human beings were friendly did make him more
vulnerable. "He has bonded with you. He knows you're nice, but imagine him flying at someone who doesn't know him. They'd just assume he
was attacking them, and they'd give him a good whack or worse. A crow
living in an urban environment around a lot of people really should be
more wary."

"I think we'd better Google to see if crows fly south for the winter,"
my husband said after lunch one August afternoon. He was watching
Russell discover the mysteries of ice cubes, which had been left behind in
our water glasses.

It would be hard to see Russell standing out in the snow, lifting one
cold foot and then the other, staring at us through the frosty window in
December, all Oliver Twisty, with that sad look on his face. I called a
neighbour. Dr. Stuart Houston is a leading authority on birds of the central
regions of North America. He's written books, articles, and has banded
and recovered a bazillion birds.

"Crows are generally the only birds that will fly directly south for the winter," Dr. Houston said, "so your guy will probably end up in Mexico." He listened to my tales and said the chance of a completely wild crow behaving as Russell had been would be extremely rare. "It would seem this one has imprinted on you or another human, mostly likely in the first few hours after hatching or at some point early on. If he's a juvenile now, someone else has probably cared for him."

Then Dr. Houston told me about my neighbour across my back alley, the one with what I thought were rabbit cages. Jan Shadick is a wildlife rehabilitator with a license for orphaned or injured small birds and small mammals. The veterinary school at the nearby University of Saskatchewan campus often asks her to foster birds, skunks, porcupines, and whatnot until they can be released into the wild.

"I'm betting your Russell may have been in her care," Dr. Houston suggested, "and when she released him, he just went to your house and made a new friend."

The next day, Jan was in the back alley so I—embarrassed to not know my own neighbour—went out to introduce myself. Russell followed at my heels.

"I see you've met Esmeralda, my abject failure," she said, picking Russell up and tucking him under her arm. Russell complained loudly and thrashed his feet.

I stared. Esmeralda? A female? The woman was obviously off her rocker. *Caw!*

No doubt Russell was protesting this affront to his masculinity.

"I call him Russell," I said in his defense.

"That's funny," Jan said, pointing to the house next to hers. "The neighbours over here call him Murray. She just seemed like an Esmeralda to me! Without genetic testing, though, we won't ever know for sure!"

After the shock wore off and Russell quit squawking, I learned the truth about "our" crow, who was found nearly dead in a local park in June and brought to the vet college. Russell/Esmeralda/Murray went to Jan's to recuperate. Most birds she releases might hang around briefly until they get their sea legs, and then move on. But when Jan released Russell in early July, he decided to simply stay on.

"Whatever I rehabilitate is kept wild, but she is going against the rule. I hope she hasn't been bothering you?"

I had a brief twinge of—what was it? Jealously? There went my theory that Russell had specially chosen me, out of all possible humans, to reach out to across the mammal/avian divide.

"Well, Russell," I said as he followed me back to our yard. "You're introducing me to some really interesting people."

Gockle.

One September afternoon as the geese were starting to V in the skies over the city, I took a break from the computer and took my afternoon tea out on the back deck. Russell sailed in. *Gurckle!* he chuckled to himself as he hopped down to the table.

An unfamiliar voice reached us from the spruce tree in the neighbour's yard. A black shape moved among the limbs and settled on a low-hanging branch.

"Russell? Who's that?"

Grock! He studied me sideways and pecked at the prism I'd tied to the patio-umbrella pole.

"You've brought a friend?" I looked up and the new crow hopped from one tree branch to the next and then lurched to the neighbour's roof, a vantage point with a good view of us below.

"Russell, you've got a girlfriend?"

Gluckle. He smiled.

I named her Esmeralda. Not long after, they both disappeared and I never saw them again. I like to think that Russell and Esmeralda enjoyed their honeymoon that winter in the Guadalajara sunshine, perhaps sharing an ice cube out of some unsuspecting tourist's margarita.

Grass Can Get Greener

Charlotte Mendel

Every day I wake up with a heavy feeling pinning me to the bed. I drag myself to the breakfast table and hunch over my cereal, praying my mother won't notice my bloody cuticles.

"Tell me what's wrong!" she sometimes says.

But I can't tell her that I am a freak. That nobody at school likes me. That every gym class is a nightmare. Two captains choose the members of their teams, one by one, while I slump against the wall, praying to hear my name next. *Just don't let mine be the last name called.* Not that anyone cares; by the time the line dwindles to three or four rejects, the teams are already turning away and moving towards the field. Still, it is a matter of pride not to be last, and my prayer is usually granted. There is one fat girl who is even more of a reject than I am.

Most of all, I can't tell my mother I spend recesses locked in the bathroom because nobody will hang out with me. Terrified that somebody will notice I'm in there all through recess, I try to convince the rotation of bodies in the cubicles beside me that I'm as busy as a bee in there. I calculate that the stall occupants change about six times, so I mete out my pee in order to give a convincing dribble for each occupant.

The ones who spend ages in front of the mirror really piss me off. I start to imagine they're onto me. They're going to stay out there until I am forced to emerge, and then they will have identified me as the pathetic person who has to spend her recesses in a smelly cubicle. So far, so good, though. They leave, next one in, I start again. Another dribble.

But today my mother says, "Daddy and I were talking last night, and we've decided that you are old enough to look after a horse."

My heart starts to pound. "You're going to buy me a horse?"

"Yes, sweetie. We've hired some men to fix up the barn a bit. We can go look at some horses on the weekend, if you'd like."

If I'd like! I've been riding since the age of seven, attending pony clubs every summer, volunteering at the local barn. The only thing my parents have ever said about horses is: "When will she switch her affections to boys?" And now they're offering to buy me a horse? I can't believe it!

I still can't believe it when Poteet joins our family a month later. She is a beautiful dappled grey Appaloosa mare, 14.2 hands high, with a scrawny mane and tail and a striking blaze down the front of her face. The wrinkles above her eyes give her a quizzical expression.

It's impossible to wake up in the morning with a heavy feeling now because there's so much to laugh at before the school day starts. First, when I open the barn door, Poteet sprints down the field like a madwoman, her scrawny tail high in the air. I always glance around the barn to see if maybe it's on fire or there's a snake, but no, she's just being ridiculous.

I fill her feed bucket with grain and call her. As though a gun has exploded, she shoots back to the barn and shoulders me aside to get to the food, plunging her head inside the trough, gobbling the grain as though I might take it back. She does everything in such a frenzy, I have to laugh out loud. Then she'll jerk her head up and look at me, grain cascading out the sides of her mouth.

It's hard to leave her, but there's the whole day to plan while I'm waiting for the bus, so I don't even notice the other kids standing there. It's not like I'm ignoring them or anything, I'm just thinking about phoning the blacksmith to trim Poteet's hooves, or reminding Dad to take me to the sawmill to get more sawdust. Maybe I'll take some lessons at the local barn so Poteet can meet other horses. There's a lot to do when you have a horse.

Recess in the bathroom isn't so bad anymore. I write to-do lists, or jot down amusing anecdotes about Poteet so I can read them to her when she gets old. I don't even notice the comings and goings in the adjacent cubicles. Who has time to mete out pee?

Sometimes I stay at my desk during recess to write my to-do lists. It doesn't matter so much if somebody sees me by myself and knows I don't have any friends. I have a horse, don't I?

Every day when I get home from school, I rush to the field, bestow a kiss on her forehead (just one kiss, because she is a snooty mare who sighs when I become too passionate), and find a good spot to sit near her.

Sometimes I saddle her up and we go for a ride in the woods, but Poteet is excitable and tends to leap about in a nerve-wracking way, so after a couple of nasty falls, I mostly just sit with her and sing. At first she ignores me, moving around the field, cropping grass. I move after her, plonking myself down in a new spot and resuming my Beatles warble. Gradually, it seems the best grass happens to be the spot I chose. As soon as I'm settled, Poteet starts to graze in my direction. Apparently I'm hogging the most succulent piece of greenery in the whole field. But if I move, there she is again, pushing her nose under my bottom so she can flap her lips at the only blade of grass worth having.

Then I realize this is affection. I am filled with such painful delight I want to cry. I allow myself a little kiss to her eyelid, and she doesn't sigh.

One day I grab her head in a bear hug and she doesn't pull away.

The vet tells me Poteet needs more exercise, so I try to ride her more. Every time we see a track leading off into the woods, we follow it to see if it evolves into a trail. The best types are the circle trails, by which we can arrive home without retracing our steps. Once we are comfortable with a trail, we can amble down it at our leisure, but the first time we try out a new trail is awful. Poteet rushes through unknown territory in great excitement, my terror keeping pace with her speed. She manages to unseat me several times by veering to the side after seeing something frightening. Since she is high-strung, verging on completely bonkers, many things are classified as terrifying, in her opinion. So I cling to the saddle, waiting for a huge rock or an old car wreck to loom in our way. The sudden appearance of such life-threatening objects results in an abrupt about-face, shooting back the same way we came. When I finally stop her by sawing at the reins (on the

Me with my beloved horse, Mahone Bay, NS, 1983.

rare occasions I don't fall off), she shudders to a stop and looks fearfully back over her shoulder, sides heaving and nostrils gaping, even though the object in question is now a mile down the road. One day we come unexpectedly across some deer, and both Poteet and the deer simultaneously leap straight up in the air and gallop off in opposite directions.

One day a few months after I start riding regularly, some kids pass us on their bikes. They all turn around to look at us, and I see that there are a couple of girls from school. My stomach feels a bit queasy, but it's nothing I can't handle.

"I didn't know you had a horse," one of them says.

"Yes. Her name is Poteet."

"Wow, you're really lucky. Can I come over and ride some day?"

"Maybe," I say, and I turn off onto a wooded trail so they can't follow me. Do I mean maybe or do I mean "Go screw yourself"? Pauline has never teased me, but neither has she been nice. She just goes along with the crowd, trying to be invisible. Like all of us.

So when she comes over to my desk the next day at recess, parks herself beside me, and bombards me with questions about my "beautiful" horse, I tell her she can come and meet Poteet the next day.

I feel a little less confident when Pauline shows up in shorts and sneakers.

"Do you know how to ride?"

"I haven't had lessons or anything, but I've been on a horse."

My heart sinks a little. It seems to me Poteet is smiling.

"Well, you pull the right rein if you want to go right, the left rein to go left, and both of them to stop."

"And I kick her to make her go forward, right?"

Poteet eyes me with amusement.

"I don't think you'll have to urge her forward. Just remember how to stop."

Pauline swings up into the saddle. Poteet's ears go back flat against her head and remain there.

"Are you sure you wouldn't like me to lead you? Just at the beginning?"

"No way. I want to ride. Open the gate," Pauline commands.

"I think it's best if you just ride around the field at first."

Poteet walks sedately around the field. Pauline gives her a little kick to get her to trot, and she mistakes it for a request to gallop. She careens around the field and I close my eyes, but there is no thud. Pauline has a lot more guts than I had when I first rode Poteet, despite my years at the riding school. She's hanging on to Poteet's scrawny mane with both hands, and she is laughing hysterically. Poteet, disgusted with her reaction, plunges her head down to buck.

"Get her head up!" I scream. "Pull on the reins!" But Pauline lost both reins long ago, and she catapults over Poteet's head and lands smack in a pile of horse dung. Poteet stops bucking and starts to graze. I stalk over in fury, and she lifts her head in an attempt to give me a conspiratorial look. "Bad girl!" I shout, grabbing her reins and jerking them "Bad girl!"

Pauline gets up and limps over to us, taking the reins and planting a kiss on the naughty beast's nose.

"That was great," she says. "Shall we try it again tomorrow?"

I come into the kitchen where Mum and Dad are having a drink.

"She doesn't bite her cuticles anymore," Mum is saying.

"Did I used to bite my cuticles?" I ask.

"Don't you remember, sweetie? You bit them till they bled. Have you forgotten?"

I look down at my cuticles. They are dirty from working in the barn. "Maybe I don't bite them anymore because they're caked in horse manure. If I ever did bite them." I grab a peanut butter sandwich.

"I can't believe you don't remember."

"That's what children are like," says my father. "They rebound quickly."

"But are you happy now at school, sweetie?" my mother asks.

"Happy? What are you talking about? I hate school," I say cheerfully, biting into the sandwich.

PRETTY BIRD

ANDREA MILLER

I

Every day after daycare, I parked myself in front of Charlo and drew pictures of different homes for him: a jungle house, an arctic igloo, a desert hut. In real life, though, Charlo lived in a cage, his two front and two back toes curled tightly around his metal perch.

I loved to look at Charlo, his brilliant green feathers, his yellow cheeks, his scarlet lores. He was a cranky green parrot that belonged to my aunt's boyfriend, and my mother and stepfather had agreed to look after him for a couple of weeks. I thought he was beautiful.

Humans are earthbound, and either earth-coloured or pale. Parrots are living bits of rainbow, playing in treetops and traversing swaths of sky. Weighted down with our plainness and heavy bones, how could we not crave all those brilliant colours? How could we not be tempted to tame them?

It's been almost thirty years since Charlo stayed with us—so long ago that none of us can remember what my aunt's boyfriend said about Charlo's origins, if he said anything at all.

I imagined Charlo was delivered to his cage by a leggy stork—his green feathers swaddled in a blanket dangling from the stork's beak. But there are actually only two ways a tropical bird could find himself caged in a cold northern country. He was either captured in the wild and shipped here, or else his parents or grandparents were.

The practice called "wild-harvesting" is carried out from Latin America to Africa to Asia. Methods, however, vary from place to place, trapper to trapper. To catch chicks, the first step is to chase off or capture the parents—not an easy task. Trappers lasso the adult birds with slings, or they string up nets between trees to catch those that are flying in the dark. The trappers may also spread a sticky combination of tree gum and coconut oil on a branch next to a decoy bird and, when a parrot lands, drawn to a faux parrot song, it gets stuck. Sometimes the glue is so strong the parrot's feet can't be pried from the branch; in this case, the trapper cuts the feet off.

Yet even when parents are trapped or otherwise disposed of, the chicks can be difficult to nab as they're often nestled in high-up tree holes. One method trappers employ is to "go fishing" using hooks attached to string, but this technique can puncture wings, throats, hearts. No matter the trapping technique, the mortality rate is high. For every bird that makes it to a buyer, more than ten can die in capture and transport.

There are a number of ways a parrot might be weaseled across the Mexican/American border by car. Smugglers, who frequently have experience as drug mules, hide birds in many of the same places they might hide bricks of marijuana or bags of cocaine. Small birds are shoved into handbags and empty deodorant containers, or they're hidden underneath the smuggler's clothes—slipped between skin and a pair of nylons or forced into a cardboard toilet-paper roll and taped to the smuggler's arm or leg. Larger birds are crammed under seats and into armrests. They're made to line the side panels of trucks or the door panels of cars. There have even been cases in which vehicles have been rigged to use alternative fuel, and parrots have been stored in the gas tank.

Smugglers tend to pack parrots as tightly as they would other kinds of contraband, but, unlike drugs and firearms, parrots can get border guards' attention by screaming, chirping, or wriggling. For this reason, smugglers sometimes choose to courier fertilized eggs, rather than chicks or adults. When that's not possible, other methods of enforcing quiet are to tape the parrots' beaks shut or to settle the birds with drugs or shots of tequila.

The sedatives, however, are sometimes lethal, particularly since, when in transport, the birds are not usually given food or water and they tend to be jammed wing to wing with a score of others in some hot, hidden place.

Officials estimate at least twenty thousand birds and eggs are smuggled into the United States each year. Some estimates are up to ten times higher, but no one knows for sure what percentage of the total number of smuggled birds is being intercepted at the border.

II

People use parrots as décor—thinking that, like Indian silk and stone buddhas, they add exotic flavour to a room. As pretty as a picture.

Gustave Courbet's *Woman with Parrot*, part of the Metropolitan Museum of Art's permanent collection, depicts a nude woman lying on her back, a sheet slipping between her legs. Perched on her outstretched hand is a colourful parrot, its wings spread wide. From the woman's tousled hair and the clothes at the foot of the bed, the viewer senses someone just outside the frame, senses that this is an image of a moist and lazy aftermath.

At the age of fifty, Courbet said: "I have always lived in freedom; let me end my life free; when I am dead let this be said of me: 'He belonged to no school, to no church, to no institution, to no academy, least of all to any régime except the régime of liberty.'"

But what about the parrot?

III

When Charlo came to stay with us, we were living in a one-bedroom basement apartment. I would fall asleep in my mom and stepfather's bed, and then later, when they were ready for bed, they'd carry me to the sofa. Their bedroom was wallpapered with images of brown birds and orange and yellow flowers. In the summer months, as I lay in bed, there was still enough light for me to make out the details of the petals, the birds' eyes, their beaks, but in the winter I could only make out dark, looming blotches on the walls.

My mother hated our apartment. Sometimes the heat didn't work and we had to wear thick jackets inside. One night, we came home to find thousands of insects crawling all over the kitchen floor. Another night, when my mother was the only adult home, a man surprised her, touching his privates in the window, watching her. But I liked the apartment just fine. It had green carpet, which made good pretend grass for Barbies and Charlo.

Charlo watched me from behind the bars of his cage as I leafed through all the pictures of different houses I'd drawn for him. Then I got out a blank piece of paper. What Charlo needed now was a castle, one with a moat around it. On the top of a turret, I drew his green body and outstretched wings, his tidy beak with its downward curve. After dinner, I decided, I'd draw Charlo inside the castle, perhaps with humongous platters of food spread out on the dining table—wedges of watermelon and whole prickly pineapples. And I'd give Charlo servants to brush his feathers and massage his toes—maybe the little brown birds from the wallpaper, only dressed as French maids. Charlo was really going to like this castle.

IV

A parrot droops her head, perhaps until it touches the branch she's sitting on. Then her partner takes one of her feathers into his hooked bill, and he delicately sweeps it clean. At the base of a parrot's tail, there is a gland that produces a fine, odorless oil that helps feathers stay supple, and the male dips his bill into his gland and sweeps another of the female's feathers. Sweeps another and another. The female has her eyes closed and is perfectly still, like she's in rapture.

For mated pairs, mutual preening is very much a part of the fabric of life, and they will spend hours alternately preening and sleeping, nestled together. Parrots are intensely social animals, and in the wild a parrot is virtually never solitary, always within earshot of its mate or its flock. Wild parrots are also engaged with the puzzle of survival—searching for food, cracking nuts, outwitting predators.

In captivity, however, parrots are routinely caged solo and left without human companionship for hours—driving them to dysfunctional behaviors, such as ripping out their own feathers. Since they cannot reach all their plumes, their bellies are stripped bare, while their backs and the tops of their heads sport colour—blue, green, red. Plucked, they have scrawny necks and legs and resemble the chicken laid out on Styrofoam platters in supermarkets. According to studies, self-plucking, which never occurs in the wild, affects ten percent of captive birds.

Another coping mechanism of captive parrots is to bond intimately with a human caretaker, as if the human were avian, capable of sharing a nest, laying eggs, understanding the language of coos and shrieks. In *The Parrot Who Owns Me*, ornithologist Joanna Burger writes about how Tiko, her red-lored Amazon parrot, courted her, how he preened her fingers and hair and jealously attacked her human husband if he dared get too close. Tiko even found nest sites for Burger, spoke to her with guttural urgency, and regurgitated for her, as he would for a parrot mate—one he wanted to fatten up for egg laying.

Parrot owners frequently choose to have only one bird, not because of issues of space in their living rooms, but rather because they don't want two bonded birds interested primarily in each other. They want to buy one bird, which is bonded to them, bending to their fingers for preening and stroking. But most people don't have time to give a lone parrot the enormous amount of attention it needs and, frequently, this drives the lonely bird to scream and act out. Frustrated owners sometimes hit or throw things at their parrots, but much more commonly they neglect them. Owners leave parrots alone all day—or longer—without enough room to spread their wings, without enrichment activities, and without a sufficient variety of food. Sometimes owners, tired of the jungle screams, shove parrots into dark closets. To shut them up.

In *Of Parrots and People*, Mira Tweti writes about a scarlet macaw that was brought to a rescue facility after spending seventeen straight years in a tiny cage—so long that he had outgrown the cage door, and the bars had to be cut in order to get him out. Due to the cramped quarters as well as malnutrition, he suffered from a curvature of the spine and bowed legs. The stationary life takes a toll on parrots' bodies. Constantly caged, their muscles atrophy and they lose the ability to fly.

V

In Yann Martel's novel *Life of Pi*, narrator Piscine Patel says that some people think animals in the wild are "happy" because they are "free" and that their happiness is destroyed when wicked men throw them into tiny jails. But this, continues Piscine Patel, is not the way it is:

> *Animals in the wild lead lives of compulsion and necessity within an unforgiving social hierarchy in an environment where the supply of fear is high and the supply of food is low and where territory must constantly be defended and parasites forever endured. What is the meaning of freedom in such a context? Animals in the wild are in practice, free neither in space nor in time, nor in their personal relations. In theory—that is, as a simple physical possibility—an animal could pick up and go, flaunting all the social conventions and boundaries proper to its species. But such an event is less likely to happen than for a member of our own species, say a shopkeeper with all the usual ties—to family, to friends, to society—to drop everything and walk away from his life with only the spare change in his pocket and the clothes on his frame.*

According to the fictional Piscine Patel, wild animals, presumably including parrots, are not pining for their freedom. And perhaps he's right; frequently, if you open the door for a parrot who has been caged for a long time, the parrot will take hours or even days to leave its "tiny jail." And the parrot will frequently return to the cage of its own volition, too, particularly if it can't find food outside the bars.

Captivity is a surefire meal. It is health insurance and safety from predators. But I become muddled when I'm not sure where the dangers are. Is the danger the hawk that could swoop down and pluck a parrot from the jungle canopy, or is it the parrot unravelling in a cage, ripping out its feathers?

VI

Parrots are dancing on command, riding bicycles, doing yoga poses, rolling over like dogs. The trainer whips out a miniature slide and a green parrot, similar to Charlo, climbs the ladder, takes a ride. I'm thirty-four now and I'm with my husband and his family, sitting on a bench, watching the show at La Casa de los Loros—"The House of Parrots"—in Monterrey, Mexico. There are palm trees circling the outdoor theatre, and the stage is lit up against a pale, purple dusk.

The trainer offers his hand to an African grey. "This is the smartest one," he says. "This kind of parrot doesn't just learn to talk. It can learn to understand the words." The trainer pulls out a toy telephone, red like the grey's shock of a tail, and the grey talks into it, its voice sometimes childlike, sometimes womanly, sometimes like a machine. "Hello," the parrot says in Spanish. "Sorry—not home. Wanna leave a message?"

Next, the trainer places a cockatoo in front of a puzzle and the bird obliges the audience, cleverly putting blue square blocks into the blue square slot, green stars into green star, red circles into red circle. I applaud with the audience and then—he looks so cute!—I laugh when the trainer gives a scarlet macaw the same job, and the macaw puts the blocks into a tiny basketball net instead. But the macaw isn't being naughty. He was trained to be funny, and he gets a nut for it.

I wish I could free every bird in the parrot show, but I can't. The terrible truth is I like to watch them do their tricks.

April Passage

Farley Mowat

I t was raining when I woke, a warm and gentle rain that did not beat harshly on the window glass, but melted into the unresisting air so that the smell of the morning was as heavy and sweet as the breath of ruminating cows.

By the time I came down to breakfast the rain was done and the brown clouds were passing, leaving behind them a blue mesh of sky with the last cloud tendrils swaying dimly over it. I went to the back door and stood there for a moment, listening to the roundelay of horned larks on the distant fields.

It had been a dour and ugly winter, prolonging its intemperance almost until this hour, and giving way to spring with a sullen reluctance. The days had been cold and leaden and the wet winds of March had smacked of the charnel house. Now they were past. I stood on the doorstep and felt the remembered sun, heard the gibbering of the freshet, watched little deltas of yellow mud form along the gutters, and smelled the sensual essence rising from the warming soil.

Mutt came to the door behind me. I turned and looked at him and time jumped suddenly and I saw that he was old. I put my hand on his grizzled muzzle and shook it gently.

"Spring's here, old-timer," I told him. "And who knows—perhaps the ducks have come back to the pond."

He wagged his tail once and then moved stiffly by me, his nostrils wrinkling as he tested the fleeting breeze.

The winter past had been the longest he had known. Through the short clipped days of it he had lain dreaming by the fire. Little half-heard whimpers had stirred his drawn lips as he journeyed into time in the sole direction that remained open to him. He had dreamed the bitter days away, content to sleep.

As I sat down to breakfast I glanced out the kitchen window and I could see him moving slowly down the road toward the pond. I knew that he had gone to see about those ducks, and when the meal was done I put on my rubber boots, picked up my field glasses, and followed after.

The country road was silver with runnels of thaw water, and bronzed by the sliding ridges of the melting ruts. There was no other wanderer on that road, yet I was not alone, for his tracks went with me, each paw print as familiar as the print of my own hand. I followed them, and I knew each thing that he had done, each move that he had made, each thought that had been his; for so it is with two who live one life together.

The tracks meandered crabwise to and fro across the road. I saw where he had come to the old TRESPASSERS FORBIDDEN sign, which had leaned against the flank of a supporting snowdrift all the winter through, but now was heeled over it to a crazy angle, one jagged end tipped accusingly to the sky, where flocks of juncos bounded cleanly over and ignored its weary threat. The tracks stopped here, and I knew that he had stood for a long time, his old nose working as he untangled the identities of many foxes, the farm dogs, and the hounds which had come this way during the winter months.

We went on then, the tracks and I, over the old corduroy and across the log bridge, to pause for a moment where a torpid garter snake had undulated slowly through the softening mud.

There Mutt had left the road and turned into the fallow fields, pausing here and there to sniff at an old cow flap, or at the collapsing burrows left by the field mice underneath the vanished snow.

So we came at last to the beechwoods and passed under the red tracery of budding branches where a squirrel jabbered its defiance at the unheeding back of a horned owl, brooding somberly over her white eggs.

The pond lay near at hand. I stopped and sat on an upturned stump and let the sun beat down on me while I swept the surface of the water with my glasses. I could see no ducks, yet I knew they were there. Back in the yellow cattails old greenhead and his mate were waiting patiently for me to go so that they could resume their ponderous court-ship. I smiled, knowing that they would not long be left in peace, even in their secluded place.

I waited and the first bee flew by, and little drifting whorls of mist rose from the remaining banks of snow deep in the woods. Then suddenly there was the familiar voice raised in wild yelping somewhere among the dead cattails. And then a frantic surge of wings and old greenhead lifted out of the reeds, his mate behind him. They circled heavily while, unseen beneath them, Mutt plunged among the tangled reeds and knew a frag-ment of the ecstasy that had been his when guns had spoken over other ponds in other years.

I rose and ambled on until I found his tracks again, beyond the reeds. The trail led to the tamarack swamp and I saw where he had stopped a moment to snuffle at the still-unopened door of a chipmunk's burrow. Nearby there was a cedar tangle and the tracks went round and round beneath the boughs where a ruffed grouse had spent the night.

We crossed the clearing, Mutt and I, and here the soft black mould was churned and tossed as if by a herd of rutting deer; yet all the tracks were his. For an instant I was baffled, and then a butterfly came through the clearing on unsteady wings, and I remembered. So many times I had watched him leap, and hop, and circle after such a one, forever led and mocked by the first spring butterflies. I thought of the dignified old gentle-man of yesterday who had frowned at puppies in their play.

Now the tracks led me beyond the swamp to the edge of a broad field and here they hesitated by a groundhog's hole, unused these two years past. But there was still some faint remaining odour, enough to make Mutt's bulbous muzzle wrinkle with interest, and enough to set his blunt old claws to scratching in the matted grass.

He did not tarry long. A rabbit passed and the morning breeze carried its scent. Mutt's trail veered off abruptly, careening recklessly across the soft and yielding furrows of October's plough, slipping and sliding in the frost-slimed troughs. I followed more sedately until the tracks halted abruptly against a bramble patch. He had not stopped in time. The thorns still held a tuft or two of his proud plumes.

And then there must have been a new scent on the wind. His tracks moved off in a straight line toward the country road, and the farms which lie beyond it. There was a new mood on him, the ultimate spring mood. I knew it. I even knew the name of the little collie bitch who lived in the first farm. I wished him luck.

I returned directly to the road, and my boots were sucking in the mud when a truck came howling along toward me, and passed in a shower of muddy water. I glanced angrily after it, for the driver had almost hit me in his blind rush. As I watched, it swerved sharply to make the bend in the road and vanished from my view. I heard the sudden shrilling of brakes, then the roar of an accelerating motor—and it was gone.

I did not know that, it its passing, it had made an end to the best years that I have lived.

In the evening of that day I drove out along the road in company with a silent farmer who had come to fetch me. We stopped beyond the bend, and found him in the roadside ditch. The tracks that I had followed ended here, nor would they ever lead my heart again.

It rained that night and by the next dawn even the tracks were gone, save by the cedar swamp where a few little puddles dried quickly in the rising sun. There was nothing else, save that from a tangle of rustling brambles some tufts of fine white hair shredded quietly away in the early breeze and drifted down to lie among the leaves.

The pact of timelessness between the two of us was ended, and I went from him into the darkening tunnel of the years.

SHIPPING DAY

CHRIS NICHOLS

Shipping out chickens was one of the most important annual events at the TP Poultry Farm, the day when my uncle's place would be bustling with farmhands and relatives. Tom (the "T" in "TP," his wife Pat supplying the second letter) grew intent and businesslike, hopeful that another year's work would pay off. We would all show up around five o'clock in the afternoon, giving those of us still in school time to change and have a quick bite to eat, and ready ourselves for a long night. I, being Tom's nephew, was on the "relative" divide of the collection of workers, though I would be paid for my work, unlike my cousin Kevin, Tom's oldest son who still lived at home. Once we entered the barn, however, we were all workers in Tom's eyes. He would flex his thumbs under his thick suspenders, scratch his bald scalp, fix us with an intent stare, and say, "Time to get to work, boys. Let's not be here all night."

Shipping chickens was all business. You would work feverishly and rhythmically, walking in the low lighting in a crouched position toward the corners of the barn where the chickens had massed in an attempt to avoid the commotion we were causing. You would swoop up two or three at a time, grasping their legs and quickly flipping them upside down, letting them squawk and thrash helplessly for a moment before shifting their legs in between your fingers on one hand, and diving back down to catch two or three more with the other. You were lost in the attempt to not get scratched, to not drop the birds you had already caught, and to keep up with the other workers who were catching chickens beside you.

You ignored the crunch of stepped-on feet and the snap of broken wings as you tore through the flock. Once you had eight or so chickens (my hands were small—the men could wedge a couple more birds between their fingers) you walked to the back of the barn where the large sliding door had been cracked eight feet across and a ramp was protruding into the barn. You would ascend the ramp to the broadside of a semi that was pulling a trailer containing hundreds of cages, where Tom would be standing, directing you to which cages could hold more chickens. You would heft the chickens up to chest height and swing them into the cages as Tom counted, usually making some dry comment about how few you had gathered or how slow you were moving. (Somehow Uncle Tom motivated people to work harder without making them resent him for it.) When you went back down the ramp into the barn, you wanted to impress him on the next trip, jumping ahead of the next person in line or collecting more than ten chickens. As the latter was not possible for me, I relied on speed.

Tom used to say with a smile that there were two kinds of animals allowed at the TP poultry farm: useful and dead. There was always one dog around, some variety of mutt, whose job it was to intimidate strangers and protect the property. The dogs' lifespans were left to chance: Sandy, a collie-shepherd cross, lived eight years before losing a fight with a pack of coyotes, whereas Sam, a husky cross, was run over by a truck a month after Tom got him from a neighbour. Dogs were trained for their roles, something unnecessary for the half-wild barn cats, which were tolerated on the farm because they kept the mice population down.

The chickens, however, were both the most-prized and least-respected animals, the most valuable yet the most expendable. There were roughly ten thousand of them at any given time, a third of them in barn one, laying eggs, a third in barn two, layers as well, but a different generation from the first, and the rest were chicks newly arrived in barn three, being raised to replace the eldest group of layers. In every group, there was a ten-to-one ratio of hens to roosters, the latter being there to ensure egg fertilization. The chickens were on a sixty-two-week cycle: in that period, they arrived, grew, laid eggs, and were finally shipped for slaughter. After sixty-two weeks, the hens would still lay eggs, but at a lesser rate, making it no longer cost-feasible to keep them. Sometimes Tom would buy two or three hundred more roosters to inseminate the older hens, but this would only help the quality of the egg supply, not the quantity. Their usefulness outlived, the old hens and roosters would be shipped. The chickens' numbers made an individual bird beneath notice, yet they were the lifeblood of the farm, the reason for the dog, the cats, and my presence on a February afternoon, in a smelly, dark chicken barn.

Having been raised and fed in the barn for over a year, the adolescent birds were ready to be sent to a large meat-processing plant, where they would be butchered, eviscerated, and ground up as meat for any products in the local supermarket that included the ingredient "processed chicken." When Tom first told me that those chicken fingers I was eating could contain meat from the TP poultry farm, I felt sick to my stomach, but the feeling didn't last long. It was just too difficult to make the connection between the food I was eating and the living, breathing birds that clucked and ran at my feet as I helped my cousins collect eggs, the roosters that would strut and peck at my boots until I kicked them, reestablishing the pecking order, and the masses of birds so stupid that herding them was a risk because the ones at the front would forget within seconds their fear and stop, allowing those following to pile on and suffocate them. The chicken I ate received barely a thought; the chickens I handled received less.

Shipping chickens was an activity that took place in the dark. The birds were docile in low lighting, so Tom dimmed the lights to the point that we workers could hardly make each other out. The only luminescence came from the cracked door that revealed the truck's ramp. The lights were flicked on only when the truck needed to move, and we would get a ten-minute break. At this time, most of us would release the chickens we had caught rather than sit with them in our hands for the time it took for the truck to reorient itself. After that, there was nothing to do, and the sights and smells of the barn would return. You would look down at your hands to see if any of the scratches you had felt while in the midst of catching had drawn blood. You would blow your nose on your shirt. Some workers would entertain themselves by chasing and killing mice, hundreds of which were always attracted to the chicken barns by the grain and the warmth. Other workers would duck outside briefly to smoke, though it was always freezing cold, and I never liked leaving because inevitably I would need to return again, and the stench of the barn would seem that much worse. Once I entered the barn I stayed because I didn't want to be reminded that there was a place that didn't stink, that wasn't too hot, that wasn't filled with stupid animals that would claw your hands and shit on you.

One time during one of these breaks, the lead farmhand Trent was in a rambunctious mood, and challenged me to a contest.

"What kind of a contest?" I asked, wary. Trent never talked to me. He smiled. "Football contest," he answered.

"What do you mean?" I asked, feeling small and foolish before this big man.

Trent swooped down and grabbed a nearby chicken before it had time to react, then held it squarely in front of him with both hands. Suddenly he dropped the chicken and booted it, football-style, into the air. It squawked as it sailed, flailing its wings in a vain attempt to fly, and landed among a hundred other birds, disappearing from view.

"Your turn," he said. Before I could respond, Tom yelled at us from across the barn. He strode towards us, red-faced.

"Don't let me catch you doing that again!" he bellowed. I struggled to conceal a smile. Trent was Tom's favourite worker, and it was satisfying to see him being chastised for a change.

"What were you thinking?" Tom continued. "You know that any bruising on the meat gets me a lower price. If I see you do that again, I'll dock your wage."

Trent mumbled something that passed for an apology, looking at me and rolling his eyes. I found myself smiling back. It felt good to share a conspiratorial moment with this man, though I was relieved I wouldn't be required to copy his action. Tom walked away and soon the truck's horn sounded, signaling that it was time to get back to work. Someone dimmed the lights, and Trent quickly ducked down beside me, coming up with five chickens, all arranged expertly in one of his massive hands.

We worked for another hour or so, catching chickens, ascending the ramp, waiting in line, then throwing the chickens up into their cages. I was badly scraped by a rooster's spur and blood was dripping down my arm, but I didn't stop to clean and bandage my cut until the next break, which, thankfully, came sooner rather than later. I showed Tom and asked where his first-aid kit was, and he told Kevin to show me.

My cousin found the kit and pulled out its two remaining Band-Aids along with a vial of rubbing alcohol, making quick work of my cut. We returned to the barn with plenty of time to spare before break was over.

"Watch this," Kevin said. He expertly plucked a chicken from the ground and held it in his lap. It squawked, but quickly settled down in his arms. He held it with one hand while slowly and gently covering its eyes with the other. It had been bobbing its head in quick, jerking motions, but when Kevin covered its eyes, it stopped. It made a low sound, almost satisfied. Soon it melted into his lap, and I realized that Kevin had put the chicken to sleep in seconds. When he lifted his hand from the chicken's eyes, it remained peacefully asleep, taking the furtive breaths of a small warm-blooded animal. He set it down carefully on the barn floor, where it continued to doze.

"Cool, let me try!" I said. I lunged for the nearest chicken. It took me longer to settle the bird in my lap, and longer to maneuver one hand over its eyes. It kept moving its head from side to side, avoiding my hand, so I applied more pressure down on its neck, trapping its head against its body. It gave a loud squawk and tried to claw at me, but I had it firmly wedged on my lap. "Sleep!" I said. "Sleep!"

But just then, the truck horn sounded again, our sign to get back to work. I released the bird, and it flapped away from me. I stood up and realized that my pants felt wet; I looked down to see that the chicken had shit on me.

I was not always the one to suffer, however. When someone new was hired to ship out, the mood in the barn would be lighter because we all looked forward to the requisite initiation. Typically, it would begin about an hour into shipping with a senior hand like Trent suddenly yelling out a number as he returned to the barn from dumping his chickens.

"Eighty-two!" he would yell.

"Seventy-four!" someone would respond, and everyone would join in, shouting numbers. Inevitably, the new hire would ask what was going on.

"What do you mean? They're just calling out their count. We need to do that once in a while."

"What do you mean, their count?"

"You know, their count. How many chickens they've caught so far. You know we need to keep track of how many chickens we've hauled if we want to get paid, right?"

This was the moment when the new worker would panic. An hour into shipping, he wouldn't have a clue how many chickens he had caught, and would rack his brain to remember the numbers that had been called out, trying to pick an acceptable number.

I know this because it was done to me, and I was nervous about making up a number in case Tom would catch my lie.

I found out later that Tom himself would sometimes participate in the ruse, asking the new worker for his number in his gruffest voice. "What are you at?" he'd say, looking at his clipboard, thumbing his scalp.

Then he would pretend that any response given was drastically inflated. "Are you trying to rip me off?" he'd say, ruddy face puffed up in anger. When the worker confessed that he had no clue as to his number, Tom would smile and say, "Good. Me neither. Now get back to work."

We all would laugh and assure the new worker that we all had endured the same thing. Then something strange would happen. Tom wouldn't shout at us to get back to work, and the farmhands like Trent would forget that we were relatives and not real workers. We still moved quickly, but not with the same recklessness as before, pausing at times to share a joke or talk about school.

The chickens benefitted too, I think, because after we all laughed together we would move slower for a while, and it was our desire for haste that caused wings to be broken and feet to be crushed. Such a strange assertion to make, as if it mattered whether or not a chicken had a broken wing while being shipped to slaughter. Dead was dead, broken wing or not; what mattered was minimal meat-bruising to ensure a healthy bottom line. You were either dead or useful. And yet, when the work slowed, and we crammed fewer chickens in between our fingers, I found myself convinced that the wings mattered, for no reason I could understand.

As the night wound down, we would turn the lights on and expose the few remaining chickens, which would instantly become far more alert and elusive. Then we would compete to catch them, the more experienced hands being far more successful, though I held my own, often catching a couple of the last dozen or so. Then we would throw them in the truck, and it would pull out for the last time. The barn would suddenly become eerily quiet, save for the humming of the fans, which had been obscured in the chaos of the night. Trent and Tom began disassembling the ramp, leaning its pieces up against the wall of the barn, where it would wait until the next shipping day. Everyone would head to the house to wash up, then sit at the large kitchen table and eat whatever snack Pat had prepared for the night, usually doughnuts and cookies. Kevin and I stayed behind to help with the ramp, and in the end there were only the four of us in the empty barn, with its whirring fans and stark smells of grain, sweat, and, of course, chickens.

Tom clapped me on the shoulder. "Let the others wash up and eat first. We've got some beer to drink, but not enough for everyone," he said. He produced a six-pack. Trent passed me a beer, and this time the smile we shared felt real.

GOOD QUEEN MAUD:
AN OTTER'S TALE

LINDA OLSON

I remember well the first time I saw Matilda. It was early morning, the
sun still blushing the clouds, when she burst from a low tunnel of leaves
beneath the wild roses. She stumbled a little just as she mounted the rise
onto the lawn, the tail of the fish dangling from her mouth caught under
a delicate front paw like the long skirt of a lady trod beneath a silk-clad
toe. She twitched it free with a noble tilt of her chin, adjusted the grip
of her teeth along its backbone, and scampered across the lawn with her
silvery treasure.

Watching through the picture window that looked out over the lawn
and the sea beyond, I couldn't see where she'd gone after disappearing up
the side of the house. But I could guess. There was a narrow strip of lawn
there between our place and the neighbour's fence, and about halfway
along the cement foundation of our house, a small gap for ventilation. I had
noticed it a few days before, when we were moving in, and had noticed,
too, the well-worn ground near the opening. I had been wondering what
might be living in the crawl space, and was pleasantly surprised that it
hadn't turned out to be the rats I'd feared.

Not that many would consider a prolific river otter bringing fish
home any better than a rat, but it didn't take Matilda long to work her
slippery ways into our life. I can't really remember, for instance, when I
began calling her Maud, after the much-loved twelfth-century queen of

England who took the name Matilda (Maud for short) when she married the son of William the Conqueror, King Henry I. I'm not sure why I chose that particular name either, save that something about her sense of entitlement struck me as aristocratic. The name proved true, however, not least because just like Good Queen Maud, whose ancient English lineage lent authenticity to Henry's Norman claim to the throne, Matilda, with her sheltered bit of waterfront real estate, won the attention of more than one powerful male.

We had been renting the house for several months when those big males first showed up. They woke me in the wee hours of the night, not with their noise, as you might expect, but with their pungent odour, so strong and musty that I could taste it, even feel it like oil on my tongue. They must have been lying right beneath the floor of our bedroom, for I soon discovered that I could literally follow them by smell as they moved around the crawl space. Fortunately they never stayed long, perhaps because Maud, a much sweeter-smelling creature, seemed as eager as we were to see them go and have her space back to herself.

This isn't to say, however, that she didn't enjoy or invite their vigorous affection, for she most certainly did, and that's where much of the noise came in. It began that morning after the musk of the males had woken me, just as my daughters were eating their breakfast.

"Who's fighting with Matilda?" my youngest asked, her blue eyes wide over the bananas and oatmeal on her spoon.

"I think she's got some friends visiting," I tried, hoping it would suffice.

"But why are they fighting? They're not hurting her, are they?"

"No, I don't think so. It's more like...she's got boyfriends visiting, and they're fighting over her." It could have been true—some of the sounds were certainly more aggressive than others—but my older daughter smiled mischievously, and such a litany of growls, snarls, moans, squeals, and caterwauls unfolded beneath our feet over the following days that it soon dawned on the younger as well. She came to be the one who most often initiated what we called the otter stomp—more, I think, to laugh and dance over what she imagined those otters doing beneath her feet than to chase the stinky males away. But I confess it was the hope of their absence for a while that inspired me to encourage the stomp, which involved playing rock 'n' roll at high volume and dancing around the living room with feet as heavy as any monster mash could demand. Worked like a charm, until nightfall came again and the males with it.

That was only for a few weeks of the year, however. Most of the time it was just Matilda herself under the house, and in the spring and summer, her young pups as well. I didn't see them much that first year—we'd come home to British Columbia from England late in the year and no doubt she wasn't yet comfortable enough with our presence and scents to let us see much of her life. I did see her swimming and fishing at times, and on several occasions watched her repeat her journey back to her den with scaly suppers for her young, but the little ones themselves remained a mystery.

By our second year at Cordova Bay, however, Maud had grown accustomed to us, particularly to me and our little grey terrier, Frodo. We took our walks along the beach after everyone else had left for the day, and we often saw Matilda eating her fill of mussels before taking fish back to her new brood. Still, it took me by surprise when we came around a tall rock one morning and found her swimming with her two pups in a small, shallow cove. We hadn't taken *her* by surprise, however—she was waiting for us, her head high in the water, and she watched carefully indeed as Frodo moved to the edge, sniffing the air for the scent of the pups just a few feet away.

There are few things more adorable than the tangled antics and slapping tails of tiny otters attempting their first dives without a hint of the silent grace their mother possesses. So joyful was their play that it took a very long time for them to notice Frodo, and I thought Maud would surely put a stop to the encounter before it really began, but she didn't—

only watched, her neck rising like a serpent further and further above the water as her curious charges swam toward the shore. The quickest had gotten so close that otter and dog had nearly touched, nose stretched to nose, when at last Matilda gave a small gurgle to call her pups back. Yet she didn't retreat, seemed even to relax with a few safe inches gained, and let her pups play for long that morning—and many a morning after it—as we sat and watched, Frodo always wagging at the water's edge.

Her instincts were dead on, of course, for she had nothing to fear from Frodo, who wore his hobbit's name with integrity and was far more inclined to reveal confusion and grief when he found some small creature injured than to do the injury himself. Yet her tolerance surprised me all the same, because she had good reason to be cautious of the little terrier. She had come across the lawn one spring day while I was pulling weeds from the strawberry patch and Frodo was resting in the shade nearby. I hadn't seen her, but I guess she must have moved between the two of us. I looked up at the sound of her feet lunging heavy on the ground, and caught the grey flash of fur hard at her heels. I could see, however, that Frodo was not giving it his all, and Maud seemed to sense it as well—certainly she passed as close by him many more times, but she never took a route between us again, and Frodo never chased her again. On those occasions when she was brave enough to let her little ones pass close on land, where they were at such a disadvantage, he would set his chin down on his paws, as if to reassure her he meant no harm, though I knew he was itching to greet them.

Such careful compromises born of mutual respect allowed this living arrangement to work for everyone. We had to accept that our lovely waterfront home would always smell a little like we'd had seafood the night before, and the neighbour who was more concerned about entertaining guests in style than enjoying the incredible ecosystem at our doorstep had to accept that I was never going to agree with her argument that "the otter could just go live down there somewhere"—an argument delivered with

Young otters peering through the old dock, Vancouver Island, BC.

a lazy wave of her hand to the monstrous houses crowding the shore. She did accept it at last, but I confess I helped her along by hauling sand up from the beach to keep the area in front of the den clean. Generally it was spotless when Matilda was home alone, but the pups made a bit of a mess as they grew, and again, it was good the big males were only around for short periods of time.

So it's true I indulged Good Queen Maud and her progeny for the few years we lived in that house—not in that questionable way of providing food better hunted, but by letting her keep to her own ways in a place otters had been living for decades. Even when the original house had burned down and been rebuilt many years before we lived there, the otters had returned after the new house was set on the old foundation. It was Matilda's place more than it was mine, and like King Henry, I could only respect and benefit from the situation.

For there can be no doubt that accommodating Maud's simple needs had its rewards. There was the night she began tapping softly on a pipe beneath the floor, with a shell perhaps. I was the only one still awake, my eyes drooping over my book, so I didn't have to explain to anyone my impulse to jump out of bed and return the taps more quietly still. I just did it—huddled down by the bathtub, tapped on the porcelain with my knuckles, waited breathless, and at last she answered. I tapped back again, then she, our patterns a little different each time, shaping the darkness with the rhythm of our complicity.

Rhythm was the essence of her life—the rhythm of the days and nights, the seasons and the sea—and she graced our lives with this primitive cycle as well. Never was this clearer to me than one morning just before dawn. I had worked at the computer far too late into the night and was shaking its hum from my head as I turned out the lights to snatch a few hours' rest before the alarms began waking everyone. I couldn't say why I glanced out the window before heading to bed, but I'm glad I did. The lawn was alive with the rhythm of the waves. Now, I'd seen a lot of otters out in the yard before. Often when the wind blew up, Matilda's progeny from previous years would seek the shelter of her den. Generally they were successful, but if the males or new pups were already in residence, they would find themselves denied entry. On those occasions, they were forced to huddle in the shadows beneath the roses.

That night, however, was calm and clear with a full moon in the western sky, and all those bright eyes had clustered in the centre of the lawn with their mother. There they were doing the most remarkable thing. They were dancing in the moonlight—if *dancing* is indeed the right word to describe their sensuous undulations. No, they were *swimming* in the moonlight—dipping their noses to the earth, curving their sleek backs, and arching their tails high to send the silvery flow of the sea along the sinuous length of their bodies. Nature and fantasy perfectly blended, they bent their liquid knees to the moon and mesmerized me. I thought of waking my husband, my daughters, to share the moment, but I couldn't pull myself from the window, so wholly had they drawn me into their urgent and timeless current. I bent my knee with them that night, stepped for the briefest moment into that rushing river of existence, and felt—really felt—its power.

How I cherish those rare and special moments now, and I often wonder what became of Matilda. The family we were renting from ended up listing the house when the market was good, and I soon got the call I'd been dreading. The real estate agent had suggested the obvious—it would be a good deal easier to sell the house without the otters. Sealing the ventilation hole would be the best way to cope with "the problem." Now, the landlady had great sympathy for the otters: the house had been her mother's, and her mother had welcomed Matilda's ancestors for many years. So when I explained that the season's pups were still in the den and I couldn't have any part in doing Matilda or her young any harm, she relented, for a while.

But I know that tiny gap was closed soon after we moved out, and when the place sold, the house was torn down to make way for one three times its size, the yard was re-landscaped, and Maud's fishy trails through the roses are long gone. It's not just there, though—almost all the old cottages along that beach have become executive houses. The tall firs that watched over the shore have been torn away, the earth once held firm by their roots bleeds into the sea, and massive walls of concrete rise to hold the precious acres against the tide. "Down there somewhere" the otters must still be, but I fear for all those young with no home to come back to in the storms, and hope that none have been lost to the sea like William, the son of Good Queen Maud, who perished in the wreck of the *White Ship*.

We may not think of river otters as threatened, of course. They are incredibly resourceful and have thrived in our shadow, so I don't doubt that some will continue to do so despite their present decline and the growing threat of environmental pollution. But each day there are fewer and fewer places for urbanized otters like Matilda to settle and raise their families, and something is always lost, I think, if we fail to see and respect the life we find thriving at our doorsteps.

My door now looks out on a different land and a different shore, but here in Newfoundland, beside the tiny trickle of a creek that adorns the piece of this earth I call my own, I saw a female river otter this morning. We watched each other a moment before she dipped her nose to the spring snow, slipped her slender body into the stream, and was gone like water through my fingers. But I thought of Matilda then, her neck stretched high and proud above the waves, teaching her young how to curve their tails at just the right angle to glide so silently beneath the surface.

LINES ON THE WATER

DAVID ADAMS RICHARDS

As a boy, I dreamed of fishing before I went, and went fishing before I caught anything, and knew fishermen before I became one. As a child, I dreamed of finding remarkable fish so close to me that they would be easy to catch. And no one, in my dreams, had ever found these fish before.

I remember the water as dark and clear at the same time—and by clear I suppose I mean clean. Sometimes it looked like gold or copper, and at dusk the eddies splashed silver-toned, and babbled like all the musical instruments of the world. I still think of it this way now, years later.

As a child, I had the idea that trout were golden, or green, in deep pools hidden away under the moss of a riverbank. And that some day I would walk in the right direction, take all the right paths to the river and find them there.

In fact, trout, I learned, were far more textured and a better colour than just golds and greens. They were the colour of nature itself—as naturally outfitted in their coat of thin slime as God could manage. They were hidden around bends and in the deep shaded pools of my youth.

I had the impression from those Mother Goose stories that all fish could talk. I still do.

My first fishing foray was along the bank of a small brook to the northwest of Newcastle, on the Miramichi. A sparkling old brook that Lord Beaverbrook took his name from.

My older brother and a friend took me along with them, on a cool blowy day. We had small cane rods and old manual reels, with hooks and sinkers and worms, the kind all kids used. The kind my wife used as a child on the Bartibog River thirteen miles downriver from my town of Newcastle, and her brothers used also, at the same time that I was trudging with my brother.

It was a Saturday in May of 1955 and I was not yet five years of age. Fishing even then could take me out of myself, far away from the worry of my life, such as it was, and into another life, better and more complete.

We had packed a lunch and had got to the brook about ten in the morning. Just as we entered the woods, I saw the brook, which seemed no deeper in places than my shoe. In we went (a certain distance) until the sounds of the town below us were left behind.

Leaning across the brook was a maple, with its branches dipping into the water. At the upper end of the tree, the current swept about a boulder, and gently tailed away into a deep pocket about a foot from the branches. The place was shaded, and sunlight filtered through the trees on the water beyond us. The boys were in a hurry and moved on to that place where all the fish *really* are. And I lagged behind. I was never any good at keeping up, having a lame left side, so most of the time my older brother made auxiliary rules for me—rules that by and large excluded me.

"You can fish there," he said.

I nodded. "Where?"

"There, see. Look—right there. Water. Fish. Go at her. We'll be back."

I nodded.

I sat down on the moss and looked about, and could see that my brother and his friend were going away from me. I was alone. So I took out my sandwich and ate it. (It was in one pocket, my worms were in the other. My brother doled the worms out to me a few at a time.)

I was not supposed to be, from our mother's instructions, alone.

"For Mary in heaven's sake, don't leave your little brother alone in those woods." I could hear her words.

I could also hear my brother and our friend moving away, and leaving me alone. In this little place we were out of sight of one another after about twenty feet.

I had not yet learned to tie my sneakers; they had been tied for me by my brother in a hurry, for the second time, at the railway track, and here again they were loose. So I took them off. And then I rolled up my pants.

I had four worms in my pocket. They smelled of the dark earth near my grandmother's back garden where they had come from, and all worms smell of earth, and therefore all earth smells of trout.

I spiked a worm on my small hook the best I could. I had a plug-shot sinker about six inches up my line, which my father had squeezed for me the night before. But my line was kinked and old, and probably half-rotted, from years laid away.

I grabbed the rod in one hand, the line in the other, and tossed it at the boulder. It hit the boulder and slid underneath the water. I could see it roll one time on the pebbled bottom, then it was lost to my sight under the brown cool current. Then sun was at my back splaying down through the trees. I was standing on the mossy bank. There was a young twisted maple on my right.

Almost immediately I felt a tug on the line. Suddenly it all came to me—this is what fish do—this was their age-old secret.

The line tightened, the old rod bent, and a trout—the first trout of my life—came splashing and rolling to the top of the water. It was a trout about eight inches long, with a plump belly.

"I got it," I whispered. "I got it. I got it."

But no one heard me: "I got it, I got it."

For one moment I looked at the trout, and the trout looked at me. It seemed to be telling me something. I wasn't sure what. It is something I have been trying to hear ever since.

When I lifted it over the bank, and around the maple, it spit the hook, but it was safe in my possession a foot or two from the water.

For a moment no one came, and I was left to stare at it. The worm had changed colour in the water. The trout was wet and it had the most beautiful glimmering orange speckles I ever saw. It reminded me, or was to remind me as I got older, of spring, of Easter Sunday, of the smell of snow being warmed away by the sun.

My brother's friend came back. He looked at it, amazed that I had actually caught something. Picking up a stick, and hunching over it he shouted, "Get out of the way—I'll kill it."

And he slammed the stick down beside it. The stick missed the fish, hit a leafed branch of that maple that the fish was lying across, and catapulted the trout back into the brook.

I looked at him, and he looked at me.

"Ya lost him," he said.

My brother came up, yelling, "Did you get a fish?"

"He lost him," my brother's friend said, standing.

"Oh ya lost him," my brother said, half derisively, and I think a little happily.

I fished fanatically for the time remaining, positive that this was an easy thing to do. But nothing else tugged at my line. And as the day wore on I became less enthusiastic.

We went home a couple of hours later. The sun glanced off the steel railway tracks, and I walked back over the ties in my bare feet because I had lost my sneakers. My socks were stuffed into my pockets. The air now smelled of steely soot and bark, and the town's houses stretched below the ball fields.

The houses in our town were for the most part the homes of working men. The war was over and it was the age of the baby boomers, of which I was one. Old pictures in front of those houses, faded with time, show seven or eight children, all smiling curiously at the camera. And I reflect that we baby boomers, born after a war that left too many dead, were much like the salmon spawn born near the brown streams and great river. We were born to reaffirm life and the destiny of the human race.

When we got home, my brother showed his trout to my mother, and my mother looked at me.

"Did you get anything, dear?"

"I caught a trout—a large trout. It—it—I—"

"Ya lost him, Davy boy," my brother said, slapping me on the back.

"Oh well," my mother said. "That's all right, there will always be a next time."

And that was the start of my fishing life.

That was long ago, when fishing was innocent and benevolent. I have learned since that I would have to argue my way through life—that I was going to become a person who could never leave to rest the *idea* of why things were the way they were. And fishing was to become part of this idea, just as hunting was. Why would the fish take one day, and not the next? What was the reason for someone's confidence one year, and their lack of it the next season, when conditions seemed to be exactly the same?

Or the great waters—the south branch of the Sevogle that flows into the main Sevogle, that flows into the Northwest Miramichi, itself a tributary of the great river. What infinite source propelled each separate individual fish to return on those days, at that moment, when my Copper Killer, or Green Butt Butterfly—or anyone else's—was skirting the pool at exactly the right angle at that same moment, and *when* was it all announced and inscribed in the heavens—as insignificant as it is—as foreordained.

The Dominant Sow

Anny Scoones

As anyone familiar with Glamorgan Farm knows, it is home to two great Gloucester Old Spot sows named Mabel and Matilda, each weighing more than seven hundred pounds. The Gloucester Old Spot is an old British heritage breed of pig, known for its large black spots. Folklore says that the spots came from fallen apples, so the Old Spot is also known as the Orchard Pig. Old Spots have huge, drooping ears that fall over their slit eyes, so they cannot see well and lumber around slowly, using their snouts to guide them from their slop buckets to their mud hole to their deep hay beds in the little board-and-batten barn in the corner of their meadow. The only thing the very proper Gloucester Old Spot breeder, Pamela Sansbury-Jones, offered when I wrote to her at her farm, Bottomly Gardens, in England, was, "They like their potatoes cooked," and she sent me a spotted fridge magnet. The breed is considered extinct in Canada, so Mabel and Matilda were imported from Oregon, and I love to show them off at the local Saanich Fair.

Mabel and Matilda both are registered with the Blueberry gene pool—their official names are Blueberry 36 and Blueberry 37—and they came with lovely, gold-sealed, parchment registration papers. There were only four gene pools left in the world, I was told, and the Blueberry sows could only be bred with the Rufus line from Dublin. That has proved quite impossible, so for now, on Glamorgan Farm, they are cross-bred.

Mabel and Matilda each had a large, healthy litter the year after they arrived with a sweet, red-haired juvenile boar named Boris. When

Boris was about nine months old, I sold him to a man with a sow named Penelope in the suburbs. I have felt guilty ever since seeing the trailer pull out of the driveway and hearing little Boris's lonely, mournful cries for his two friends. I was sure the man who bought him would never scratch his pink belly, which he loved, or pick him tender broccoli leaves.

Mabel and Matilda grew larger and larger. Their great sagging pink teats swayed as they moved around their meadow, eating fallen apples and the tender blackberry shoots that grow out of control up the side of the rotting log barn at the lower part of their large fenced area. On hot days, I'd leave the hose running and the girls wedged their powerful pink snouts into the soft black earth and made a voluptuous, cooling mud bath that they flopped their great bulks into with happy grunts and sighs. On those hot days, I had to rub sunscreen on the tender skin behind their ears.

In the cool evenings, after they ate their warm mash mixed with cooked potatoes and cabbage leaves (Mabel and Matilda love cooked vegetables—everything except carrots, which they separate by neatly spitting them out between their picket-fence-like teeth), they ambled outdoors to do their business in the corner of the meadow and then retired to their deep straw beds in their little barn. Mabel and Matilda always sleep close together and leave enormous indentations in the straw—outlines of their rotund bodies.

They snore quietly—if only I could sleep as deeply! Matilda, particularly, sleeps *so* deeply that sometimes in the morning when I arrive with their buckets of mash, I look at her lifeless body and think, *Oh my god—she's dead!* and it's a shocking feeling for a moment or two. My heart stops, and I sort of freeze, and then I see an eyelash twitch or hear a muffled grunt followed by a rising puff of dust, and I relax, but what a terrible feeling it is for the moment, to think she has died in the night!

Matilda is the slower, more thoughtful pig, and she always plods over to me for a scratch and, yes, a loving kiss on her wet pink snout after her dinner. That's why I always have a towel in my pocket, in case she's a bit muddy from rooting in the clay soil for grubs and roots. The pigs have a lovely smell, especially around their eyes—it's a delightful fresh smell, far better than a fabric softener or plug-in candle. When I bend down and tell Matilda that I love her, she leans into me and gives a soft grunt in appreciation. I am sure that pigs are not only affectionate and sensitive, but intuitive as well.

There have been times when I kissed Matilda and half an hour later had on my diamond earrings and was making a political speech on food security and farmland assessments to the local Chamber of Commerce—if they only knew! People always ask me, "Are pigs really intelligent?" and I have two answers: "What exactly do you consider intelligent? Sensitivity? Memory? Outsmarting others to get your warm delicious slop?" And, "Well, they must be intelligent because all they do all day is eat and sleep and get scratched, and I'm totally exhausted slogging around in the mud, picking up their dung, mixing their slop, and scratching their backs—so who is the intelligent one?" But my *real* answer is this: they know something—something that I admire—something that, when their little glassy slit eyes stare at me, goes right through me. I know there is another intelligence, another something going on.

Well, the time came for Matilda and Mabel to be bred again. It's difficult to borrow a boar, and we missed a breeding year after Boris left, but I came in contact with a nice country farmer, Tom, with a fresh English wife, Vio, who wore green rubber boots with buckles on the sides (like Prince Charles) in the rural municipality of Metchosin. Tom and Vio had a small farm of rambling golden meadows and evergreens near the William Head prison. Tom was interested in pigs and had a boar named Buster, a Berkshire, as rare in Canada as our dear Gloucester Old Spots. Buster had come from Winnipeg as a piglet in a cold, crowded, metal livestock truck. As you drive along the highway sometimes one of these livestock trucks passes and you see countless resigned little snouts pressed against the air holes.

Buster was delivered to Glamorgan Farm in a lovely white horse trailer. Tom said he was well endowed and ready to go ("like a surfboard" were his exact words, I think). Mabel and Matilda trudged out through the buttercups to meet their arranged husband.

Buster was no oil painting (though he *was* well endowed). He was built like a box, skookum, as the local farmers would say, with grizzled whiskers and caked mud clinging around his tiny squinty eyes; his great leathery ears had square bite marks out of them from when a larger boar had bullied him, no doubt over a young pink sow. As Tom herded him off the ramp with a board, Buster slipped and fell clumsily, but slowly got up, looking perplexed. Then he stumbled over to the girls, who were waiting with curiosity. I couldn't help but think that he really didn't look as good as dear Boris, all sleek and handsome with his shining copper coat, bright eyes, and inquisitive expression. Buster was black, as Berkshires are, with a white snout, white tail, and white lower legs.

I gave him a scratch and thought, *As soon as Tom and Vio leave, I'll give him a good brush down and clean him up.* Tom told me to never turn my back on Buster, or any boar. "He could tear off your thigh with those tusks." I looked at Buster, who was sniffing the spring air, his eyes half closed, contemplating life in this new place, and I thought he looked like a kind and gentle soul. His tusks were a rich ochre yellow, thick with tartar and broken off unevenly, jutting from his muddy lips like old branches.

Tom and Vio left. I took a horse comb and curried it through Buster's coarse, filthy bristles as the dust rose. He leaned into my legs with pleasure, and I said, "Now, Buster, I know you like this, but you are here to do a job with Mabel and Matilda, so as soon as I clean you up, you go and do your duty." Oh, how Buster loved his rub! Then he retired for a nap with the girls in their deep straw bed. At dusk I took them a bucket of russet apples, which they devoured—great strands and gobs of saliva hung from their broad jowls as they chewed and grinned with joy. Pigs really do grin!

Night fell across the red metal roofs of the barns, the Garry oak wood, the gnarled branches of the apple orchard, the sleepy, clucking hens tucked into their boxes of deep hay, the rockeries full of poppies and marigolds, and the meadows damp with dew and spiderwebs, strung from a cherry tree to an evening primrose. The frog chorus rose in its nightly symphony, and the bats swooped over the pond and in and out of the willow trees.

The next morning I carried out three buckets of warm mash and cooked chard for the pigs. Buster was at the gate at the crack of down. I poured his breakfast into the new red dish I'd bought from the feed store, White House Stables, down the road. He slopped it up with delight, and then I gave him another rub. He squealed with joy during his rubs and gazed at me longingly for more when I had to go and do the other chores. I visited him throughout the day and slipped him apples and ear scratches, and he was always at the gate, resting his massive, bristly face through the page wire until I returned. Mabel and Matilda usually rose at noon, gave a few grunts, lay in their mud bath, and then returned to their beds until dinner.

Spring slowly turned into summer. The poppies faded and dried like sticks in the rockeries, the sunflowers replaced them with their enormous yellow faces, and the graceful, pale pink hollyhocks bloomed on the hot side of the barns. The peaches began to ripen and the meadows dried hard underfoot. I thought by this time the girls must be pregnant, and it was time for Buster to return home. I'd miss him—we had come to have great affection for each other.

"That pig sure loves you," said the neighbour over the fence. "He gets anxious when you go into town, pacing up and down, giving worried little grunts. I've never seen a pig like that before."

One morning I was cleaning out the horse barn as usual, and out of the corner of my eye I saw Buster trot past the doors and head toward the house. Damn, I thought, I had left his gate unlatched, and pigs are difficult to round up because there is nothing to grab on to. But Buster would follow me anywhere, so I finished the barn work and wasn't too concerned. I thought it might be a nice change for him to wander around the farm anyway, and maybe he'd root out some blackberries around the septic tank.

Boris and me.

When I finished I called, "Buster," but to no avail. He had looked as if he were on a mission, head down, a steady pace, past the clay pots of nasturtiums, the ceramic pig that my friend Lorna had given me as a house-warming present when I bought the farm, the lichen-covered gargoyle, the woodpile, the little grave of Willy, the old ginger cat from the SPCA who died of renal failure, the white enamel buckets full of freshly picked drying onions. I found him on the porch by the blue front door under the sticker that says, "Well-behaved women never make history," which my friend Patsy had given me. (She got it at a peace rally in New York.) And there he remained, and I couldn't budge him.

In one way, it was good that he didn't want to go back with Mabel and Matilda, as it meant they were probably pregnant. Also, Matilda, who suffers badly every month from PMS (I have to hand-feed her apples in her straw bed for half a day because she won't get up), didn't seem to exhibit this problem anymore, so I deduced that if she had no PMS, she must be pregnant. I called Tom and explained that Buster had done his manly duty. The arranged marriage had been a success (albeit it had taken a few extra months) and although it would break my heart (both our hearts), Buster was now in the porch, wouldn't move, and was ready to return home. Tom said he would come within the week. He had a younger Yorkshire boar that he had to pick up, and Buster should probably go for bacon.

"*Bacon!*" I gasped. "Tom, promise me that you will tell me if Buster needs a new home. I'll pay you whatever the butcher would."

That evening I managed to lure Buster onto the lawn, about three steps from the door.

I thought about inviting him into the house, but I was worried about my Moroccan rugs. I gave him a clean, fresh bale of straw, and he made a bed under an ornamental plum tree beside the badminton net. He had his warm mash and went to sleep under a lovely summer moon. I sat with him, his filthy ochre tusk on my thigh, and I remember thinking that although animals sometimes suffer in nature, and often at our hands, they are lucky in that they do not anticipate the pain. Buster didn't know that Tom might have made bacon of him.

Dear Buster left in a day or two in the clean white trailer, and the cooler autumn weather arrived. The purple asters and garden mums replaced the now-mildewed brown hollyhocks, and the garden birds had a great feast on the sunflower heads decomposing in a heap in the garden. Green tomatoes that were too late to ripen were ready to be made into relish or Nova Scotia chow chow.

I calculated that Mabel and Matilda should be due to have piglets any day, and I hoped that I could take them and their adorable spotted litters to the Saanich Fair, a grand annual event that marks the end of summer on the Saanich Peninsula. They didn't produce, but my old friend

Fred hauled them to the fair anyway, where they had an airy pen full of fresh hay. I had made a terrific display above their pen from swaths of pink cloth and garlands of plastic maple leaves from a local craft store. I painted a large corkboard deep red and in gold letters wrote:

Glamorgan Farm—North Saanich
Rare Heritage Breed
Gloucester Old Spot
Extinct in Canada

Mabel and Matilda were entered in "Best Sow—Has Been Bred" (thank goodness for Boris!). They lay in their hay beds like two pink spotted slabs.

Next to them were the 4-H pigs, younger, squealing pigs being raised for the auction by local youth. One little boy (I never knew his name) had no front teeth and was one of the nicest boys I have ever met. He offered to clean and feed Mabel and Matilda for me, and at the end of the three-day fair, our girls, being the only entries in their class, had two rosettes pinned on their sign: "Champion" and "Reserve Champion." This little boy said to me, "Well, your thowth came firtht and latht, Mithith Thcoonth," and then he took a big breath and said, "Thank you for bringing your thowth." I plan on finding out who this boy is and giving him a spotted piglet from the next litter to raise next year in his 4-H Club.

The last day of the fair was cool, grey, and hazy, the low clouds hanging below the distant dark hills. The fairground showed a weekend's worth of wear: potholes were forming, and grass was flattened into a mud pancake. The turquoise porta-potties were full, litter was piling up in the trash bins, and the fruit and vegetables in the produce barn were dry, wilted, and sagging over their rosettes. Paper cotton-candy funnels were squished in the gravel. Farmers and pioneers and gardeners were slowly packing up as the last of the public wandered through.

At five o'clock, when the fair officially ended, a thunderclap ruptured the sky right above the Tilt-A-Whirl, and torrents of rain pelted down in the approaching dusk. Everyone rushed to load their trucks and live-stock trailers. Women in overalls were shoving nervous, bleating sheep up ramps into wooden crates; the 4-H mothers were yelling, "Get those pigs loaded—you have school tomorrow!" and backhoes were moving in to pile up three days' worth of cow dung and straw from the livestock barns. Young men in green slickers carrying clipboards and walkie-talkies were driving little mud-splattered golf carts in all directions, just organizing things. The Ferris wheel was dismantled in about ten minutes. The Lions hamburger trailer pulled out behind the Bavarian sausage cottage.

And Mabel and Matilda refused to go into their trailer. Fred had agreed to transport them as a favour to me—I knew he didn't really want to do it—I had promised him a martini and some free pork if I ever got any. Fred wasn't known for his patience.

"What kind of a gong show is this?" he asked in total frustration when Mabel and Matilda lay down on the ramp in the teeming rain. I thought he was going to explode! "I have to haul to Vancouver in the morning," he said, controlling his exasperation.

I couldn't make my big girls get up. And then this nice, thin, friendly man came by and said, "I can load those pigs," and he put a cardboard box over their heads and backed them into the trailer in about two min-utes. I thanked him and climbed into Fred's hot, steamy truck with the new pink feed buckets and ropes that I had used at the fair as the rain beat against the truck windows. Fred's face was red!

Weeks later he had coffee with my friend Ellen, a local cat veterinar-ian—they always had morning coffee at a local café—and Ellen reported, "Fred said the loading of the pigs was a real gong show!" I told her that it wasn't that bad and that Fred just has to know that you can't rush two seven-hundred-pound pigs who can't see up a trailer ramp in a thunderstorm. And I added, "But just wait until next year when I want to take their piglets, too!"

A month passed. Mabel and Matilda lounged in their straw beds and the winter rains began to arrive. The drooping old cedars dripped, streams of water ran off the red metal grooves of the barn roofs, and the white field mushrooms pushed through the damp dirt. The horses grew thick coats and had to wear their nice new canvas Burberrys on stormy days; they clustered together under the Garry oak trees in their meadow until I called them in for hot bran mashes for the night. They loved their wet, warm bran soaked in molasses; it dripped off their hairy chins, and the steam from their warm bodies rose off their damp skin. The chickens stayed in their dim house and stared out at the thick, low, wet sky, their scrawny pink legs clutching their roosts. And still, no piglets.

There was a new pig veterinarian in town named Meg, who agreed to come out and give Mabel and Matilda their annual tetanus shots. She arrived in a fancy maroon truck. She was just a tiny thing in light blue overalls. Her assistant, Joey, was a dear man. That was my first impression of him: just a really sweet man who loved animals, quite dark and handsome and quiet, and while Meg asked questions, he stroked Daisy, our old farm dog who has a gigantic fat deposit on her belly. It's so large that it drags on the ground, but she doesn't care—we always say she's going bowling. Our dog vet, Nigel, in nearby Sidney, said it was best to leave it alone since the fat deposit doesn't bother her. I love vets who say, "Leave it alone."

Mabel and Matilda scream when they have to have their annual shots. "They're drama queens," said Meg. What relaxes them is to be squeezed in the snug wooden chute, not too tightly, just snugly—there's something about the squeezing action on their bulk that calms them. I can't explain it, but squeezing would calm me too: it's as if when squeezed, all your body parts, internal and external, and your emotions, come together into one little pressurized ball.

I told Meg about Buster and how there must be something wrong with the girls, that he was here for five months and nothing happened. I explained the bond that Buster and I had, and how he loved his rubs and apples and scratches all day, and that I thought it was a cruel and unfair rumour that boars are dangerous and mean and aggressive.

Meg listened and then said, "Anny, Buster thought *you* were the dominant sow. He loves *you*, not Mabel and Matilda."

"Well, what about his sexual urges?!" I asked in an anxious defence. "He must have had those."

"He didn't *have* any the way you mollycoddled him. If you want piglets, leave the boar alone. There's nothing wrong with the girls."

I thought about the lovely summer days that Buster and I had had in the shade of the plum tree, sharing a banana, enjoying the peace of nature together, and I decided that it had been worth it, and that I *liked* being the dominant sow. Mabel and Matilda were probably very happy about it too, although it seemed their Blueberry line had come to an end.

FINDING SOPHIA

JUNE SMITH-JEFFRIES

The sounds of coastal Carolina awaken me this morning: the ceaseless turning of the tide against the shore, the brush of palmetto across my window, gulls calling as they swoop low over the sea. The early autumn air is crisp and salt-scented.

Coming here alone is something I have never allowed myself. However, now it is not an indulgence; it is something I am compelled to do. This is a gift of time I have given to myself so I can to listen to the wisdom I know is somewhere deep inside me—wisdom that began to surface after I witnessed a spectacular wonder of nature when our family visited this island in June.

Last winter, when my doctor gave me the news, I was stunned. She insisted I hadn't been listening to my body: how else could I have missed the signs of a life-threatening illness? I had attributed my symptoms to a too-busy life: a full-time career, four teenagers, and an unhappy marriage.

Although my doctor has now given me a clean bill of health and I have recovered physically, emotionally I am shattered. The effort of facade—of constantly keeping thrusts of self below the surface like the persistent shoots of seaside sawgrass—has left me exhausted.

Here on the island there are no expectations. I do not have to say yes when I mean no, smile when I want to cry, give my full attention to double-booked patients, remain silent when words, like surging waves, rise in my throat. A whole week of solitude stretches before me with only a nothing-to-do list.

I rise early, and after doing a few yoga stretches, I descend the steps, bleached pale by sun, wind, and salty air. I walk toward the south end of the beach. The molecules of the sky form an azure arc as the sun appears to ascend from the mouth of the Atlantic. I want to see if the turtle nest is still in the dunes or if the hatchlings have already made their way into the ocean.

Our family has come every summer for the past five years to this island wildlife sanctuary where we regularly see deer, bald eagles, wood storks, blue herons, and egrets while walking or biking along the paths of the salt marshes. Loggerhead sea turtles lay their eggs along this area of the Southeastern Seaboard from late May until the end of June.

When I was here with my family in June, we arrived late. The night was clear, and the moon was slung low, suspended over the sea like a giant opal. After I had settled my family into the cottage, I walked alone on the beach, deep in thought, listening to the voluptuous rise and fall of the waves. Moonlight shone on the water, making it gleam phosphorescent. As I approached the south end of the island, I saw a small gathering of people. When I looked toward the ocean, I spotted the dark mound of a loggerhead's back rising like a mountain out of the translucent foam at the shoreline. For a while, I stood transfixed. Eventually, I jogged back to the cottage to tell my family.

The boys flicked off the TV and rushed to the door, competing, with their gangly adolescent limbs, to reach it first. Both girls abandoned their books and followed their brothers.

My husband was already in bed. When I walked into the room his back was turned, but I knew by the stiffness of his shoulders that he wasn't yet asleep.

"There's a loggerhead down at the south end. Want to come with us?"

"Not interested," he answered.

"The children are excited. I'm sure they would like you to come...*I* would like you to join us."

"Not interested, I said."

His words lodged somewhere in my midsection, and a recognition washed up, a truth I had not allowed to surface before this moment. I thrust it down.

I pulled my arms around myself, and knowing the consequences of persistence, left the room and walked out into the humid night air. I paused on the wooden steps that led down to the beach and took a deep, slow breath. I said a silent prayer that another holiday not be ruined. My daughters ran back and took my hands.

The boys were together just ahead. When we caught up with them, one of them asked, "Dad's not coming?"

"No, he's tired. He was almost asleep." Did a lie count when spoken to protect my children?

We laughed together as the children speculated about how a pregnant turtle might look. We were about forty feet from the water when, with a sharp intake of breath, one of the girls pointed. "There it is! It's ginormous!"

They ran toward the gathering of people, talking all at once, pulling me along in their excitement.

An elderly man approached us and introduced himself as Charlie. He asked us to stand with the group at the bottom of the dunes and to go no closer than twenty feet to the turtle as she made her way up the beach. He was wearing a floppy red hat pulled low over shaggy hair. He was gaunt and his back was bent, but he spoke with a passion that belied his fragility. He told us he'd been a volunteer with the Turtle Project for eleven years, since his wife died, and that this sighting was the fifty-seventh on the island this year. He explained that part of his responsibility as a volunteer was to count and record the number of eggs the turtle would leave. One of the bystanders asked how he was able to do that. He pointed his index finger skyward and said with a chuckle, "The full moon helps and I still have excellent eyesight." He pulled a small pad and a pen from his shirt pocket. "I make note as each egg goes into the nest."

I was mesmerized by the loggerhead, but I listened while Charlie explained that sea turtles, which can live as long as seventy years, are a threatened species because of fishing trawls and natural predators. They reach maturity and begin mating around age twenty. They can grow up to seven feet in length and weigh as much as four hundred pounds. The males never come ashore, but each female returns year after year to lay her eggs on the same beach where she herself had hatched and scuttled into the sea. The turtles always lay their eggs when the moon is full. This phenomenon has been studied by marine biologists, but no plausible explanation has been found. Charlie's hypothesis, though, was that the full moon, like a beacon on the water, beckons the female back to her first home.

I tried to concentrate on what Charlie was saying, but the turtle's heavy breathing distracted me. I was struck by her determination. Like a rower intent on the finish line, she pulled her mass across the beach, making deep, wide tracks in the sand. Even though the tide had brought her high, it took over an hour for her to move her bulk to the dunes where the sand was soft enough for her to dig. She was powerful—a magnificent creature—and she seemed certain as she moved toward the place she knew she must go: the place that would take her into the pain of giving birth to new life and then deliver her out of it again.

Once she found a spot that satisfied her, she began digging, alternating one flipper and then the other. I was barely able to breathe for fear of disturbing her. I was enthralled as I watched dry white sand slash past her body. She laboured for almost two hours, digging a deep, narrow hole. Her raspy breath changed into rough huffs.

By the time she began releasing her leathery eggs, the size of Ping-Pong balls, into the earth, the group of a dozen or so people had dispersed, my children included. Only Charlie and I stayed until the last egg was deposited. No words passed between us as we watched this sacred act.

Exhausted, the turtle finally thrust sand back over the nest and tamped it down by thumping her shell over it. Then with agonizingly slow movements, she turned in the direction of the sea and pulled herself toward the moonlight on the water.

I startled when Charlie spoke, having had the feeling of being alone with this amazing creature. "Thanks for staying. I enjoy company on these nights. Most people get bored and don't hang around."

"I was spellbound! I couldn't have left!" I said.

As the turtle made her painstaking journey across the sand, Charlie covered the nest with mesh wire for protection and placed a stake beside it with the date, the sighting number, and the number of eggs this turtle had deposited. He told me the eggs would hatch in about eight weeks, providing, of course, that they remained unharmed in the meantime.

Then Charlie patted my shoulder and tipped his hat, which caused his hair to fly like a white flag in the wind, as he walked across the dunes.

"Thank you, Charlie," I called.

Although it was well past two in the morning, I stayed, unable to leave. I watched the old woman until her great humped back sailed beneath the surface of the waves. The topography of the sea shifted and washed over her body.

I looked toward the heavens, my heart full and grateful. Even though the night was luminous, I was able to see the faint outline of Pleiades. I remembered that the derivation of the name was from the Greek, meaning "to sail."

While walking back to the cottage that night, questions and chaotic thoughts about my own life arose in my mind. At the same time I felt serene, a feeling I hadn't had for a long time. I became aware of a vague feeling of connection with the loggerhead.

How is a sea turtle able to find her way, summer after summer, back to the very place where her life came into being? *Instinct!* She knows when she's reached the place she needs to be. She trusts herself, no second-guessing. That would be too dangerous for her.

The sun rises higher as I walk this morning. Light glitters off the waves like scattered jewels, and seagrass ripples and unfurls in a strong offshore breeze. I watch a V of pelicans fly just out over the breakers. As the lead bird dives into the ocean, the others dip in sequence, a game of follow-the-leader. How often, I wonder, do I follow just to keep peace? For so long now, my tenet has been *don't rock the boat,* while I have been a slowly sinking ship.

After a while, I arrive at my destination. My intuition tells me this particular nest is the one for which I am searching. When I am close enough, I see that the stake Charlie put up is still here; it reads *June 30—133 eggs—sighting #57.* Any day now, these eggs will break open, and the hatchlings will scurry into the ocean.

Sea oats toss and bend their heads on the dunes around me as I sit cross-legged facing the nest. In the weeks since I watched the mother turtle pull herself out of the water and lay her eggs, my mind has returned again and again to her voyage. I think of her as Sophia—from the ancient Greek, the etymology of which is "wisdom."

Something inside me becomes unmoored, slips its anchor and rises. A single sob escapes the depths of my chest and is swallowed by the breath of the sea. Beneath my breast bone there is an ache, a longing for my life to be different, an understanding that I must overcome my reluctance to change.

Why have I allowed my physical life to become a vortex of activity with no regard for my spiritual life? When did I stop trusting myself? What do I truly fear?

I do not know how much time passes as I sit, still in awe of Sophia's journey. Then a realization comes to me. I have to do what all female loggerheads do. I must cast myself into the waters of the unknown. I must fight the undertow with the same strength that Sophia does. I must swim this current and reach the other shore. I must swim home, home to myself.

RAISING NELLIE

MARY ELLEN SULLIVAN

in memory of Miss Isobel Cunningham

Miss Cunningham lived with her bachelor brother Rob just down our side road, on the other side of the Fergus highway. Like most of our neighbours, the Cunninghams lived in a large, brick farmhouse that had been in their family for generations. And, like most of our neighbours, they ran a mixed farm of animals and crops—the diversity a defence against hard years. The Cunninghams, however, were the only ones of our neighbours who raised sheep.

Miss Cunningham was the volunteer librarian for our tiny Ennotville Library, which had been founded by the Scottish and Irish settlers of our rural Ontario community. Many of them had donated treasured books they brought with them on the ships during those tragic and deadly migrations from Europe to North America.

Mom would call Miss Cunningham on Saturdays to make sure she could be there to open the library for me. That musty little building lined with bookcases up to the ceiling was my second home. Sitting on a deep, padded windowsill, my back and feet pressed against bookcases, I read my favourite book, *Paddle-to-the-Sea,* over and over. Miss Cunningham may have noticed the reverence with which I handled books, stroking the textured covers, and the bright face on one so often solemn. She was a person who knew how to watch.

Miss Cunningham was also the informally appointed hostess for community events held at the library. After spending much of her time alone with her brother, she clearly savoured an opportunity to socialize. She'd move through that room, creating an easy flow of conversation, guiding people towards a new audience, and teasing farmers a decade younger than herself.

She had the solid, square build of many farm women, but there was also an impression of softness. Her hair had that bluish tint popular among greying women at that time, but which still seemed strange enough to be fascinating to kids.

At these events I stuck by my mom. It must have been difficult for my extroverted mother to see how painfully shy her daughter was. In that limbo land of shifting childhood, I watched the moving mouths, the wordplay between people, the air-slicing gestures, people chatting in a natural way I envied. How did they do it? What did they talk about? I stood awkwardly in their midst, self-consciously poking my left ear, that darn ear that stuck straight out from the side of my head, back under the cover of my red pigtail.

Perhaps Miss Cunningham noticed my shyness, noticed how my more boisterous siblings overshadowed me. Why she took notice was a mystery to me. She'd make her way over to talk, without any pressure on me to respond. She regarded me with a gentle attention that gradually eased me into talking.

One day, she invited me to visit the Cunningham farm, and before long my visits were a weekend ritual. Some days we'd have tea using real china cups and saucers, and she'd serve me dainty squares. She told me tales about trips she'd taken and showed me the seashells she'd gathered on Florida beaches. Questions built up inside me, and finally curiosity burst out: "What are their names?" "What is Florida like?" "Is it really hot?" "Are the shells still alive?" Each time I visited, she let me choose a shell to take home.

What I loved most about the Cunningham farm was the herd of sheep. They were Suffolks, a popular breed favoured for its meat, which had been brought to Upper Canada from the British Isles in the late

1800s. I thought sheep were the most wonderful creatures in the world. They always seemed delighted to see me, shuffling for position when they saw me approach. I'd hold a fistful of grass out to one, my fingers held tightly together so they wouldn't get nipped. The sheep's lips tickled my hand, and I laughed as the grass disappeared into its mouth. Other sheep crowded around, each wanting my attention and some of that sweet grass they couldn't reach from their side of the fence. I loved to bury my fingers in the sponginess of their wool. They'd tilt their heads skyward and lean into my fingers in a state of rapture as I scratched behind their ears. The affection of animals chips away at a kid's shyness.

I'd heard people talk about how dumb sheep were, how they were easy picking for wolves and wild dogs, but at eleven I was in love with them, especially the lambs. I loved their gentle eyes, their wobbly, wide-based attempts to stand, and the thin, soft layer of wool covering them. How could you not love such sweet little things? I knew that lambs were special. After all, I'd seen pictures of Jesus holding a lamb, but I'd never seen Him holding any other animal.

One Saturday in March, I biked over to the Cunningham farm, jumped off, and ran towards the barn. I was eager to see the spring lambs. In the barn, I found Miss Cunningham leaning over the side of a sheep pen. She was wearing dusty green overalls and rubber boots. Her blue-tinted hair was as impeccable as ever as she picked up a tiny lamb. "Poor thing," she said. "Its mother abandoned it. She's saving her milk for the stronger twin."

In the pen I saw one lamb nursing. Two other lambs, which had been born a few days earlier, were playing together, their small bodies perched on incredibly long, black legs. They chased each other, jumping forward with their front legs, hips kicking up as their rear legs followed through. It was as if the cement floor was a trampoline they were leaping on, twisting their bodies in the air, thrilled with their new freedom. Their mother munched hay nearby. Miss Cunningham stood beside me watching them play. "They're such imps," she said with a laugh.

I looked at the small lamb she was holding, lying quietly in her arms. "What will happen to it?" I asked.

"I'll just have to try to bottle-feed it. I don't know. It doesn't look very healthy." She rubbed it vigorously with a rag.

The thin lamb shivered in her arms, its head supported on her forearm. Its thin layer of wool was greyish and damp, with slack wrinkles that would fill out as it grew. I could have sworn its large, dark eyes were looking right at me.

I watched as Miss Cunningham finished cleaning the lamb and set it on its feet. Its steps were tentative. Finally it swayed and plunked down on its bottom. I laughed at its startled look.

"I'll take care of it," I said in a voice that startled me with its strength. "I want to raise it."

She looked at me with surprise. Her eyes were troubled. "It's not very strong, but I guess if it makes it through the week it should be okay. Well, only if your parents say it's okay."

I grinned and took the lamb into my arms. I was exhilarated! Soon it would be healthy like the other lambs. I imagined taking my new friend into the hayfield to play. At first it might get tangled in the alfalfa and red clover, but soon its head would poke above the plants. It would leap after me on the paths I'd tramp down. I wondered how long it would be before it could outrun me.

Rob Cunningham drove me home in his farm truck, my bike thrown in the back and the lamb on my lap. I didn't take my eyes off of it. When we got home, Rob helped me down from the high seat so I wouldn't drop my lamb. I ran gingerly into the house, calling for Mom and Dad as Rob trailed behind me. They looked up at me from where they sat at the kitchen table, and then their eyes dropped to the lamb.

"It's the runt of twins and the mother wouldn't nurse it," Rob said. "Isobel said she can keep it if it's okay with you two. She said she wasn't sure about it, but then she'd never heard Mary Ellen speak up like that."

"That Isobel," Dad muttered. He came over to look at the lamb. The tiny body was cradled in my arms, its little black head resting in the crook of my elbow. Its eyes were closed and the little body trembled. I hugged it protectively, and it let out a weak bleat as it struggled against the pressure.

"By the way, it's a girl," Rob said quietly.

"I want to take care of her, Mom. She needs me!" Mom was the easier one to convince, and after she'd made up her mind, there wasn't much Dad could say.

My parents must have realized there was no going back. "Okay, Mary," Mom said, "but you've got to keep up your homework and chores. Now, that lamb looks like it needs a bit of tending to. We'd better get some food into it. Jack, get that cardboard box from the basement and some old rags." At some point, Rob slipped out.

The word was out, and my brothers and sisters ran into the house and gathered around me, chattering and asking if they could hold my lamb. "Now isn't that the cutest little thing!" said Tim.

"Don't scare her, you guys!" I said.

My parents taught me how to care for my lamb. Mom found an old bottle and a nipple that had been used for piglets. She warmed some milk on the stove until the temperature was just right and showed me how to test its warmth on the inside of my wrist, just like I'd seen her do when she fed my baby sister, Irene. Soon I was sitting in the rocker holding my lamb on my lap, aiming the nipple towards its mouth.

My lamb pushed the nipple around as if not knowing what to do with it. She finally latched on to it and began to drink weakly. I looked up triumphantly, only to catch a look of sadness pass between my parents.

Dad came and sat beside me, his large fingers gently scratching the lamb's side, and began to explain what I had to do. It needed to be fed four times a day—breakfast, lunch, dinner, and bedtime. I panicked when I realized I would be in school at lunchtime, but Dad said he'd take that shift. We lined the box with soft rags and placed it on the open oven door, the oven's heat taking the place of its mother's warmth.

At suppertime Dad said grace. "Bless us our Lord for these Thy gifts. And bless our fuzzy new family member." We laughed as the lamb poked her head over the box's top and bleated as if on cue. I kept an eye on it while I ate, feeling so thrilled and proud to have a lamb of my own.

Having a farm animal as a pet was discouraged in our family. Even our faithful dog, Calo, knew she was not allowed to stray off her mat just inside the kitchen door. Our barn cats were wild—their job was to catch mice, not to be pets. As soon as we lifted the barn door latch you'd hear a swish, and the adult cats would be hidden by the time we got inside. If we were able to catch one of the kittens, it would rasp our hands with its razor-sharp claws and teeth. But it was clear from the start that my lamb would be treated differently, that I could raise it as my pet.

I wanted to name my lamb. I had been named after Mom's mother, and I liked my name. It always reminded me of how safe I felt when Gramma had rocked me—in this very same rocking chair—and sang hushed songs to me.

I looked at my lamb long and hard to see if she reminded me of someone. I came up with several girls' names I liked—Maggie, Heidi, Sadie—but none of them seemed right. Finally, I thought about my Great-Aunt Nellie. She was a strong woman who always spoke her mind, and she was really funny. Yes, I'd call my little lamb Nellie. "Nellie?" I said. The lamb looked up at me. I knew it was the right name.

The next morning I woke early and, avoiding the board in the upstairs hallway that always creaked, hurried downstairs. My lamb was standing in the middle of the floor, and I ran to hug it.

"Your little one has been trying to help me," Mom said. "She's been so curious, I have to watch that she doesn't trip me!"

Nellie stepped towards me, her little hooves making staccato sounds on the linoleum as she followed me back and forth as I set the table for breakfast. I scratched her between her long, narrow black ears. Her legs slowly slid out, and she landed on the floor.

On Sunday, as everyone was getting ready to go to town for church, I trailed after the others, giving my lamb a last-minute hug before the eight of us packed into the station wagon. After Mass, Mom and the other women gathered to chat in the parking lot. Dad sat in the car, drumming his fingers on the steering wheel. I knew it was a highlight of my mother's week, as if she was starved for the pleasure of talking with other women, but I wanted to get home. I tugged on her sleeve. "The lamb!" I whispered, "Please!" She sighed and got into the car.

We ran into the house, Mom calling after us, "Get out of your good clothes!" I heard a wavering bleat. When my lamb saw me, she stood up and wagged her tail so vigorously her hindquarters wiggled. I lifted her up, burying my nose into the lamb-scented wool.

Dad made me put her back in the box so we could have lunch. Nellie didn't like that very much and got her leg caught over the top of the box trying to get out. I ran to straighten it up.

I ate as quickly as I could until Dad caught on. He rapped his fork on the table. "Slow down, Mary! Show some manners." I looked at my lamb and rolled my eyes.

I spent most of that Sunday with my lamb. She lay on my lap as I worked on my homework, slept while I did the dishes. When I sat in the rocking chair to rock and feed her, her little body molded into my lap. The sucking sounds seemed so dear. Sometimes she'd drift off, then startle herself awake and resume pulling on the nipple. Finally, she fell into an exhausted sleep. She was so precious, lying there. I didn't think I could love more than this.

In the next couple of days between doing my chores and homework, I'd lift my lamb up and cuddle her. I was getting up earlier to help Mom make the school lunches, so I had time to feed my lamb. I'd hold Nellie until the very last moment before I had to run for the school bus.

Day and night lost their sense of order as I cared for my lamb. Sometimes I wasn't sure if I was awake or asleep. I watched for the moments when Nellie would open her eyes and look up at me, nuzzling her tiny nose into the warmth of my freckled arm. I'd sing softly and Nellie would look up at me with those dark, liquid eyes as if she really was listening.

Mary had a little lamb, little lamb, little lamb,
Mary had a little lamb, its fleece as white as snow.
And everywhere that Mary went, Mary went, Mary went,
And everywhere that Mary went that lamb was sure to go.

Once, my brothers overheard me and began singing a falsetto version, howling with laughter as they fell all over themselves. I smiled tolerantly.

As the week went on, I noticed that Nellie was not herself. Thursday morning when I slipped downstairs, she didn't bleat as she usually did, and when she tried to stand she collapsed. I wrapped a towel around her and promised I would take care of her, not to worry. She sucked weakly at the bottle.

"I think she's sick, Mom." Mom sat down beside me and gave me a hug.

I held Nellie on my lap. She shivered and looked up at me. Occasionally a strong shudder shook her body. I tried to convince Mom I wasn't feeling well and should stay home from school. But she said no.

At school the teacher's muffled words floated around me, I scratched *Nellie* into my wooden desk-top with my pen. Fear was building inside me. I knew my lamb was very sick, that I had to do something. But I didn't know what. That night, when I finally dozed off, I had fitful dreams of finding Nellie's box empty and desperately searching for her.

The next morning, the sixth day since Miss Cunningham had given me the lamb, I found Nellie lying flat out in her box. Diarrhea soaked her woolly flanks. Her sides were heaving. I cleaned her up and changed the rags. My hands trembled as I prepared her milk. She would not take her bottle.

When I got home from school that afternoon, she was still lying on her side. She looked up at me, but she didn't lift her head. I sat on the floor beside the box and scratched behind her ear, talking softly to her.

I was peeling potatoes for supper when I heard Dad walking towards me. He placed his huge hand on my shoulder. "I'm sorry, your lamb has died." I pulled away from him, my face hardening, focusing on my reddened hands, raw from working in the hard water from our well.

I ran up the back stairs to my room, my safe place. On the bookshelf were my rock collection and the shells Miss Cunningham had given me. Above my bed was a drawing of Nellie and me. When Mom came in I was lying on my bed, sobbing so hard it hurt my ribs.

She sat down on the bed beside me and sighed. "Hush, Mary," she spoke softly. "That lamb started out pretty sick. She couldn't have had a better, more loving little mother than you. That's the way of God's world—every creature, human or beast, has its time." She patted my back, and shifted to her practical voice. "Now." She slapped her thighs. "Supper will be ready soon, I'll call you."

It was a sombre meal: everyone was subdued. Dad did not have to whack his fork once to make us behave. I asked him if he would help me bury Nellie and if I could ask Miss Cunningham to come to the burial.

The next day the Cunninghams and my family stood with me around the hole Dad had dug under my favourite spruce tree. The sky was brilliant and the wind played in the tree branches. We buried Nellie there. It would not have been proper to place a cross over an animal's grave, so I laid my favourite seashell, an abalone, on top of the rich soil that covered Nellie. Miss Cunningham gave me a hug, and her brother awkwardly patted my shoulder. I'd done my crying; the acuity of pain had drained out of me. I was exhausted, but surprisingly tranquil, cushioned by those around me.

One Christmas, many years later, my brother-in-law Joe, a mill-wright, made me a gift, not realizing the significance it would have for me. Now, many years later, as I look out the dining room window of my Halifax home, I can see the weathervane he made on top of the garage roof: a young girl in a full skirt, reading a book as she walks. Prancing behind her is a tiny lamb.

Freeing the Pike

Richard Wagamese

As a boy I loved nothing better than a solitary wandering along the serpentine lengths of a river. I'd study the water, searching out the places where fish might be hiding, or lie on the riverbank, lost in thought under an endless blue sky.

Back then a river felt like an opportunity. Within it lay the lunker fish of my dreams or the magic passage away from the world that had me snared. Only in the aloneness the land and rivers represented could I find the freedom to dream and create. Many of my stories were born along a river.

In my adopted home there were no fishermen. Nobody spent time in the outdoors. Camping for that family was a travel trailer parked on a cultured lot with a convenience store a short walk away, laundry facilities, and public showers. I could walk for miles through the bush. I could sit for hours in a thicket of trees and watch things. I could feel at ease with nothing but the land. They could never do that.

So I fished alone. What I learned on those solitary jaunts I kept to myself. No one was interested anyway, so they never knew how much I learned of life and nature and the universe on the riverbanks of my youth. More importantly, they never understood how the land, rivers in particular, fleshed out my insides, soothed me, comforted me. They would never know that I was born into the Sturgeon Clan, or that the teachings of that clan membership would define me and give me purpose. Instead, they found me odd and left it at that.

We camped once beside a river outside a southwestern Ontario town called Tara. The family parked their trailer in a small roadside area along a gravel road. There was an iron bridge over the river, and I stood on it reading the water. It was shallow and weedy without much current. I could see cow-pies and horse dung along the rocky shore. It didn't look hopeful except for the clumps of lily pads dotting the surface whenever the river got deep enough.

They laughed when I said I would fish it. But that didn't matter. It was a river. Along the shoreline on the opposite side of the bridge I turned over rocks and logs looking for insects. There weren't many, so I opted for worms.

I cast to different parts of that river. About a mile downstream I reeled in a few small bass. That excited me. Even as a kid I understood that the presence of small predator fish meant the presence of huge predator fish. I moved on, rounding a wide curve where the current carved a trench that looked dark and promising. Submerged timber angled into the depths. I chose a bobber and a long leader that would allow me to drift my bait along the entire length of the trench. It was about three feet deep, just over the top of those fallen trees.

My first casts came up empty. But on the fourth cast I watched an enormous shadow glide out of the darkness and aim for my bait. The fish gulped the hook and swam off almost casually. The weight of it arched my rod, and when it felt that pressure the fish exploded, threatening to tear the rod right out of my hands. I backpedalled to get more secure footing.

That fish gave me the fight of a lifetime. It breached the water four or five times, jumping clear and rattling the bobber in the air. The splash it made when it landed was awesome. When it sounded, as it did a half-dozen times, I could feel its weight like a truck pulling away. Reeling it in took forever, and whenever it got close enough to the shore to see me it took off again.

I had to step into the river finally. I couldn't lift the fish over the bank without snapping the line. Standing thigh-deep in the water, lifting a pike far longer than my arm, I felt totally alive. As I removed the hook and rested the fish against my other palm, I knew I'd landed a monster. I shook with excitement.

But something happened to me then that's taken years to fully understand. Seeing that huge fish gulping at the water, straining for life, its power ebbing, its beauty already beginning to fade, I lowered it, let it rest in my hands and then watched it swim away.

I never spoke of it, even though they laughed when I came back empty-handed. I ate supper silently, and when I got to bed that night I thanked that fish for the challenge. They would never have understood. They would never have appreciated the enormity of that encounter or how sitting on the riverbank, after it was over, I could cry and feel incredible joy at the same time.

That river pike was freedom in my hands. When I chose to let it go, I chose life. For the Indian that lived in me, that fish was honour and respect and love. They never would have gotten that, either.

APPARITION

DAVID WEALE

I can't even remember what it was I'd forgotten. A book? My coffee mug? It doesn't matter. What I do recall is that when I pulled my truck back into the yard behind the house, I glanced across the field to the east and spotted at the edge of the woods a big yellow dog that I took to be a Labrador retriever.

My place is on Five Houses Road in Ft. Augustus, and as the name suggests, there aren't many of us living there. Because I was almost certain no one on the road had a dog like the one I was looking at, it roused my curiosity and sent me scurrying off in search of my binoculars. I hurried, binoculars in hand, to the bathroom window, from which vantage point I knew I would have an unobstructed view of the spot where I had seen the dog. I feared it would be gone, but a quick glance assured me it was still there, standing motionless and looking across the field in the direction of my house. Good! I dropped to my knees on the floor, placed my elbows on the windowsill to steady myself, and raised the binoculars to my eyes.

"Lord Liftin' Jesus! What do we have here?"

It seemed impossible I was seeing what I was seeing—but there was no mistake. What I had assumed was a large dog was not a dog at all. It was, incredibly, a very large cat of some kind—large enough to be mistaken for a full-grown Lab. I noted the small pointed ears, the squared face, and especially the long thick tail with a succession of dark rings along its length. It was magnificent, whatever it was, and it took my breath away.

Islanders, of course, aren't very good at identifying large cats, since for as long as we can remember there haven't been any living here. I knew there had been lynx and bobcats on the Island when the European pioneers arrived, but the pioneers had killed the big cats off as quickly as possible, with the last of them disappearing in the late 1800s. Just a few months before my sighting, I had heard at Dave Wakelin's store in Ft. Augustus that someone's dog had been badly mauled in the woods by what, they speculated, might have been a bobcat from the Cape Breton Highlands that had found its way to the Island across the ice during the previous winter. But bobcats aren't yellow, and they most certainly don't have long ringed tails. No, it wasn't a bobcat. More likely a cougar, also known as a mountain lion, and it was fifty or sixty metres away, on the edge of my field, staring at my house. Perhaps at me. I was dumbfounded.

After about fifteen seconds, the big cat turned gracefully, moved off toward the woods, and disappeared. Its motion was so smooth it seemed to be gliding. I thought briefly about heading across the field for the chance of getting a better look or of seeing some tracks, or perhaps some scat, but prudence prevailed and I stayed put. I waited at the window a short time hoping for a reappearance, but after a few minutes I put away the binoculars, gathered up whatever it was I had forgotten, and headed for town.

I knew I had a great story to tell but realized I might not be able to share it without raising questions about my mental state or perhaps my use of some consciousness-altering substances. Would even my closest friends believe I had locked eyes with a cougar at nine o'clock in the morning on Five Houses Road? Did I want to run the risk of being known as a person who saw things that weren't there or who made up fantastic stories to fabricate a more interesting life? Not especially. But, on the other hand, how could I possibly keep such a thing to myself? It was just too good a story. I would surely explode if I attempted to keep something like that inside.

Before the day was over, the raconteur in me had won out, and by the time I headed home that evening I had related the event a number of times. Predictably, my hearers were largely incredulous. No one came right out and questioned my sanity or my sobriety, but I think there were a few who had doubts about my eyesight. On balance, however, the pleasure of relating the account outweighed the risk of possible blotches on my reputation, so I told it often, and here I am telling it again.

Over the years, the core facts of the story haven't changed in the telling, but I have drawn meaning out of it, which is what storytellers do to make a good story better. I still am not willing to concede that, for some reason or other, I wasn't seeing clearly that morning and that what seemed at first a yellow Lab was, in fact, a yellow Lab. My inclination is to interpret the sighting as a sign, a reminder of all the animals that have been driven off this island and, in some cases, off the very face of the earth. When I tell the story that way, I get to remind myself and others of the disappearance from our island of the walrus, sturgeon, black bear, otter, bobcat, deer, moose, passenger pigeon, and great horned owl. I get to remind my listeners, and myself, how vain and short-sighted we were to leave no place for the animals and how, in doing so, we diminished the landscape and impoverished ourselves by removing the genius and grace of their wild ways and the haunting reminder of their wild calls. And the more I tell the story, the more inclined I am to view that big cat as an apparition or visitation, and to recognize that if I don't understand why it appeared, it can never come back.

A few days after spotting the big cat, I called the Fish and Wildlife department to report what I had seen and, I hoped, to possibly to have my sighting confirmed. The officer on the other end seemed a bit uncomfortable, and I was imagining the look on his face and how he was probably gesturing for his secretary to pick up the other phone, all the while pointing at his receiver as if to say, "This is a weird one!" However, after a short silence he told me that, oddly, there had been a similar report from the same area a year or two before. And that was the end of it.

Maybe.

Frogality

Jacqueline Windh

The frog sits on the tip of the mossy log. Her skin loses its roughness as it warms. It relaxes, becoming smooth and shiny, its bright green hue turning even more brilliant. Her eyes gleam in the sunlight, glossy black and flecked with gold.

My frog enjoys the warmth. I can tell this from her posture: how she flattens herself against the log, her sides bulging and her head curled downward, her front toes turned in so they touch one another under her chin—a contrast to the tense arched position of a frog about to jump. Other than the ceaseless pulsing of the creamy membrane of her chin, she is motionless. Her expression is one of permanent surprise, with her head facing stiffly forward and her eyes wide and bulging—or so it appears, if we can use human facial expressions to interpret what a frog might think, or feel.

I have an insect in my hand, a housefly, one of those big ones that glints blue like metal. I have it by one wing, and it vibrates impatiently.

I rest my elbow on the rim of the terrarium to steady myself—I've already removed the screen lid—and position the fly in front of the frog's nose. This one is about a quarter of her size, it will be easy. On mild summer evenings, I have seen her gulp down plump soft-bellied moths that are as long as she is, and nearly as wide.

The frog and I know the routine. She hears the buzzing, perks up, and stiffens. I hold my hand steady—as steady as I can with the fly fluttering and struggling in my fingertips—so she can fix on its movement. She lunges, grasping it with her open mouth. Her moist front feet touch my fingers for a moment. Then she pushes off me, and shovels the fly's flailing wings, its twitching legs, into her wide frog-mouth.

I place the screen lid back on the tank. After all these years, I still chuckle with every feeding: at the frog's earnestness as she darts at the insect; at the bulge of her eyes as she crams it into her mouth; at how she blinks as she gulps it down. Maybe it's just me—maybe I'm easy to amuse—but, after all of these years, I am still unabashedly charmed by my frog.

I've always loved amphibians. When I was a child, growing up in Ontario, I foraged along the reedy shorelines for frogs, and under rotten boards for salamanders. I read nature books and learned about the different species and their habits. I kept a pair of salamanders in my bedroom for an entire school year. My parents never knew. Along with the other neighbourhood kids, I made an annual attempt at raising tadpoles—attempts which, year after year, ended in disaster as somebody always knocked over the jar— squirming black tadpoles skidding across the back porch.

But it was never my plan, as an adult, to have a pet frog.

Here in the Pacific Northwest, for a few months of the year, tree frogs become one of most obvious creatures in our landscape. They seem to be everywhere; the irony is that they are almost never seen. In late February or early March, they descend to ponds and ditches, where males begin an incessant chorus. It is a cacophony of *ribbets*, in tones high and low and in-between, that continues until midsummer.

I had lived on the west coast for nearly a decade when, one dusky evening, I heard a lone frog calling from a puddle in a wheel rut on a construction site. Thinking that this might finally be my chance to *see* a Pacific tree frog, I squatted by the puddle for a half hour. I saw nothing but a flattened gelatinous mass of eggs. I went back home for a plastic cup, returned, and scooped them out.

Ten days later, the eggs I had rescued hatched: thirteen tadpoles. I had become a tadpole mother.

They ate algae, I found out—a lot of it. I learned where, around town, to scoop the best algae. I got in the habit of waving to passing motorists from the ditches, to let them know I was okay.

The tadpoles grew, and a friend donated an old aquarium for my project. I filled it with a few inches of pond water. I had to learn my parenting skills all over again when the tadpoles metamorphosed, one by one, into tiny, perfect frogs, gleaming like emeralds the size of my baby fingernail. As their lives transformed from aquatic to terrestrial, I placed rocks in the water and planted moss and ferns above, turning the aquarium into a terrarium. I constructed a lid from a scrap of window-screen, fitted into a frame of wood that I built to size so it rested precisely upon the inner lip of the tank. I raised eleven tadpoles to froghood.

I would have let all of the froglets go. But the last one to metamorphose, the runt of the brood, had a defect: where her right eye should have been, there was only a sunken socket, overgrown with glimmering green skin. This frog would not survive in the wild. I decided to keep it. I considered the ethics of keeping one frog all alone. Would it get lonely? Of the runt's ten siblings, only one froglet seemed to like the tank, even hopping back into it when I took it out. So I kept the sibling, too, as company for the little runt. (I did not yet know the gender of my frogs. It wasn't until two years later, when they reached maturity but had uttered not a peep, that I realized they were both females.)

Conscious of the significance of the decision I had made—keeping wild creatures in a situation in which they had no choice about their surroundings, or the circumstances of their lives—I resolved to give my frogs a quality of life at least as good, if not better, than they would have had in the wild. As I designed the land areas in the terrarium, I did my best to create a varied habitat, so the frogs would be free to choose: a section of sphagnum moss and peat bog; a mossy stretch of forest floor planted with ferns and a tiny salal bush; and a mossy piece of damp wood angled upward so it grazed the tank's screen lid. A small section of pond remained, beneath the climbing log and beside the bog.

I researched amphibian nutrition, and learned that many captive frogs and lizards end up with deficiencies as a result of being fed only pet-store crickets; their owners must roll the insects in vitamin powder before feedings. So I made sure that my frogs received a naturally varied diet. I caught moths and flies, their favourites, over the summer months. I plucked green caterpillars from my broccoli patch, and spiders from my woodpile. I dug earthworms from the compost heap when insects were scarce.

And for several years we got along fine, the two frogs and I. I kept the tank outside since, as native species, they would be healthiest exposed to natural seasonal cycles of temperature and light. An overhanging shed-roof sheltered the tank from the rain.

Wild Pacific tree frogs burrow under the ground to escape the coldest temperatures of winter. My frogs were in a tank on a shelf, though; they could not burrow far before reaching the bottom of the tank. So when temperatures plunged much below freezing, I brought the tank inside for a few days. At that time, I lived in an upstairs suite. My downstairs entranceway was the perfect place for the frog tank during a cold spell—not as warm as the living space upstairs, which would have shocked the frogs, but warm enough to safeguard them from the freezing temperatures outside.

I became accustomed to the frogs' routines. They stayed up late and slept in until noon. To my visiting friends, the green frogs were as good as invisible against the greenery of the tank. Even when I pointed them out, my visitors often could not see them. But the frogs were such creatures of habit that I never had trouble finding them. I knew—by the time of day, by the time of year, by the temperature and the humidity, by whether the sky was cloudy or clear—exactly where each frog could be found in the tank. The vegetation I had planted years before had grown into a dense mass of ferns and grasses and salal, which now occupied the entire tank, covering the old climbing log and pushing upward against the screen lid, forming a three-dimensional landscape that the frogs moved through, around, and over. In cool weather, the one-eyed runt preferred to sit on the moss under the sword fern, while the other frog lurked in a cave she had excavated in the mosses beside their miniature pond. On sunny days, both frogs climbed the salal bush to bask in the sunlight. They were most active on mild damp evenings, prowling the vegetation at the top of the tank, then descending before dawn to hide under the moss until noon.

When the weather was cold, the frogs would disappear under the mosses for days, or even weeks. I worried the first few times they disappeared, but I soon learned that this was their normal response to the cold. However, in our fourth summer, I became concerned when I hadn't seen the runt for several days. Had she died somewhere under the mosses? Or had she got out? Then I noticed the lid: one corner of the netting was curled up and away from its wooden frame, as if pushed up from inside. The runt had escaped.

Here was a dilemma. I had only kept the second frog to accompany the one-eyed runt. What should I do now?

This frog seemed happy in the tank—to the best that I could tell what "happy" was to a frog. Content, at least. I didn't know how she would adjust to the wild after four years—her whole life!—in captivity. She was habituated to me, accustomed to being handled and hand-fed; I didn't know if she had the proper instincts to flee predators. I didn't even know if she had the stamina and strength that a wild frog, ranging over distances of hundreds of metres, would have. I decided to keep her, resolving once again to ensure her quality of life and, to the best that I could tell, her "happiness." But, as part of my decision, I chose not to repair the hole in the lid. Instead, I tucked the torn screen back down against the wooden frame. If she really wanted to go, she could push her way out, just as her sister had done.

Now that I had the one frog, alone, somehow my responsibility to her seemed even greater. I wondered about this concept of "happy," or if she could be "wanting" something. In the early years, I had assumed that the frogs were not capable of much in the way of thought or feeling. They are tiny, cold-blooded creatures, after all, with reptilian brains hardly larger than a grain of barley. But, the winter following the runt's escape, I started to get an idea that perhaps there was more to frog consciousness than I had assumed.

It was during a long cold spell. I carried the tank into my downstairs entranceway and set it on the lowermost step. I wondered again about how lack of exercise might affect my frog—in her confined quarters, with bugs being delivered literally to her nose and, especially in this cold weather, when she didn't move much at all.

That evening, after her tank warmed up, I decided to give her some exercise. Trusting in a frog's natural instinct to hop upward, I placed her on the bottom edge of the banister. For a frog the size of my thumb-tip, ascending to the next floor seemed a reasonable workout.

I sat on the stairs to watch, sliding myself upwards a few steps at a time as she hopped and crawled her way towards the top. Once she reached the top, I coaxed her onto my finger and carried her back to the tank. Mission successful: the frog had a new exercise program.

The next day we repeated it. However, on the third day, she paused, turning her head left and right, as if thinking: "Not this again..." She started up the banister but, a third of the way up, turned around and crept back down. I returned her to the tank.

The fourth day, she paused again. She looked to the right towards the stairway, then to the left at the wall. She arched her back, tipped her head to nearly vertical. She jumped to the wall, plastering her belly against it. Using her sticky skin and her toe pads, she began to climb up the wall. When she had ascended as high as I was able to reach, I lifted her off and returned her to the tank.

By the fifth day, it seemed clear to me that she knew what this routine was about. My frog did not want to climb the banister, and she did not want to go up that wall again. She looked to the right, then the left, then she spun around and contemplated jumping down from the bottom end of the banister. She turned to the right again. That's when she spied her tank on the step below.

Her frog body language was clear. She crept to the edge of the banister. She aimed her head downward, towards the tank. She tensed, adjusting and repositioning her hind legs as she prepared for the leap. Then she launched herself, flying spread-eagled to land squarely on a springy bundle of fern leaves in the centre of the tank.

My frog had recognized her tank—from above! The "home" this frog knew had always been viewed from inside: a three-dimensional mesh of greenery which she moved *through*. Yet she had recognized it from above, this black plastic rectangle framing a tangle of fern leaves and salal. I know *people* who would have trouble recognizing their neighbourhood from above. Yet my tiny, cold-blooded, reptilian-brained frog had recognized hers.

I wondered what else she might know.

"Of course your frog recognizes you," my friends assured me. "How couldn't she, after all these years?"

But I wasn't so sure. What does a frog see? What does a frog know? I know that she is not able to recognize an insect as food unless it moves. Pick a dead one up and wiggle it, and she'd bite. Give her a dish full of dead flies, though, and she would starve to death.

Kermit.

What does she think of the hand that comes down and feeds her? This tiny frog—could she conceive of something as large as my hand? And how about what was attached to it? What could she know of me?

The frog and I moved house when she was six. Many of my friends, coming to check out my new home, were shocked to find out that I still had her. None of us had known that frogs could get so old.

The frog tank now sat on a stand outside my sliding glass back door. I could keep an eye on it from inside the house. I moved it out to the back deck if it was sunbathing weather, and placed a sheet of plastic over it if it was raining. That was the disadvantage of this house: there was no good place for the tank that was sheltered from the rain. I had to be extra vigilant to keep from flooding my frog.

By now, feeding my frog had become an easy routine. I was as attuned to the seasons as she was: to cycles of darkness and light, of warmth and cold, of dampness and drought. I no longer spent an hour or more hunting for insects; I now let them come to me. I knew instinctively which nights the moths would flit about in the darkness of the garden, and when to leave my windows open by day to bring in the houseflies, or by night to attract crane flies. I'd scoop the insects out of the air with a net and feed them to my unblinking frog.

Surely she saw me coming and going, with the tank now outside the back door. Surely she was aware of the sequence of my actions: as she watched me step outside; as she saw the lid lift off above her; as she saw the hand descend with the bug. But if she did, she gave me no sign.

I recalled why I had selected *her*, of the ten froglets, to accompany the little runt. It was her personality, or "frogality," as I had come to think of it: how easygoing and contented she had seemed compared to some of her more jumpy siblings, who were more wary and difficult to feed. One of them, the second frog to metamorphose, could almost be called aggressive, always aware when the lid was removed, always looking for a chance to escape. But this frog, the one I kept, had always seemed to appreciate the tank. Even then, at a few months of age, the frogs had had unique habits, had possessed individual temperaments: each one a distinct frogality.

But for every sign I saw of some greater frog consciousness, another sign denied it. One summer, a week of warm weather raised her metabolism. I could not satisfy her hunger, no matter how many bugs I caught and delivered to her. She snapped at the slightest movement. She turned agitatedly when I lifted the tank lid, leaping at the insect in my hand before I had even lowered it to her. One evening, I walked past her tank. She turned to face me. *Finally,* I thought, *recognition!* But then she leapt at me through the glass, her mouth open. Instinctual actions and nothing more: a hungry frog snapping at movement. Did she not know it was *me*?

I sat with her, sunny days and cool evenings, entertaining myself as I fed her moths and flies and earthworms. She was a creature of habit; I always knew where to find her. I wondered what consciousness made her movements so predictable. Did she "decide" where to sit, or did each combination of conditions—warm and sunny, or dark and damp—simply trigger a more unconscious, instinctive reaction that directed her to a specific spot?

And my frog sat, too, as I watched—motionless but for the gentle pulsing of her chin, her goggle-eyes staring outward, revealing nothing.

The spring that she turned eight, I had to leave town for a weekend. Sunshine was forecast, so I left her tank on the back deck; I would only be gone two nights. But the second day, an unforeseen storm hit, drenching the west coast in pounding rain.

I returned home the following day. I ran through the house, out the sliding glass door to the back. The tank was flooded, two-thirds full. The climbing log had collapsed under the greenery years before; only the tips of the fern leaves and salal fronds protruded above the water. Rain whipped around my head and shoulders as I grabbed a plastic cup and started to bail. Although I couldn't see the frog, I wasn't worried about her: she wouldn't have drowned. But I worried about my commitment to her, the quality of life I had promised her. She would have spent an uncomfortable night clinging to the tips of the branches instead of in her preferred late-night hideaway under the moss.

I squinted into the rain as I tipped cupful after cupful of water from the tank, trying to be careful not to bail the frog out as well. Cold raindrops pelted against my back. I finally got the water down to the level of the mossy forest floor. I slapped the screen lid on, laid the plastic rain-lid on top, and bolted back inside.

I lay down on my couch, shivering from the cold rain and exhausted from my journey. Grey raindrops streaked across the glass. After a time, a movement near the bottom of the window caught my eye. The frog!

The frog was out. She was climbing my back window. I leapt up. She quivered and trembled as she struggled to ascend the rain-pelted glass, working her way up, step by shaky step. Her eyes goggled out with an expression that seemed to cry: "Help me!"

I carefully slid open the door, scooped her up, and put her back in the tank. I placed the lid on, tucking the curled-up part of the screen back against the frame to cover the hole that the runt had escaped through years before, and replaced the plastic rain-guard.

How had she got out? I had watched for her as I bailed. But it had been raining hard, I had been squinting, I had been rushing. I could have missed her, tossed her out in my hurry. Or had she been out all along? I hadn't seen her in the fern-tips as I bailed. Perhaps she had used the runt's escape route when the tank flooded, earlier today, or even the day before.

How she got out was a mystery. But the greater mystery was: *Why did she come to me?*

The frog had not gone out to the back deck or to the flower pots. She had not hopped beyond, into the rainforest. She had leapt down to the concrete walkway, she had hopped over to my house, to my sliding glass door, and she had climbed up my window.

It might have been random—she had to hop in *some* direction. Perhaps it was pure coincidence that she happened to hop towards me. A 1 in 360 chance, after all.

But maybe it was deliberate. Perhaps she really did know me, did know the door that I always emerged from, did recognize me as her care-giver and protector. Perhaps she had come to me for help.

I watch her. For nine years I have watched her. She sits motionless for hours at a time, her gold-flecked eyes staring, staring. She doesn't respond to my voice. I pass my hand beside her and she doesn't flinch. At times, it seems there is nothing there—that aside from the moment the fluttering of an insect's wing catches her attention and she perks up to lunge at it, there is nothing. She swallows her bug, she retreats to her nothing.

But I wonder. We humans look for gestures and expressions that we are attuned to, that we can understand. We can read the face of a dog. A frog, however, is a different creature.

In the absence of facial expression, it is easy to assume that thought and emotions are absent, too. But I wonder if my frog might experience some rich internal life, some level of hope or desire, some emotional world that *I* simply am not capable of accessing. Perhaps she even carries some sort of affection for me.

How would I ever know?

RED EFT ROAD

JESS WOOLFORD

Mid-afternoon on a warm spring day in central Vermont and my father and I are escorting red efts across the road that runs past his house. It's a back road, but there's more traffic than you'd expect, mostly half-ton pickups hauling wood or hay or livestock to and from the homesteads tucked into the folds of the hills, and the young efts, with their soft orange bodies, stubby legs, and tentative movements, are sure to be crushed. So when we spy one picking its poky way over the hard-packed dirt, it seems a small mercy to pluck it up, cup it close, and carry it to the shelter of the bracken and Jack-in-the-pulpit and jewelweed jostling for space on the opposite side. Apart from the occasional exclamation of "There's one!" it is quiet work, and that is for the best because Dad and I have never quite gotten the hang of exchanging words. Still, as we shuttle the juvenile eastern newts to the next stop in their quest to locate the vernal pools lying high up in the sugar bush, a frond of memory unfurls in my mind and with it a question I would like to ask: *Dad, do you remember that time, all those years ago, when you showed me my first salamander?*

I couldn't have been more than three the day my father led me into the woods behind our house in Lyndeborough. Across the stone wall we scrambled, the rocks pale green with lichens that felt scaly to my clutching fingers. As I stretched one foot and then the other down to meet the ground, Dad took my hand to steady me. Then he turned and slipped between the stout trunks of a pair of ancient maples standing in line with countless others, and I followed him. Once past those sentries, we peered into shadows. As my eyes adjusted, I noticed sunlight filtering through the branches cross-hatched above us. The light mottled the spongy mat of leaves beneath our feet, the scent of its decay strong and complicated. Here and there broad clumps of ostrich fern arched their lithe necks, and emerald patches of moss lay thick. Perhaps a shy trillium trembled in the shadows but if so, I did not notice: my eyes were fixed on my father who had let go of my hand and strode on ahead, twigs snapping beneath his work boots. Pumping my legs, I tried to catch up, my red shoes flashing like busy cardinals.

After a while, Dad stopped at a fallen log and crouched beside it. As I drew near, he slowly rolled the log to one side and the wood was so soft with rot that chunks of it broke off and lay pale on the ground. Where the log had lain, the leaves were dark with damp and from their midst Dad quickly scooped up something bright. A cortège of small black beetles fled to safety underneath the log, and a millipede reared up and flailed its legs in protest before scuttling after them. Several pill bugs curled their armored bodies tight and pretended invisibility. Slugs the dull hue of sodden mushrooms clung to a few twigs that had been pinioned beneath the log.

"Look," my father whispered, and he brought his cupped hands close to my face. Peeking in, I saw what looked to be an orange ember pulsing against his palm. "It's a salamander," he said. Smiling, he gently stroked the creature's back with one finger. "Want to touch it?"

I nodded.

"Go ahead."

As I had seen my father do, I placed one finger against the creature's back and slowly petted it. "Gentle now," Dad said. I nodded again and repeated the stroke. The salamander's skin felt like cool silk, and to my eyes each speckle on its bright flanks seemed a gem. Watching the mysterious creature's sides slowly expand and contract, expand and contract,

I became aware of the gradual filling and emptying of my own lungs, as well as my father's. The woods seemed to fall silent then. Squirrels neither scampered nor scolded and the leaves of the maples hung mute. As we three breathed together, it seemed to me that this was all there was. Nothing more was needed.

I don't know how long we remained like that but after a time Dad said, "We have to put him back now. It's not good for wild things to be held for too long." He set the salamander back down where he had found it and carefully replaced the crumbling log. Then he held out his hand to me. I took it and we turned for home.

Do you remember that, Dad? I want to ask, but instead I keep quiet. This is my one perfect memory of my father, and I cannot risk exposing it to his dismissal. Besides, when it comes to my father, I am well aware of the trouble with questions. Not long ago, when the snow lay thick on the ground, I flew from Winnipeg to Montréal and then made my way south to Dad's house where he'd quickly reminded me of his aversion to scrutiny. He must have sensed that I was heavy with memories of our shared past, and before I could begin to find the words to ask *What?*, never mind *Why?*, he brought me up short.

It happened late one afternoon when he hauled a pail of feed to the edge of the driveway where we scattered it before retreating inside to watch from the sunroom. A clan of deer soon clambered over the lumpy lip of the drive and began to jostle for the chance to gobble the food.

"They come every day," Dad said, and there was pride in his voice. In that moment it was easy to love him. He reminded me of his mother who used to delight in coaxing squirrels and chipmunks up the steps into her kitchen to take peanuts from her warm hands. So trustworthy had she proven herself that the creatures stayed close by while they ate, their black eyes glinting as the bulbous shells fell to the linoleum.

As Dad and I watched the deer, I noticed one of the yearlings standing apart from the rest of the raucous group. He kept his head down and
refused to fight for access to the food. I wanted to shoo away his relatives
so he could eat his fill, but that was impossible. The slightest noise of the
doorknob turning would have sent all of them bounding back down the
hill and into the woods. Pointing to the outsider, I said, "Do you think
that one will survive?"

Dad shrugged.

"But what if he dies?" I pressed.

My father crossed his arms. "Shit happens," he said. Then he turned
and stumped off to the kitchen.

I watched him go but didn't follow, and soon I turned my gaze back
to the herd. With the exception of the young buck, the deer grazed until
chaff was all that remained of the feed. Then they ambled through the
lower field, their exclamatory tails bobbing, and cloaked themselves in
the trees below. As blue shadows began to reach across the snow, I stood
quiet and tried to fathom my father. He wouldn't bother to feed the deer
if he didn't care about them, that much was obvious. Yet his concern was
tempered by shit. Because when shit happened, well, what could anyone
do? It reminded me of what he'd said when I'd described my difficulties
navigating out of Montréal, and then Québec itself: *The best thing to do is
just forget about it.* Maybe that was a Life Lesson, a bit of wisdom passed
from father to child to smooth the latter's path. I had always hoped for
something more, but perhaps this was it: *Shit happens. The best thing to do is
just forget about it.* The advice had a certain appeal. If I took it, I could shake
off the past and its hold on my heart, maybe even seize the day and get
happy like the chorus of all the self-help books. Yet even as I considered
adopting Dad's philosophy, my recollections and questions surged to the
fore and began pestering me anew. Though there was much I longed to
forget, I could not.

Now, watching my father gentle the red efts, I sense time collapsing as it often does in his company, so that once again I am simultaneously in two places, the present drawing the past near as I try to reconcile what lies in front of me with what has gone before.

Little more than a year after Dad showed me my first salamander, Blackie and Snowball disappeared. Balls of fur with needle claws, they were the kittens a neighbour had bestowed upon my sister Annie and me, and we delighted in their zany antics and, when they'd stay still, the feel of their warm bodies soft against our faces. The last time I saw them they were curled tight together, asleep on the white chenille spread that draped my parents' bed. When Mom said Blackie and Snowball were gone, I couldn't fathom what she meant, even when she added that they'd wandered off. I cried then, along with Annie, and together we worried for them and hoped they would return, but they never did. Eventually the pain dulled, and I didn't think about those dear pets again until many years later when my parents' marriage came asunder. That was when Mom told us that Dad had in fact killed Blackie and Snowball. Some time after Annie and I had left them to their nap, they had mistaken the pristine bedspread for a litter box and fouled it with their tarry shit. When my father discovered the mess, he'd whisked them to the barn, plunged their tiny bodies into a bucket of water, and held them under until they went limp. I didn't want to believe my mother's story, but at the same time I knew there was a cruelty to my father and that he often used the bodies of animals to express it.

I was about eight years old and Annie six when I overheard my mother tell my father that he should spend more time with us. "Why don't you try reading them their bedtime story for a change?" When Dad agreed, I was so excited I felt like a can of soda that had been shaken and then set back in the refrigerator. I could hardly wait for bedtime, and when it finally arrived I launched myself onto my bunk. As my mother tucked the covers in around me, smoothed my hair, and kissed my cheek,

Me, age 3, near the woods where I meet my first salamander.

attentions that I usually welcomed, I wished I could wave her away. I wanted my father. As he settled into the chair and opened the book he had chosen, I kicked my feet in anticipation. *"The Call of the Wild,"* Dad intoned, and then he began to read. Within ten minutes my delight was dead, clubbed insensible just like poor Buck. That first chapter was the start of a nightmare in seven parts, and its dark pictures included one of a man who, like my father, wore a moustache and smoked a pipe. It made my heart hurt to hear the words that fell from Dad's lips and I tried to shut my ears against them but despite my efforts, a vivid and sickening picture of a piteous creature choked, caged, poked with sticks, and smashed until his coat was bloody took root in my mind. Thirty years on it is still there. I don't know what my father was thinking when he selected *The Call of the Wild* for us and, close on its heels, *White Fang*. Annie and I were accustomed to our mother's choices, stories like *The Secret Garden* and *A Little Princess* in which beauty, goodness, and hope always defeated despair and loneliness, the very qualities that saturate Jack London's books. Perhaps Dad deliberately chose bleak texts as antidotes to Mom's gentler tales. I can imagine him reasoning that a good dose of misery and death would toughen us up. Perhaps that was what drove him to take us fishing.

One Friday night, Dad was late getting home from work, and when he finally pulled into the driveway, he lifted two miniature Zebco Rod'n'Reels, the same ones we'd seen advertised on TV, out of the back of his truck and presented them to Annie and me. The next morning, he led us to the compost pile where we watched him dig for worms. When he'd collected enough to fill an old green tobacco can halfway, Dad gathered the rest of the fishing tackle and we walked to the neighbourhood pond. To reach it we had to wade through a field awash in tall grasses and as we went the sun warmed my face and the sharp scent of wild mint filled the air. At our approach a red-winged blackbird scolded and fat green frogs flopped into the water, their skin glistering. It was springtime, and pollywogs flickered and hung in the water, some with tails and some already developing back legs, while others were caught halfway between fish and frog. Cupping my hands together, I tried to scoop them up, and it would have been great fun to linger at the pond if only my father hadn't kept saying, "Be quiet or you'll scare the fish away." It was almost unbearable to have to keep my mouth shut when each new impression made me want to exclaim in delight.

If only Dad hadn't insisted that I fish. Trying to run my hook through a worm while it did its utmost to wriggle away was unsettling, and watching my father finish the job was worse. Once the fish started biting, I hated looking into the old pickle bucket Dad put them in. With a stick pushed in through their mouths and out through their gills they swam in place, fins stirring water pink with their own blood, their eyes open and unblinking and their mouths gulping repeatedly as though begging for resuscitation. Later their iridescent bodies ended up suspended in blocks of ice stacked in the big chest freezer, but no one ever got around to cooking them. Which in a way was good because the thought of having to swallow the sad suffering of the fish made my stomach shrink. To me the whole experience seemed a waste of beauty and life, and I wondered why my father couldn't or wouldn't give me his time alone, without adding a darker note to the mix. Though I am a grown woman now with a child of my own, I still don't know the answer.

Pulling myself back to the present, I see my father fretting over the red efts, and I think that he is partly right. Yes, shit happens. But, whatever the reasons, we also *choose* shit, and we *make* shit, and we *do* shit. Yet through all the shit I can't forget and, what's more, refuse to forget, I hold tight to the memory of the salamander secret and those few moments when my father was both revealer and protector of mysteries.

They say that amphibians are an indicator species: their health mirrors the health of their environment. This is perhaps true of the red efts in more than one sense. As I watch my father scoop up another mild young newt, the fragile orange ember flickering in the bowl of his cupped hands gives me small hope. Crossing the road, Dad carefully shelters the creature beneath the glossy fronds of a dagger fern. I wait, and while I wait I work to slow my breath, *inhale-exhale, inhale-exhale,* as though by doing so I might catch the slow pulse of the woods. When Dad finishes, we continue on, silent, but side by side.

ACKNOWLEDGEMENTS

I'm grateful to my father and my grandmother for sharing their love for animals, and I'm grateful to Pamela Banting for teaching me to think about animals. Many thanks to Merle Henderson and Stephanie Howe for providing childcare while I worked on this manuscript. I'm grateful to Laura Best, Sara Chamberlain, Laurie Elmquist, Cathy Fenwick, Rose-Marie Lohnes, Karin Melberg Schwier, and Marianne Stamm for their feedback on the introduction. Many thanks to the staff at Nimbus Publishing, particularly Patrick Murphy and Jenn Embree. Above all, I'm grateful to the authors who so generously shared their stories and photographs for this book.

Photo Credits

Photo on page 62 by Eeva Miller
Photo on page 85 by Evelyn R. Firby
Photo on page 106 by Dave Brosha
Photo on page 133 by Krista R. Mallory
Photo on page 166 by Richard Schwier

Photo of Leslie Bamford by Robert Bamford
Photo of K. Bannerman by Shawn Pigott
Photo of Pam Chamberlain by Lena Gilje
Photo of Catherine R. Fenwick by Kristin MacPherson
Photo of Penny L. Ferguson by Portraits by Johanna
Photo of Donna Firby Gamache by Luc Gamache
Photo of Mark Ambrose Harris by Dallas Curow
Photo of Joanna Lilley by Marten Berkman
Photo of Rose-Marie Lohnes by Trudy Johnson
Photo of Christine Lowther by Marlene Cummings
Photo of B. A. Markus by Nathan Markus
Photo of Catherine McLaughlin by Pauline Waugh
Photo of Karin Melberg Schwier by Richard Schwier
Photo of Andrea Miller by Adán Cano Cabrera
Photo of Farley Mowat by Peter Bregg
Photo of David Adams Richards by Bruce Peters
Photo of Anny Scoones by Mikki Richards
Photo of June Smith-Jeffries by R. Drew Jeffries
Photo of Richard Wagamese by Debra Powell

PUBLICATION CREDITS

Leslie Bamford's "A Perfect Ten" includes a quotation from *By the Grace of the Sea: A Woman's Solo Odyssey Around the World* by Pat Henry (International Marine/Ragged Mountain Press, 2002).

Paul Beingessner's "Old One-Eye" is published with permission of his family.

Andrew Boden's "Mad King Grover" was first published in *Descant* 143 (Winter 2008). Reprinted with permission of the author.

Pam Chamberlain's introduction includes quotations from Jane Goodall, quoted in David Quammen's article "Jane: Fifty Years at Gombe" (*National Geographic*, October 2010, p. 117) and Richard Wagamese's "The Animal People" in *One Native Life* (Douglas & McIntyre, 2008, pp. 141–143). It also refers to John Berger's "Why Look at Animals?" in *About Looking* (Pantheon, 1980).

Catherine R. Fenwick's "*Ein Gutes Gespann*" includes quotations and statistics from *Hoofprints and Hitchingposts* by Grant MacEwan (Saskatoon: Modern Press, 1964, pp. 76–77).

Penny L. Ferguson's "The Only Time" was first published in *Cormorant* (Spring 1999, pp. 71–80). Reprinted with permission of the author.

Donna Firby Gamache's "Daisy" was published in a different version in *Farmers' Independent Weekly* (July 28, 2005). Reprinted with permission of the author.

Melody Hessing's "Home Invasion" was first published in *Up Chute Creek: An Okanagan Idyll* by Melody Hessing (Kelowna: Okanagan Institute, 2009, pp. 161-164) and is reprinted with permission of the author. It includes a quotation from *Mammals of Canada* by A.W.F. Banfield (U of Toronto Press, 1974, p. 178).

Bud Ings's "Bessie and the Young Vet" was first published in *Mud, Sweat, and Tears: Tales from a Country Vet* by Bud Ings (Charlottetown: Acorn Press, 2008, pp. 11–15). Reprinted with permission of Acorn Press.

Linda Johns's "Discovery" was first published in *Sharing a Robin's Life* (Halifax: Nimbus, 1993, pp. 1–8). Reprinted with permission of Nimbus Publishing.

Christine Lowther's "Living Light" was first published in her memoir *Born Out of This* (Halfmoon Bay, BC: Caitlin Press, 2014). Reprinted with permission of the author.

Michael Lukas's "Discourse with a Mountain Lion" was published in a different version in the journal *Camas: The Nature of the West* (Winter 2008). Reprinted with permission of the author.

Charlotte Mendel's "Grass Can Get Greener" was first published in *The Healing Touch of Horses* (Avon, MA: Adams Media, 2007, pp. 43–49). Reprinted with permission of Adams Media and the author.

ABOUT THE AUTHORS

 Jean Ballard grew up in White Rock, British Columbia, and taught at the University of the Fraser Valley before retiring to Vancouver Island. She is a columnist and photographer for the *Chemainus Valley Courier* and has been published in Chicken Soup for the Soul's *O Canada: The Wonders of Winter* and elsewhere. She has volunteered with animal rescues and shelters since 2005 and has a passion for senior dogs and potbellied pigs. She can be contacted through her blog at mylifewiththecritters.blogspot.com.

 Leslie Bamford was born and raised in Montréal and now lives in Waterloo, Ontario. Her short stories, creative non-fiction, poetry, and plays have been recognized in local literary competitions and published in several national and international anthologies. She has been the caretaker of many adorable cats throughout the years and now has a new puppy in the family. While learning about canine nature, she teaches memoir writing and is at work on a book about her wacky husband, a feisty black cat, and her mother's ghost. Visit her online at lesliebamford.ca.

 K. Bannerman's short stories have appeared in publications worldwide, including *100 Stories for Queensland* and *Paraspheres Anthology*. She has written four novels: *The Tattooed Wolf*, *The Wolf of Gilsbury Cross*, *The Fire Song*, and *Bucket of Blood*. She lives on Vancouver Island with her husband, two children, and a mischievous dog named Loki. Visit her at kbannerman.com.

Paul Beingessner was born in 1954 and spent most of his life on the family farm at Truax, Saskatchewan. He helped found Saskatchewan's first short-line railway, and from 1991 until his sudden death in 2009, Paul wrote a weekly column on farming and transportation issues with a social justice focus, which was featured in newspapers across Western Canada. His true passion was farming, the land, and community. He loved hunting, birdwatching, camping, gardening, and searching for fossils while walking countless miles of railroad track and fence.

 Andrew Boden's stories and essays have appeared in *The Journey Prize Stories: 22, Prairie Fire, Descant, Vancouver Review,* and the anthology *Nobody's Father: Life ·Without Kids*. He co-edited *Hidden Lives*, a collection of personal essays about mental illness. He works in Burnaby, British Columbia, where he lives with three low-maintenance cats. His website is andrewboden.ca

 Sandra Cherniawsky has been writing all her life and worked as a reporter for local weekly newspapers. She is currently a county councilor for Yellowhead County in west-central Alberta. When she isn't busy chasing Ellie from her garden, she can be found in her greenhouse planting, pruning, and producing tomatoes and cucumbers. She lives with her husband, three dogs, and two cats near Evansburg, Alberta.

 Vivian Demuth often brought home snakes, frogs, and crayfish from the woods surrounding her childhood home in Ontario. She studied biology at the University of Western Ontario and worked for many years as a park ranger, warden, and outdoor educator in western Canada, where she fell in love with the mountains. For the past twenty summers, she has lived on a mountain in Alberta where she works watching for forest fires. She has published a novel, *Eyes of the Forest,* and a poetry collection, *Fire Watcher,* and has a forthcoming novel, *Bear Warden.* Her work is online at viviandemuth.wordpress.com

Ruth Edgett has been writing for most of her life and has had careers in both journalism and public relations. Her writing has been published in *RED: The Island Story Book* and two Maritime Christmas anthologies. She is the author of *A Watch in the Night: The Story of Pomquet Island's Last Lightkeeping Family.* Born and raised on Prince Edward Island, Ruth now lives in Ancaster, Ontario. When she is not writing, she can be found riding her second horse, Whisper (therein lies a whole other story), on the trails through the Dundas Valley.

Catherine R. Fenwick was born in Indian Head, Saskatchewan, and raised on a mixed farm nearby. She is the eldest of ten children and mother of two daughters and two sons. Her articles and stories have been published in several magazines, journals, and anthologies. She has written two books, *Healing with Humour* and *Love and Laughter,* and is currently working on a collection of poems. She continues to have a great fondness for horses.

Penny L. Ferguson was born in Storeytown, New Brunswick. She has published two poetry collections, *Clarity That Is Darkness* and *Runaway Suite: Two Voices.* Her poems, short stories, articles, and drawings have been published in Canada, the United States, and England. She has been writer-in-residence at the Nova Scotia Teachers' College, co-founder and editor of *The Amethyst Review,* vice-president of the Canadian Poetry Association, and is a member of the Writer's Council of the Nova Scotia Writer's Federation. A former teacher, Penny lives in Valley, Nova Scotia, with her husband and two dogs, Sophia and Kestrel.

Donna Firby Gamache is a writer and a retired teacher from MacGregor, Manitoba. Her childhood was spent on a farm north of Minnedosa, and she fondly remembers exploring the hills and valleys, horseback riding along the river, helping with barn chores, playing with kittens, and attending a one-room school. She has published fiction for children and adults, articles in farm newspapers, and short verse. She has published four books: *Spruce Woods Adventure, Loon Island, Return to the River,* and *Sarah: A New Beginning,* a fictionalized story about her grandmother's immigration to Manitoba in 1891.

Mark Ambrose Harris lives, writes, and teaches in Montréal. His essay "Beautiful Books" received the 2012 *Songe-de-Poliphile* award from *l'Académie de la vie littéraire au tournant du 21e siècle.* His work appears in the anthologies *I Like It Like That* and *Men on the Make* and in the online journals *Revolver* and *No More Potlucks.* He has written about parasitic STI stigma, as well as gender, otter identity, and body hair. His arts and culture pieces appear in *Lickety Split, 2B Magazine, Nightlife, Cornershopstudios, The Lost Boys, Xtra,* and *Empty Mirror Books.* For more information, visit markambroseharris.com or follow @homosonic on Twitter.

Melody Hessing frequents the Okanagan for the neon blue of western skink, the blink-of-an-eye of bobcat, and the gaze of bighorn sheep. As a sociologist, she explores the connections between society and environment, and she teaches at UBC, SFU, TRU, and many BC colleges. She has co-published the textbooks *Canadian Natural Resource and Environmental Policy* and *This Elusive Land: Women and the Canadian Environment,* as well as many scholarly articles about biodiversity. Her most recent book, *Up Chute Creek: An Okanagan Idyll,* describes making home with "others" in a unique but endangered ecosystem.

Bud Ings grew up on a farm near Mount Herbert, Prince Edward Island, where he helped with the dairy herd and learned about animal care from his father. He studied at the veterinary college in Guelph, and then returned to PEI in the 1950s as one of the Island's first professionally trained veterinarians. In the 1970s, he sat in the PEI legislative assembly as the minister responsible for agriculture, health, and social services. Ings has written two memoirs: *Mud, Sweat, and Tears* and *Vet Behind the Ears*. He lives in Montague, PEI.

 Marcus Jackson grew up in central Alberta, where he spent much of his time drawing and writing. He has a BA in English from the University of Calgary and a BFA in print media from the Alberta College of Art and Design. He lived in British Columbia for ten years before moving to Yellowknife in 2010. As an artist, he explores the relationships between people and the wilderness. He published a story in *Coming Home: Stories from the Northwest Territories,* and his artwork has been exhibited across Canada and in the United States, Mexico, Poland, and Australia. You can see his work at luckyjackpress.com.

Linda Johns is a writer and artist who lives in rural Nova Scotia. She has published several books, including *In the Company of Birds, For the Birds, Wild and Wooly,* and *The Eyes of the Elders. Sharing a Robin's Life* won the 1994 Edna Staebler Award for Creative Nonfiction.

 Shannon Kernaghan has published two books, and her stories have appeared in journals and newspapers across Canada and the US. Through the years, she watched her parents rescue and cherish an array of furred and feathered creatures. She is forever grateful to the compassionate example Donna and Leon set, and for the memories—and stories—they helped create. Her website is shannonkernaghan.com.

 Joanna Lilley was born in England and lived in Wales and Scotland before settling in Whitehorse, Yukon, where she's lived with her husband, a cat, and a dog since 2006. Joanna has published a poetry collection, *The Fleece Era,* and a chapbook of animal poems called *They Bring It on Themselves,* which she published as a fundraiser for animal-welfare organizations. Joanna has been vegetarian since her thirteenth birthday, but wishes it had been even longer. Visit her online at joannalilley.blogspot.com.

Rose-Marie Lohnes grew up on a small farm in Upper Northfield, Nova Scotia, and in nearby Pinehurst, in a time when animals were considered useful, but expendable—certainly not pets. Her thirty-seven-year teaching career included volunteer work in Barbados with her daughters, Krista and Toni, and in Bolivia with her husband, Corwin Hirtle. She has published educational manuals, a short story in the anthology *Country Roads,* and an article in *Saltscapes.* She is a reader, gardener, beach walker, ukulele player, and lover of life. She enjoys her family—especially granddaughter Mallory and great-grandsons Noah and Oliver—and animals, especially cats.

Christine Lowther lives in Clayoquot Sound on the west coast of Vancouver Island. She is the author of three books of poetry and the co-editor of two collections of essays. Her writing has appeared in literary magazines, anthologies, and periodicals including *Crowlogue, Wild Moments: Adventures with Animals in the North,* and *Animal Studies Journal.* Visit her online at christinelowther.blogspot.ca.

Michael Lukas, who was raised in the American Midwest on the banks of a Wisconsin River tributary, is a former fly-fishing guide, Alaska bush nanny, and environmental educator who now makes his home in Victoria, BC. He is a lecturer, writing tutor, essayist, and dedicated steelhead fisherman who teaches composition, literature, and cultural theory at the University of Victoria, where he is completing his PhD. His dissertation is a book-length series of essays entitled *The Rhetoric of Wolves,* which theorizes responsibility in human-animal encounters by tracing and tracking wolves through literature, media, policy, and popular culture.

B. A. Markus is a writer, teacher, performer, and mother who grew up in Toronto and lives in Montréal. She teaches English, writes book reviews for the *Montreal Review of Books*, and writes song lyrics for Michael Jerome Browne, Bob Walsh, and Eric Bibb. Her songs are found on three Juno-nominated CDs, and she has been on the QWF/CBC Literary Prizes shortlist twice and on the CBC Creative Non-Fiction Prize longlist once. Her stories have appeared in various literary journals and anthologies, and she has written and performed one-act plays across Canada.

 Catherine McLaughlin is a poet, freelance writer, essayist, and photographer who is inspired by the natural world. She was born and raised in the Georgian Bay area of southern Ontario and has lived in the Peace River Country in northern Alberta for many years. She co-wrote the *Grande Prairie Century Play* (2014), a community play with a focus on the last hundred years of Grande Prairie's history. Some of her poetry can be seen at dailyhaiku.org

 Karin Melberg Schwier grew up on a farm near Seattle and dreamed of being a zoologist. Later, on the family farm near Fairview, Alberta, Karin milked cows and hand-cranked the cream separator, which was good training for a later stint on a dairy operation in New Zealand. Now a Saskatoon-based freelance writer and illustrator, Karin contributes to several magazines and has published eight books, the most recent of which is *Flourish: People with Disabilities Living Life with Passion*. Visit Karin's blog at karinschwier. wordpress.com. To watch a video of Karin and Russell Crow, search for "russell crow + schwier" on YouTube.

 Charlotte Mendel was born in Nova Scotia and has lived in England, France, and Israel. She has also travelled through the Far East, the Middle East, South America, and Europe. Since returning to Canada, Mendel has worked

as an instructional designer and a teacher. Her short stories have been published in a variety of literary journals and anthologies. Her first novel, *Turn Us Again,* won the H. R. Percy Novel Prize and the Beacon Award for Social Justice. She lives in Enfield, Nova Scotia, with one husband, two children, three cats, two goats, and eight chickens.

Andrea Miller is the deputy editor of *Shambhala Sun* magazine and the editor of the anthologies *Buddha's Daughters: Teachings from Women Who Are Shaping Buddhism in the West* and *Right Here with You: Bringing Mindful Awareness into Our Relationships.* She has an MFA in creative writing from the University of British Columbia, and her poetry, fiction, and creative non-fiction have been featured in a variety of publications, including *The Antigonish Review, Prairie Fire, The Best Women's Travel Writing* series, and *The Best Buddhist Writing* series. She lives in Halifax and is a member of the Nova Scotia Bird Society.

Farley Mowat (1921–2014), the iconic Canadian nature writer, was born in Belleville, Ontario, and grew up in Ontario and Saskatchewan. He wrote dozens of books for adults and children—including *The Dog Who Wouldn't Be, Owls in the Family, Never Cry Wolf, People of the Deer,* and *A Whale for the Killing*—which were translated into more than twenty-five languages in over sixty countries. He earned dozens of awards for his writing and conservation work, as well as a star on Canada's Walk of Fame, and he was an Officer of the Order of Canada.

Chris Nichols grew up near Pigeon Lake, Alberta, and earned a BA from the University of Alberta and an MA from the University of Victoria. He lives and writes in Vancouver, where he also crafts furniture from recycled lumber through his company, Lazarus Upcycle (lazarusupcycle.com).

Linda Olson grew up on Vancouver Island and studied medieval literature and history in both Canada and England. She has worked at many jobs, including teaching, editing, and proofreading, but her passion is writing. Most of her published work is academic and includes several articles and two co-authored books—*Voices in Dialogue: Reading Women in the Middle Ages* and *Opening Up Middle English Manuscripts: Literary and Visual Approaches*—but she has also written fiction, poetry, book reviews, and distance-learning courses. She lives on three wooded acres in Newfoundland, where she loves to feed the chickadees and grow Brussels sprouts—even when the moose get to them first!

 David Adams Richards was born in Newcastle, New Brunswick, and attended St. Thomas University. He has written over a dozen novels, several plays, and the memoirs *Facing the Hunter: Reflections on a Misunderstood Way of Life* and *Lines on the Water: A Fisherman's Life on the Miramichi*. Richards has won two Geminis for scriptwriting, the Governor General's Award in both fiction and nonfiction, and the 2000 Giller Prize for *Mercy Among Children*. Each year, the Writer's Federation of New Brunswick awards the David Adams Richards Prize for Fiction. A Member of the Order of Canada, Richards lives in Fredericton.

 Anny Scoones grew up in Fredericton, New Brunswick, and spent summers with her grandmother on Galiano Island in British Columbia. She spent several years on the Glamorgan Farm north of Victoria restoring the farm's historic buildings, raising heritage breeds of livestock, and growing heirloom produce. She also served as a councilor for the District of North Saanich. Scoones has written four books—*Home: Tales of a Heritage Farm; True Home: Life on a Heritage Farm; Home and Away: More Tales of a Heritage Farm;* and, most recently, *Hometown: Out and About in Victoria's Neighbourhoods*. She lives and teaches in Victoria.

June Smith-Jeffries grew up in South Carolina, moved to Edmonton in 1995, and now lives in London, Ontario, where she develops curricula and instructs online for a local technical institution. She has had a life-long fascination with animals of all types, particularly with their innate instincts. When she was eight, she conversed regularly with a squirrel in her backyard and wrote her first poem about those encounters. Her writing has been published in a variety of literary journals in Canada and the US. June was shortlisted in the Writers' Union Writing for Children Competition, and her fiction has been aired on CBC.

 Mary Ellen Sullivan grew up near Elora, Ontario, on a farm that she has been writing about ever since. She is published in *All Rights Reserved, The Canadian Messenger of the Sacred Heart, Rural Delivery* magazine, *Open Heart Forgery: Year One Anthology,* and by the Organic Agriculture Centre of Canada and Canadian Jesuits Overseas (online). She is committed to sharing her respect for farmers and has collected poems by Nova Scotia poets in two issues of *Open Heart Farming,* an annual special issue of *Open Heart Forgery.* She lives in Halifax.

 Richard Wagamese is from the Wabasseemoong First Nation in northwestern Ontario. He has worked as a newspaper reporter, a radio broadcaster, and a documentary producer. His books—including the memoirs *For Joshua: An Ojibway Father Teaches His Son, One Native Life,* and *One Story, One Song* and the novels *Keeper 'n Me, Runaway Dreams,* and *Indian Horse*—have won many awards, and he has received an honorary doctorate from Thompson Rivers University and a National Aboriginal Achievement Award. He leads writing and storytelling workshops across Canada and now lives near Kamloops, British Columbia. His website is richardwagamese.com

David Weale, a self-described mystic, is the editor of *RED* magazine and has authored more than a dozen books, including four for children and a memoir, *Chasing the Shore: Little Stories about Spirit and Landscape.* Well known on the Island as a storyteller, Weale hosted the award-winning program, *Them Times,* for CBC Charlottetown and has been featured as a guest contributor on the CBC radio program *Tapestry.* He lives in Charlottetown.

Jacqueline Windh grew up in Ontario, and after living in Montréal, California, Australia, and Chile, finally settled on Vancouver Island in 1995. She brings her background as an earth scientist and her passion for nature and the environment into both her writing and her photography. Her first book, *The Wild Edge,* was a Canadian bestseller. Her articles, stories, and photographs have been published in magazines and newspapers around the world. Find her at jacquelinewindh.com

Jess Woolford is an essayist, memoirist, and prize-winning poet whose work has appeared in *Contemporary Verse 2, Prairie Fire,* and *Social Politics.* A poem and memoir are forthcoming in *Canadian Abortion Experience: Voices on Choice(s).* She is also the author of *Lumping It: A Breast Cancer Blog,* which you can visit at lumpingit.wordpress.com. Though Woolford now calls Winnipeg home, she grew up in Vermont, and she often returns there to teach her daughter to guide red efts across the road.